Dear Reader:

W9-BSE-417

The book you are about to read is the latest bestseller from the St. Martin's True Crime Library, the imprint *The New York Times* calls "the leader in true crime!" The True Crime Library offers you fascinating accounts of the latest, most sensational crimes that have captured the national attention. St. Martin's is the publisher of John Glatt's riveting and horrifying SECRETS IN THE CELLAR, which shines a light on the man who shocked the world when it was revealed that he had kept his daughter locked in his hidden basement for 24 years. In the Edgar-nominated WRITTEN IN BLOOD, Diane Fanning looks at Michael Petersen, a Marine-turned-novelist found guilty of beating his wife to death and pushing her down the stairs of their home—only to reveal another similar death from his past. In the book you now hold, IF IF CAN'T HAVE YOU, bestselling authors Gregg Olsen and Rebecca Morris explore the horrific case of Susan Powell and her little boys.

St. Martin's True Crime Library gives you the stories behind the headlines. Our authors take you right to the scene of the crime and into the minds of the most notorious murderers to show you what really makes them tick. St. Martin's True Crime Library paperbacks are better than the most terrifying thriller, because it's all true! The next time you want a crackling good read, make sure it's got the St. Martin's True Crime Library logo on the spine—you'll be up all night!

Charles E. Spicer, Jr.
Executive Editor, St. Martin's True Crime Library

If I Can't Have You

Susan Powell, Her Mysterious
Disappearance, and the Murder
of Her Children

Gregg Olsen and Rebecca Morris

St. Martin's Paperbacks

IF I CAN'T HAVE YOU

Copyright © 2014, 2015 by Gregg Olsen and Rebecca Morris.

All rights reserved.

For information address St. Martin's Press, 175 Fifth Avenue, New York, NY 10010.

ISBN: 978-1-250-06668-8

Printed in the United States of America

St. Martin's Press edition / May 2014
St. Martin's Paperbacks edition / May 2015

St. Martin's Paperbacks are published by St. Martin's Press, 175 Fifth Avenue, New York, NY 10010.

10 9 8 7 6 5

FOR SUSAN'S UTAH SISTERS

Kiirsi Hellewell
Debbie Caldwell
JoVonna Owings
Rachel Marini
Michele Oreno
Amber Hardman
Barbara Anderson

Prologue

In every way Chuck Cox is an unassuming man. He wears tan Dockers and plain, buttoned-up shirts, usually white or pale blue. He keeps his once-sandy hair, now gray, combed neatly. His eyeglasses are more about function than style. Chuck even drives a suburban mainstay, a minivan. As an accident investigator for the Federal Aviation Administration, he has seen some of the worst tragedies imaginable, but he has kept the grim mental images of crash sites separate from his life as a husband, father, grandfather, and active member of the Church of Jesus Christ of Latter-day Saints. If you passed Chuck on the street, he would have been just another pleasant face. A smile. A nod. A quick wave.

Judy Cox, like her husband, is in her mid-fifties. She wears her graying hair long, and has a light touch with makeup. Judy is the neighbor lady who always makes sure that the mail is picked up when someone is on vacation. Who watches out for others in her church ward. Who makes sure a missing dog is found, every letter is answered, and every phone call is returned. Judy lives with diabetes, but that doesn't mean that she won't make a double batch of chocolate chip cookies for her grandchildren.

Yet, these days, doing that is so very, very hard.

The Coxes live in Puyallup, Washington, a town that epitomizes suburban sprawl at its best and worst. Pockets of the city of 37,000 retain the small-town vibe of a once-burgeoning farming community. Most of those areas, however, are cordoned off by an array of franchise restaurants and strip malls like many once bucolic communities across the growing Puget Sound region.

The town with the tongue-twister name is named for the Puyallup Tribe of Indians. It is known for three things: as the site of the largest fair in the state; the two hundred varieties of daffodils sold around the world; and—less pleasantly—as the location of a temporary internment facility called Camp Harmony, where Japanese-Americans were interned before being sent to camps in California and Idaho during the Second World War.

Four years ago, life changed for the Coxes. It will never change back. Judy knows it every time she looks over from the compact kitchen at a table that will always have three empty places. No reminders are necessary, but they are everywhere. A strange black rock that Chuck keeps by his computer. A faded purple ribbon on the lamppost on their street corner. A continuous flow of sympathy cards and e-mails of support.

No one—least of all Chuck and Judy—could have guessed where their lives would go when their daughter went missing in December 2009. Neither could have imagined the horror that was in store for them, or that they would find purpose in enduring the greatest tragedy a parent can face.

Susan Powell, the third-youngest of the four Cox girls, disappeared from the West Valley City, Utah, home she shared with her husband, Josh, and their sons, Charlie and Braden. A few days later a friend of Susan's told Susan's distraught father about a secret diary Susan had been keeping. That she kept a diary at all didn't surprise Chuck—she'd done so on and off through her teenage years and young adulthood. Susan wrote romantic fantasies as a teen and later, her dreams for the future. Writing helped her process what was going on in her life.

The friend, a coworker of Susan's, told Chuck that Susan kept the secret diary in her desk at work.

"Where Josh can't see it," she said.

Chuck felt his stomach, already wrenched with pain, drop.

He had no doubts that whatever Susan was writing had to do with her husband—or maybe her father-in-law, Steve. There wasn't enough paper in the world for Susan to write down everything she thought about Steve. More than anything, however, Chuck hoped that the diary would hold some clues to her whereabouts.

Judy, a woman of unshakable faith like her husband, prayed the diary would lead the police to wherever Susan was in time to save her.

Based on the tip relayed by the friend and the worried father, West Valley City police investigators found a small key in Susan's purse during a search of the Powell residence. The key fit a safe-deposit lock at a bank a block from her office.

A detective slid the key into the lock and lowered his eyes into the open box. Inside was a single piece of lined notebook paper, folded over and crudely stapled. As if it had been done in haste.

The words on the paper would send a chill down the spine of even the most seasoned investigator. It was like a message from the afterlife. In Susan's loopy, sweetly girlish handwriting, it said:

If I die, it may not be an accident even if it looks like one. Take care of my boys.

If that wasn't enough, there was also a caveat, a finger-pointing accusation toward her killer.

Susan asked that whoever found the note *not* show it to her husband, Josh.

> *For mine and my children's safety I feel the need to have a paper trail at work which would not be accessible to my husband . . . it is an open fact that we have life insurance policies of over a million if we die in the next four years.*

It was dated June 28, 2008.

Over time that cruelly stretched for years, Chuck and Judy and others who loved Susan would discover secrets and lies that would plunge all of them into the darkest places imaginable. They learned firsthand that the most startling depravity in the world can come from places close to home, even from a house in a gated community just a few minutes' drive away.

1

Every moment I step back and take stock of what I'm dealing with, it feels like a never ending cycle but I'm too afraid of the consequences, losing my kids, him kidnapping [them], divorce or actions worse on his part . . .
—SUSAN POWELL E-MAIL, JULY 5, 2008

Debbie Caldwell pulled up in her Ford Club Wagon—the one with fifteen seats to carry all the children who attended her day care—and observed how quiet her friend and neighbor Susan's house seemed. It was 9:00 A.M. on Monday, December 7, 2009, and West Valley City, a suburb of Salt Lake City, was in the middle of a three-day winter storm. Freezing temperatures and four inches of new snowfall made the roads so icy that the local news described the streets as "mayhem."

Susan, twenty-eight, and Josh, thirty-three, usually dropped Braden and Charlie at Daydreams & Fun Things Child Care as early as 6:00 A.M. When they didn't appear that morning, Debbie started trying to reach the young parents. Susan was always prompt and conscientious. Josh was another story. He tested Debbie's patience regularly, bringing the children late—which complicated the morning, since Debbie needed to know how many children needed breakfast.

He also neglected to pick up the boys on time in the evening, cutting into Debbie's time with her own family.

The other day-care parents avoided Josh because he talked incessantly and acted as if he was an expert on anything and everything. They had a nickname they called Josh behind his back: *Rocks for Brains*. One day, when Josh had given Debbie a hard time because Braden had lost his socks, one of the mothers said, "That idiot must have rocks for brains." It stuck.

Charlie and Braden, ages four and two, respectively, had been attending Debbie's day care for a year and a half, and like many women who had met the outgoing Susan, Debbie had become a confidante. Susan and her circle of friends were young, committed Mormon wives. Their children and their marriages came first. The friends had heard, because Susan told them, that Josh wouldn't give her money to buy groceries and diapers, wouldn't have sex with her, and wouldn't go to counseling. One friend joked that Josh treated his pet parrot better than his wife and sons. Susan also voiced displeasure that he was spending too many hours on the phone talking with his father, who had left the Mormon church. Steve Powell, Susan told her friends, had been inappropriate with her—disgustingly so. Susan was so open with her complaints that her friends were feeling a bit apathetic. They'd heard it all so many times.

That morning, Debbie, forty-seven and the mother of four daughters, was on her way home from dropping the older children at school. She still had three toddlers in the car, and as she parked the van in front of 6254 W. Sarah Circle she told them she would just be a minute. She knocked on the front door several times. No answer. She expected to find Josh, harried anytime he had the slightest responsibility, getting the boys dressed, or more likely sequestered on his computer in the basement where he liked to hide. In any case, Susan would have phoned Debbie if there had been a change in plans.

By the time Debbie was at the Powells' front door Monday morning, she had already called Susan on her cell phone.

When there was no answer, she tried Susan's work phone at Wells Fargo Investments and, finally, their home landline.

Again, no answer.

Debbie dialed Josh's employer, Aspen Distribution, a trucking and shipping firm where he did computer programming. They said that Josh hadn't shown up for work. When no one answered the front door of their house, she phoned the name listed as Josh and Susan's emergency contact, his sister, Jennifer Graves.

"Hi Jennifer, this is Debbie Caldwell, Josh and Susan's day-care person," she said when she got Jennifer's voice mail. "It's nine o'clock. I'm at Josh and Susan's house. No one is home, and they didn't drop Charlie and Braden off this morning. Do you know what's going on?"

A few minutes later, Josh's mother, Terrica (Terri) Powell, heard the message. A quiet woman who never really got back on her feet after the divorce from her husband Steve, she lived with her daughter Jennifer, her son-in-law Kirk Graves, and the couple's five children fifteen minutes south in West Jordan, Utah.

Terri conferred with Jennifer and they went over to the house. Finding it locked up tightly they tried both Josh's and Susan's cell phones, which went to voice mail. Then Terri phoned the West Valley City police to report the family missing.

The Powell residence looked like hundreds of others in West Valley City; maybe thousands. It was a white tract home with blue trim and blue shutters, and some stonework in the front. There was a tiny porch, a bay window, and a two-car garage. In the front yard was a wooden swing Josh had built for their two little boys. In back was playground equipment a neighbor had lent the family and a dormant vegetable garden. The garden wasn't a mere hobby for Susan, it was a necessity. Occasionally its produce was the only thing Josh allowed his family to eat. Susan sometimes called friends to ask if she could borrow some hot dogs.

"The boys are hungry," she'd say.

Within minutes of Debbie's call of concern, Josh's sister Jennifer met the police at the Powell house. The police logged it as a "welfare check" call. Jennifer, a soft-spoken woman with long, brown hair and her father's blue eyes, was shaken. There was fresh snow on the driveway and the steps to the door. After accounting for Debbie's tracks, it was clear that no one had been in or out of the house for at least several hours. When police knocked and got no answer, she gave them permission to break a window. They all braced themselves. Salt Lake City had just had several deaths attributed to carbon monoxide poisoning caused by faulty furnaces and that was on their minds as they entered the house. There was loud music blaring from a stereo and two box fans were angled to blow air on a damp spot on the carpet and a love seat near the front window.

At first there was a sense of relief: Josh and Susan and the boys were *not* dead in their beds. But something was wrong. *They weren't home at all. Where were they?*

Jennifer went into the master bedroom. Despite the clutter, she noticed Susan's blue leather purse on a table by the foot of the bed. It contained her wallet, credit cards, and keys. There was no cell phone. The house was messy, but that was normal. There was no sign of forced entry or a robbery, home invasion, or struggle. Susan's red nylon snow boots, which she wore whenever she left the house, were in the living room.

West Valley City police issued a statewide attempt-to-locate bulletin so that law enforcement in other jurisdictions would be on the lookout for the Powells' 2005 light blue Chrysler Town & Country minivan. The police sent Jennifer home so they could search the house.

Jennifer called Susan's father, Chuck Cox, in Puyallup, Washington, nine hundred miles to the northwest, to ask if he had heard from Susan or Josh. He hadn't, but he wasn't alarmed. Josh was known to make impulsive, last-minute decisions and the family liked to go rock hunting or camping. Yet, Chuck agreed it was odd that neither Susan nor Josh had called their places of employment or day-care provider to say that they'd be away.

Jennifer phoned her father's house, also in Puyallup, and talked to her younger sister, Alina. Jennifer believed that Susan had moved to get away from her father, Steve, because Susan said he had made sexual advances toward her. In the background, Jennifer could hear her father talking while she asked Alina if they had heard from Josh and Susan. Alina asked everyone in the house, but no one had heard from Josh or Susan.

Jennifer called Kiirsi Hellewell, Susan's best friend, who lived down the street from the Powells. Kiirsi hadn't talked to Susan since Sunday, when they had walked home from church together.

"Susan didn't say they were going anywhere," Kiirsi told Jennifer.

Kiirsi then phoned the Relief Society president—the head of their ward's women's group—and the two of them joined Jennifer at the Powell house and talked to the police.

"I was still thinking at that time that maybe they went for a drive because Susan had posted on her Facebook page that they had gone to a work party on Saturday night and Josh had won a camera," Kiirsi remembered some time later. "I thought, 'Well, it would be just like them to drive up in the mountains and take pictures.'" Then she began to imagine a different kind of threat than the carbon monoxide poisoning Jennifer and the police had feared. "Maybe they slid off a cliff and they're all dead at the bottom of it or stuck on some back road. Because knowing Josh, he'd drive on some back road in fresh snow."

Word spread among friends and church members that the Powell family was missing. In the early afternoon Kiirsi sent a text message to JoVonna Owings, who knew Susan from the church choir.

Susan, Josh and the boys are missing. We don't know where they are. They haven't been seen since church.

* * *

But JoVonna Owings *had* seen the family. She'd been with them Sunday afternoon and would be critical to piecing together Susan's last hours.

If our lives can be read in our faces, JoVonna's said she had lived a tough life. Although she was about the same age as Susan's mother, JoVonna was thin and wizened and appeared older. She had a huge heart and wore big glasses that nearly gobbled her face. After church on Sunday she had helped Susan with some crocheting and had supper with the family. Josh had even cooked—an unheard-of event. JoVonna was the last person to have contact with Josh and Susan on Sunday—and would be the first to have contact with Josh on Monday.

At about 3:00 P.M. on Monday JoVonna phoned Josh. There was no answer. Her son Alex, who occasionally babysat for Charlie and Braden, punched in Josh's number on his phone. Josh answered, but Alex panicked and hung up without speaking. JoVonna grabbed her son's phone and redialed. He answered again.

"Josh, where are you?" JoVonna asked. "What are you doing? The police are looking for you."

Josh, who could be an absolute motor mouth, was silent for a moment.

"We're driving around."

JoVonna felt her heart race. "Where's Susan?"

Josh paused a beat. "She's at work." He went on to stammer out that he and the boys had gone camping overnight without Susan.

JoVonna was frustrated. "No, she's not at work. We're really worried, Josh. You didn't go to work."

"I got confused," he said. "I thought it was Sunday."

JoVonna felt he was lying and pressed him.

"No, you didn't," she said. "You knew it was Monday. Don't you tell me that. You need to get home, Josh, right now."

Immediately after getting off the phone with JoVonna, Josh checked his voice mail. Two minutes later he left Susan a message on her phone, which was on the seat beside him.

For the next two hours he answered no calls and drove nearly twenty miles around West Valley City, stalling. He washed his van at a do-it-yourself place where he could soap and scrub the car over and over, far more thoroughly than a drive-through car wash would.

At 5:27 P.M. Jennifer tried to call Josh but got no answer.

At 5:36 P.M. Josh left Susan a message on her phone—still on the seat beside him.

At 5:43 P.M. Josh called Susan's phone again to say he was in the parking lot of the Wells Fargo building where she worked and asked if she needed a ride home.

At 5:48 P.M. Jennifer finally heard from her brother. She was home, talking to Chuck Cox at the moment, and she told him to listen in and stay quiet while she put the call on speaker.

"Where are you, Josh?" she asked.

"I'm at work," he said.

"You're lying," she said, knowing he hadn't gone to work. "Where are the boys?"

"They're safe," he said.

"Where's Susan?" Jennifer continued.

"I don't know. Work, I guess."

"No, Josh," Jennifer said. "We know that's not true."

"How much do you know?" Josh asked.

Now she felt real fear.

"Why would you ask that? Josh, what have you done? What did you do to her?" Jennifer asked.

Josh hung up.

Just then Chuck, whose job with the FAA had taught him to question much of what he saw and heard, went into full-on investigative mode.

"Write down whatever you heard," he said to Jennifer. "I'll write down what I heard, and we'll have our notes because we have to document this."

Jennifer drove back to Josh's house in West Valley City, hoping to confront him as soon as he arrived.

Chuck immediately started to log notes about what he had

overheard. He thought Josh's end of the conversation was peculiar.

The boys were safe? What kind of answer was that to where he'd been?

Chuck and Judy Cox, parents of four daughters, grandparents of nine children, married thirty-five years and no fans of Josh or his father Steve, were alarmed. Something bad had happened.

Maybe Josh and Susan had a fight, he hurt her accidentally, Chuck thought. *Maybe he stashed her somewhere and someone is going to find her. She'll come home and we'll deal with it then.*

As soon as Jennifer arrived at the house and told West Valley City Police Department Detective Ellis Maxwell of her conversation with Josh, he borrowed her phone and called Josh, and when Josh answered, Maxwell told him to come home. Josh said that he needed to stop and get his children something to eat first.

At 6:40 P.M. Josh finally pulled his minivan into the driveway. The police kept father and sons in the vehicle while they questioned him. Josh said he and Charlie and Braden had left just after midnight to go camping and Susan was in bed. He had no idea where she might be now. He repeated that he had been confused and thought it was Sunday. Once he realized it was Monday, he hadn't called his employer because he was afraid he would lose his job if he admitted he had mixed up the days.

When asked why he hadn't answered his cell phone during the day, Josh said he had kept it off to preserve the battery. He said he didn't have a cell charger. Plus they were out in the desert where there was no service. Detective Maxwell, a solidly built man with a dark crew cut, mustache, and ruddy complexion, had fifteen years on the force but this would be the most complicated and trying case of his career. Maxwell leaned through the window of the minivan and saw one phone on the center consul plugged into a charger. He also noted a second cell phone—later determined to be Susan's—in the van. Josh didn't have an answer as to why his wife's phone was in the car.

Jennifer called Chuck to tell him that Josh and the boys had returned from a "late night camping trip." And, Jennifer told Chuck, Josh didn't know where Susan was.

After being trapped by the police in his driveway, Josh followed Detective Maxwell to the West Valley City Police Department to tell his story once more. The police wanted Charlie and Braden to come to the station, too.

The recorded interview began at 7:15 P.M. with Detective Maxwell, Josh, Charlie, and Braden in a room. During the two-hour interview, Braden and Charlie can be heard in the background wanting a soda, which Josh forbids. Finally, a victim advocate takes the boys out of the room to watch them and keep them occupied.

Asked to relate the events of Sunday, a nervous Josh couldn't remember what Susan was wearing, and explained again how she had been tired and had laid down. Later she had gotten out of bed and they had hot dogs and watched *The Santa Clause 2*. Or maybe it was *The Santa Clause 3*. Braden had fallen asleep, so Josh took just Charlie sledding at a park near Whittier Elementary School, although in one version of his story both boys went sledding. When they got home, Susan was watching TV. Josh read the boys a story, then he began to clean the couch with his new Rug Doctor, a vacuum cleaning system he had spent several hundred dollars on a couple of weeks before.

Then Josh had decided to take the boys camping. Susan didn't want to go. He'd "gotten a late start" and left after midnight. Despite the warnings of cold, snow, and ice, Josh said he, Charlie, and Braden had gone to Simpson Springs, about two hours southwest of Salt Lake City, elevation 5,100 feet. They had slept in the car, tried out a new electric generator for heat, and taken firewood with them so they could make s'mores. They made them, but without the chocolate. He'd forgotten that ingredient.

Ellis Maxwell: So where do you think she's at?

Josh Powell: I don't know.

EM: Has she ever done anything like this before?

JP: No, not missing work.

EM: Has she ever left like this, left you and abandoned the kids?

JP: I mean, you know for, for the day but not, not when it's a work day.

EM: Um, huh, okay . . . why would you, why did you miss work?

JP: Um . . . Somehow I was thinking I didn't go to church therefore tomorrow would be Sunday and therefore I didn't find at that time I realized it, I was already stuck in a snowstorm so . . .

Detective Maxwell is alternatingly friendly and incredulous of Josh's story.

EM: Did you guys have any arguments, any fighting the day before, the night before?

JP: No . . .

EM: Explain your relationship to me, then?

JP: Really, um . . .

EM: Explain to me how . . . what about your guys' relationship . . . what it consists of and stuff like that.

JP: I mean, you know it's pretty good. I mean, we sometimes have disagreements but . . .

EM: Yeah, everybody has disagreements, right?

JP: I think so.

EM: So nothing.

JP: It's not like, it's not like we get into screaming fights or anything.

EM: Yeah.

JP: Well, not usually . . . it's happened a couple of times.

EM: Yeah.

JP: But you know it's very, very rare. . . .

EM: Do you think she's in danger right now, do you think she's hurt?

JP: Don't know . . . I don't think she would do that.

EM: You don't think she'd do what?

JP: I don't think she would miss work.

Maxwell, who more than once mistakenly refers to Susan as "Sarah," tries to get Josh to tell him who Susan's friends are. But Josh can't seem to think of anybody.

EM: Let me tell ya something. You're, I mean, you're kind of being helpful but you're not helpful, 'cause I mean I've been married and I know who . . . I can tell you who my wife's closest friends are.

JP: Ah, she talked to . . .

EM: You know what I'm saying? And I actually know who her closest friends are and you're telling me that you can't tell me.

JP: Okay, she talks to [redacted] a lot.

Maxwell asks Josh more pointedly if he is worried about Susan. For years to come, the West Valley City police would say that Josh never acted concerned about Susan, didn't ask about the investigation into her disappearance, and never helped look for her.

EM: . . . If you last seen her at midnight that's the last time you've seen her, um, nobody else has seen her or talked to her since, so she's basically been missing for about twenty hours.

JP: Okay.

EM: So where would you think she would be at? Does that concern you at all? I mean, just 'cause . . .

JP: It, it does.

EM: It does concern you?

JP: Yes.

EM: Okay, so help me try to figure out. I don't live with

you. I don't live with her, okay. You guys have been to-
gether for what, seven years?
JP: Um . . . it seems like maybe eight.
EM: Okay, eight years. You know her a hell of a lot bet-
ter than I do. First we're taking a report at ten o'clock
[in the morning].
JP: Well, I think she would go to work.
EM: All right, but she didn't go to work, dude!

Josh was like a broken record. No doubt he'd been taken
by surprise that he, Charlie, Braden, and Susan were discovered to be missing early that morning by Debbie Caldwell.
He probably planned to arrive home before anyone knew he
was gone, maybe dispose of Susan's purse to make it look like
she had left voluntarily, and later he would report her missing. He would have time to come up with a story. He'd lost
that advantage.

EM: What do you think? I mean we've talked quite a
bit. What are you thinking? You thinking, where do
you think she's . . . you think she's at a friend's house,
think she's okay?
JP: I don't even know what to think . . .
EM: Hum, I don't know either . . . you didn't take her
out to Pony Express with you guys?
JP: No.

Josh finally signed a consent form authorizing a search of
his van. In the vehicle they found the electric generator, blan-
kets, a gas can, tarps, and a shovel. They also recovered a
circular saw, a humidifier, at least two knives, a tripod, a
newly opened box of latex gloves, and a rake, but did not disclose the existence of those items for more than three years.

Except for the generator, there was no camping equipment.
No sleeping bags, no provisions such as diapers or food—
except for a few snacks—for a father taking his two young
sons camping in a snowstorm.

At 9:00 P.M. on December 7, twenty-eight hours after

JoVonna Owings last saw Susan, the police let Josh and the boys leave the police department, take the minivan, and return to the house on W. Sarah Circle. When he arrived home Josh backed the van up to the garage door. Neighbors reported that he spent all night and early the next morning cleaning the vehicle and made dozens of trips from the van to the garage.

Down the street from the Powells', Kiirsi Hellewell sat at her computer in a downstairs playroom filled with crafts and toys that shouted to the world she was a mother—and a busy one at that. Surrounded by her children's photos, she went onto Facebook to see what, if anything, anyone had reported about the Powells.

Nothing.

Something did come, however, a little later that evening in the form of a phone call. It made her heart beat faster, her stomach turn somersaults.

"Josh is back," a neighbor said.

"Are they okay? Are they okay?"

There was an uneasy pause.

"Susan is not with them," the neighbor said.

Kiirsi felt a horrible, heart-sinking dread take over.

"Oh no," she said, her voice shaking. "What has he done?"

It was a question that would be asked over and over for years.

Far away in Puyallup, Washington, framed photographs of Salt Lake City's Temple Square adorned the Coxes' split-level house, panoramic reminders of their faith. On Monday night, Susan's parents, in addition to keeping in touch with Jennifer Graves, were also working the phones and the Internet. They knew that Josh had returned home with the boys, but had no idea of Susan's whereabouts. The police told Chuck that they weren't sure if a crime had been committed. If he thought the worst, even in that moment, Chuck didn't tell Judy.

Susan's father had faith that things would be all right. His daughter would be found safe and sound. He promised Judy. He believed it. He prayed for it.

Three miles southeast of the Coxes' home, in Steve Powell's two-story house in a modest, gated community called Country Hollow, Josh's father, his youngest sister Alina, middle brother Johnny, and youngest brother Mike, must have heard about the call that morning from their oldest sibling, Jennifer. How they reacted is unknown. Maybe they weren't concerned at all? Josh, it was true, could be impulsive and disorganized. It was part of who he was. He'd always been the kind of person who would come up with some grand scheme and then try to conjure a way to make it work—even though his track record was less than stellar.

Upstairs in thirty-year-old Johnny Powell's bedroom, a carefully coiled rope noose hung on the wall along with disturbing renderings of a woman with a knife running through her vagina and exiting her stomach. Johnny, whom his father and sister Alina considered an artist, had a history of mental troubles.

That wasn't all that was upstairs. In Steve's bedroom down the hall from Johnny's was part of a cache of more than a dozen computers. Inside those computers, and also in scores of notebooks and stacks of homemade music CDs, was incontrovertible documentation of an obsession the likes of which had seldom been seen by even the most experienced police investigator. In image after image, in song after song, diary entries that went on for reams of pages at a time, was the object of Steve's obsession: a blue-eyed beauty, now the missing mother of two, Susan Cox Powell.

Moments after logging Josh's and Susan's cell phones into evidence, investigators discovered that both phones were missing the SIM cards—the data recorder of calls made and received.

If Josh Powell had thought he could thwart the detectives and the investigation with this obvious deception, he was wrong. It would take some effort to gather billing records from the service providers, but it could be done.

Evasive?

Lying?

Unconcerned about his wife's fate?

Josh Powell didn't know it, but he'd just nailed the trifecta, the traits of those who kill their spouses. It was so obvious.

But apparently it was not obvious to the West Valley City police.

That night, Jennifer Graves woke up in a panic. The phone was ringing. She knew it was Susan. Jennifer groped wildly for the phone by the bed, struggling to get to it in time to talk to Susan, find out where she was, and get her home. As she became more awake, Jennifer realized that the phone hadn't rung. It was a dream.

She stayed up for hours, reliving the vivid scene over and over and wondering what her brother had done to his wife.

2

He will go to counseling for himself and/or meds to deal with his mental issues and if he refuses I will not ruin mine and my boys' lives further and we will divorce and I hope it's not as ugly as he claims it will be when we've talked about it in the past.
—SUSAN POWELL IN E-MAIL, JULY 11, 2008

Life in any home is a crazy quilt and sometimes the edges are frayed. The Coxes had experienced their ups and downs like any family. Long before husbands and children, the Cox girls tried their parents' patience as teens often do. There was some sneaking around. There were alliances and feuds. There were the cover stories that sisters sometimes tell for one another. Susan and her sister Denise were especially tight. Susan, though younger, stuck up for Denise, who was the "wild" one of the Cox girls. When Denise found herself unmarried and pregnant at eighteen, her parents and her other sisters were anything but happy about it. Susan took a different tack.

"I'm going to be an aunt!" she said. "I'm so happy and excited, Denise!"

Susan's move to Utah and the troubles in her own life had put distance between the once very, very close sisters. But still, when Denise heard that Susan was missing, she felt a surge of uneasiness. Susan was fun, but responsible. She would never run off and leave her kids. Denise recalled her last conversation with Susan the month before. It was small talk mostly. Later Denise would sit in a chair in her Bonney Lake, Washington, home and try to piece together all that had been said. Try as she might, she came up with nothing, except regrets.

She wished that she'd called her sister more often, that she had probed deeper into what was going on. Denise herself had been in an abusive relationship. She knew that it took a great deal of strength—and often the helping hand of another—to get out.

But by the time Susan and Josh had settled into married life in Utah, the pattern had been established. Talking on the phone with Susan often felt empty, one-sided. It wasn't that Susan wasn't an outgoing person with lots of news to share, but she didn't. It was all surface conversation.

Denise knew the reason. Josh was always hovering nearby, listening to every word, making sure that his wife painted the picture of their lives that he wanted to believe was true.

That they were normal, happy, and safe.

When Denise heard that Josh and the boys had gone camping in the middle of the night, she gave her head a quick shake.

Who does that? Where is my sister?

She remembered a letter Susan had written to her in 2007, saying that she was afraid Josh would kill her before he agreed to a divorce.

Susan's Utah friends said she would never have permitted camping in winter. A trip in the fall when it wasn't nearly as frigid had been a dismal failure: the boys were cold and hungry and crying to go home, forcing Josh to cut the trip short. Susan, who had stayed home, didn't say "I told you so."

While camping in the middle of the night in record cold temperatures sounds unlikely at best, Chuck Cox was not surprised when he heard about the trip. Susan's father knew

Josh had a tendency to lose track of time and act on the spur of the moment. In the immediate days after Susan disappeared, Chuck called Josh "a super father" to the boys and said there was no doubt in his mind that they were safe with him. Chuck had helped the family financially when one or the other of them was unemployed. As far as he knew, the couple had worked through their problems. A family friend said there was no indication that the marriage had ever been abusive.

If Josh could play a game, denying any knowledge of what had happened to Susan, so could Chuck. When Chuck called Josh "a super father," he was doing so to try and keep the lines of communication open with Josh. He didn't really believe it.

On Tuesday, December 8, 2009, two days after Susan was last seen, Chuck finally received a phone call from Josh. His son-in-law's voice was soft and he seemed upset. He said that Susan was missing and that he didn't have any idea what happened to her. He made no mention of the Sunday dinner he had fixed or the late-night camping trip.

Chuck looked at the time. It was 12:30 P.M. He knew that Josh was late for a meeting with the police, but purposely did not ask him any questions. If he did, he might tip Josh off to what the police were sure to ask. If Josh had done something to Susan, then it would be a mistake to give him a chance to come up with a lie. Chuck began to feel a sense of dread.

What had Josh been doing all morning? Why hadn't he gone down to the police station first thing, like any other husband would have?

For his part, Josh didn't know that his father-in-law had been on the phone with Jennifer the day before when he tested his excuses on her.

After the call ended, Chuck took a couple of calls from reporters inquiring about the circumstances in Utah. He had no idea at the time, but over the course of the next couple of years, he would be on every major network and in newspapers around the world. And no matter the airwaves or the newspapers, his message would always be the same: "Where is my daughter? Where is Susan?"

Josh stalled his second interview with the police. Jennifer and their mother arrived at the house. The boys hadn't eaten. Josh kept going back and forth from the garage and putting items in the washing machine. Jennifer offered to help him, and vacuumed up the broken glass from the window. She tried to see what he was up to in the garage. She saw a sled with a pile of things on it, including cheap work gloves. Later, she asked herself, "Did he pull her body somewhere on the sled to get rid of her?"

After hours of delaying—his call to Chuck, his clean-up, reminder calls from the police, and his mother and sister nagging him—Josh finally arrived at the West Valley City Police Department, four hours late for his appointment.

While Detective Maxwell talked to Josh, other officers with search warrants arrived at the house and sent the two women away with Charlie and Braden. They went to Jennifer's house in West Jordan, and later to a children's center where child advocates talked to Charlie and Braden. It would be days before Jennifer saw or heard from her brother again.

Police removed boxes of potential evidence, including computers and a large piece of the carpet where the box fans had been aimed. They loaded a rocking chair and Susan's love seat—where Susan and JoVonna had sat and crocheted on Sunday—into a truck to take to a lab for testing. They bagged a pancake found in the kitchen garbage and dirty rags in the bathtub. They took dozens of photographs: Susan's purse, still waiting for her on a table in the bedroom; the pancake on a yellow plate; an artificial Christmas tree in the living room; the wooden entertainment center Josh had built; the orange and yellow yarn Susan had been making into a blanket for Braden; and a bag of oranges on a kitchen counter just waiting for a mother to hand out to her young children. A photo of the refrigerator shows family pictures; a note reminding someone to make lasagna on Thursday; and seven magnets with Josh's photo on them, reminders of his failed career in real estate.

They also took photos of drops of blood on the tile near the front door.

The police photographs told the story of the young Powells' lives: a child's potty seat in the bathroom; Susan's beauty salon chair in the basement, waiting for the day she could open her own business; some of the Mary Kay products Susan sold when Josh let her invest in supplies; Josh's parrot in a cage; and gaping holes in the bathroom walls where Josh had intended to install shelves—just one of his many unfinished projects around the house.

Like the evening before, Josh sat slumped in a corner of the windowless room at the WVCPD, as far as possible from Detective Maxwell, who was again questioning him. This time Josh was alone—Charlie and Braden wouldn't be running in and out because they were with his mother and Jennifer. Josh never took off his jacket or the stocking cap on his head. He looked and acted cornered and lethargic and took long pauses before answering questions.

Josh was upset, but it wasn't about his missing wife. Again and again during his second interview with the police Josh returned to the fact that they had broken a window in his house the day before—the day the entire family was missing and who knew what terrible tragedy had befallen them.

Several times Josh lamented the broken window. It was unnecessary, he said, because the day-care provider, Debbie Caldwell, had a key. Josh was also mad because he hadn't known until the day before that Susan had given Debbie a key, just in case. He didn't care that Debbie wasn't at the house when Jennifer Graves and the police arrived and were trying to find a way in.

As with the prior interview, when he was fixated on telling the police over and over that Susan would never miss work, he was obsessed now with the broken window—and photos the police took of his hands.

On Monday night his hands were red and chapped and there was a cut on one knuckle when the police photographed them. On Tuesday, he brought it up with Detective Maxwell.

EM: I [already] took photos (inaudible) photos of your hands.

JP: Well, I thought you were implying you're, you're saying, you know, you really made a big deal out of this . . .

EM: By asking you where you got a nick on your hand?

JP: I thought you were trying to say I got some kind of defensive wounds, you know.

EM: I never said that though, did I?

JP: It seemed implied.

EM: OK, but all I did was inquire about a nick on your hand and (inaudible) kinda get, um, you know, I mean you've been worried about that ever since we got here today. You want me to take photos again of your hands?

JP: I kinda do.

EM: OK, well . . .

JP: 'Cause . . .

EM: A what does (inaudible) . . .

JP: I want to have both photos available, you know?

EM: Well, what does it tell you? I mean, I haven't come in here with a camera. I haven't even worried about your hands but you're still worrying about . . .

JP: Well, I just want my second photos, you know, because, I was just to prove that there [sic] . . . they do it on their own.

Josh informed Detective Maxwell that he had talked to a legal aid service, which suggested he get an attorney. "They said that, I'm, you know, pretty much in over my head," Josh said. "I can't even think straight."

But there was a long list of things Josh hadn't gotten around to yet. Calling an attorney was just one of them. He hadn't talked to Susan's manager at Wells Fargo. He hadn't talked to his own employer. He hadn't talked to his sons about where their mother was. And he hadn't called the couple's friends to inquire about Susan.

EM: Did you talk to anybody last night?
JP: (inaudible).
EM: As trying to find out where she could have been? No? OK.
JP: Um, I talked to my dad and my family.
EM: Last night?
JP: Yeah.
EM: Why? Did he have any help?
JP: Um, I think, you know, I, they just updated me the same things as other people did.
EM: OK. All right. Um. Have you called any other places where she could be? I mean, have you checked any places where she could be?
JP: I haven't had much of a chance to do any of that yet.

Josh apparently hadn't done one thing to try and find his wife—he'd been busy cleaning the van.

Josh did suggest that Kiirsi might be hiding Susan at her home. Police followed up by phoning Kiirsi about it, a phone interview that left her stunned by the suggestion.

Josh had no explanation for why Susan had left without her purse and keys, or how she might have made it to work—since Josh had the family's sole vehicle.

EM: OK. Why would she leave her . . . any thought on why she would leave behind her purse?
JP: Well, she doesn't always take her purse 'cause its bulky, you know?
EM: Women go everywhere with their purses. That's where their hair spray . . .
JP: She . . .
EM: . . . and their makeup and their money . . .
JP: She doesn't always take it.
EM: OK.
JP: I mean . . .

EM: What are some examples of some times when she wouldn't take her purse?

JP: I don't think she took it to that party. I don't think she takes it to church. You know, most of the time if she doesn't . . . you know, she's just going somewhere . . .

The detective asked Josh about the wet spot on the rug and the two fans that he'd left running in the living room. Josh explained Susan had asked him Sunday night to do the cleaning.

EM: OK. So when, um, so when you cleaned the couch? And she wanted you to . . . what, was the couch dirty? Was there a stain on the couch or something?

JP: It's just all goobers and stuff from kids who wipe their noses on it and . . .

EM: OK.

JP: They just, they just do brutal things to the furniture. Like the other couch needs it, too.

EM: OK. And when you talk to, um, Susan about taking the kids and doing s'mores and generator, tell me more details on that conversation.

JP: She just, you know, I told her that I wanted to and she just said (inaudible) heater . . . you can't take the boys out in the cold without a heater. I'm like, yep, I got my generator.

EM: Um-huh, K, and that was it?

JP: That's basically . . . I mean, it wasn't a long conversation.

EM: She didn't inquire as to when you'd be back, when you were going? Where you were going?

JP: I told her, I told her I'd be back. I said I'll come back tomorrow morning.

EM: Um-huh, OK.

JP: And then with the snowfall it . . . I got up a little later in the morning.

The detective asks Josh if Susan had ever been suicidal or depressed.

JP: She was suicidal.
EM: She was?
JP: Yeah.
EM: When's that?
JP: Well, I thought that was over.

Josh admits he was partly to blame for Susan's moodiness.

JP:. . . I don't always do everything that she wants and, you know, for a while we were not affectionate, you know.
EM: Um-huh.
JP: I guess that was depressing and I don't know if maybe she was upset about work or something but I don't know it all. I mean, like I say, we didn't do a whole lot of talking about it and I thought she was over it, you know . . . sometimes she thinks I'm lazy or something, you know?
EM: Caused her to be sad? Are you saying that you caused her to be sad?
JP: Um, I don't know.

As far as Josh having Susan's phone in the van, he said he had been looking up a number on it Sunday and accidentally put it in his pocket.

Ever the cheapskate, when Josh was offered a soft drink during the interview, he said he'd like to take it home to his boys. But Detective Maxwell didn't have any cash and his inability to buy a soda for Josh prompted a discussion between the two about outrageous prices and the merits of bottles versus cans.

Josh stood up to leave and said he would like a "couple of days to think about answering questions." Maxwell reminded him his wife was missing *now*.

Maxwell told Josh that he wasn't going to cuff him and take him to jail, but then after explaining that he wanted to continue the interview but had to follow procedure, Maxwell read Josh his Miranda rights, because "that lets me know that you understand that we're just having a conversation here and you are free to go at any time."

At the same time at the South Valley Children's Justice Center a West Valley police detective named Kim Waelty had questioned Charlie.

> **KW:** Okay, Charlie, when we talk today it's really important that we talk about things that are true, okay?
> **CP:** Okay.
> **KW:** Okay, and if I ask you a question, Charlie, and you don't know the answer, it's okay to say I don't know, okay?
> **CP:** Okay.
> **KW:** Okay, well what did you do Sunday night?
> **CP:** Um . . .
> **KW:** Before you went to bed?
> **CP:** Go camping.
> **KW:** You went camping? Tell me about camping.
> **CP:** Camping is where we have s'mores.
> **KW:** Who were you camping with?
> **CP:** Um, my dad and my mom and my little brother.
> **KW:** So you went camping with your mom, your dad, your little brother, and you had s'mores?
> **CP:** Ya.

Although Charlie seemed to understand telling the truth, there were some fanciful elements to his story.

> **KW:** Okay, how did you guys get to where you were camping?
> **CP:** Um, we got in the airplane and the airplane went to Dinosaur National Park.
> **KW:** Oh you went in an airplane yesterday?
> **CP:** Ya, and our airplane brings us to Dinosaur National Park.

In the past, Josh had probably taken his boys to visit Dinosaur National Monument, 250 miles east of Salt Lake City. It's nowhere near Simpson Springs, where Josh said they had camped. Although Josh hadn't talked to his boys about where their mother was, he had told them he was talking to the police and even managed to blame the Coxes.

KW: Okay. So Charlie, have you talked to your mommy today?

CP: Nope.

KW: Where's Mommy at?

CP: Um, at work.

KW: Mommy's at work?

CP: Ya, and my dad is seeing the police.

KW: Your dad is?

CP: Ya.

KW: How do you know?

CP: Um . . . we had a broken window. That's why he see the police . . . two times.

KW: How'd your window get broken?

CP: Um, my grandma and grandpa throwed a rock at our window . . . at our window.

KW: Charlie, when you guys came home from camping, who came home with you?

CP: My dad.

KW: And?

CP: And my mom stayed at Dinosaur National Park.

KW: Your mom stayed there?

CP: Ya.

KW: Do you know where at the park?

CP: No, she . . . my mom stayed where the crystals are.

KW: How come Mommy stayed?

CP: 'Cause it had so much pretty . . .'cause it has so much pretty where the crystals grow.

Detective Maxwell returned to the room where Josh waited.

EM: Um. I just spoke with some of our other detectives, um, and you're gonna have to wait here with us. You're not gonna go anywhere. Um, one of our detectives just interviewed your children and your children are telling our detectives that Mom went with you guys and that she didn't come back.

JP: She did not go with us . . .

EM: K, well, with that, just getting that information, you're not gonna go anywhere. I'm not gonna let you leave. I'm gonna detain you. You sit right here. If you want a lawyer and you want to talk, or you want to change your mind and talk, or take a CVSA [Computer Voice Stress Analyzer] test, um, then we can do those things, but . . .

JP: They know that she didn't go with us.

Another police officer, Detective Tony Martell, who is identified as CM in the transcript—and who seems to play the bad cop to Maxwell's good cop—joins Maxwell and Josh.

CM: Well, here's the thing. Kids, kids are very honest. That's one thing I've learned in the years of doing this job. That when kids talk to us we listen because there [sic] honest and they they, they, they never lie. They don't make things up. So there [sic] sayin' they were with you, they were with you, OK? So that means she was with you. So I have to believe the kids. So now it's gonna be up to you if you want to help us find her and help us get to the bottom of what really happened here. That's what we're here for, K? We're gonna find out either way, with your help or without your help.

But within just a few minutes, the police said Josh could leave if he wanted to. So he did. He couldn't have his phone—the police had it. He couldn't go home—search warrants prevented that. He couldn't have his van back—there was a search warrant for that, too.

He simply stood up and walked out.

At a news conference, police captain Tom McLachlan faced the television cameras and said it was too early in the investigation to presume that a crime had occurred.

"Could it be that she has taken off on her own? It possibly could," he told reporters. "Could it be something else? It possibly could. We just don't have enough to nail it down one way or the other." McLachlan said that it was still officially a missing-person case, but that it had become suspicious.

They described their meeting with Josh as "not very productive," and said that he seemed unconcerned about Susan's welfare.

3

... that night we had a huge hour long yelling fight (amazed that my voice still works) I even had to threaten calling the police b/c he was being so irrational and unpredictable. I told him he needs to change, counseling or something.

—SUSAN POWELL E-MAIL, JUNE 30, 2008

At fifty-four, JoVonna Owings was two decades older than most of Susan's friends. Mother of seven and stepmother to four, JoVonna had lived in Utah since 1979 but had moved recently to West Valley City to be closer to her daughter. JoVonna and Susan were sopranos and sat next to each other in the church choir. They became immediate friends.

"She had a wonderful voice. Really angelic, just beautiful," JoVonna said later. "So we were starting to find a lot of things we had in common. And I thought, 'This is really cool! I've got a friend and she is right around the block from me. This is going to be so neat!' I was looking forward to the future and doing stuff together."

A shared love of music, their faith, and Mary Higgins Clark novels cemented a deepening bond.

JoVonna, in fact, had seen more of Susan during the previous two weeks than anyone else had. Susan and Josh seemed to have exhausted their other friends with their never-ending neediness—child care, rides, money, food. Emergencies created by Josh. Teenagers in the church who used to babysit complained that Josh was "creepy" and paid them a measly two dollars an hour.

JoVonna didn't meet Josh until the Tuesday of Thanksgiving week, thirteen days before Susan disappeared.

"It was her day off, the boys were at a sitter, and Josh had the van," she said later. "She was supposed to pick the boys up at six o'clock because her sitter [Debbie Caldwell] had a training class. He wasn't home and she couldn't get ahold of him. So she came to my house and I took her to pick her boys up. And then we came back and I stayed for a while."

JoVonna had heard that Josh was unpredictable and argumentative. She knew that Susan was alone in her semi-tolerance of her husband. Most of their friends rolled their eyes at Josh's antics. JoVonna was curious about him.

He didn't disappoint. Immediately upon arrival at the house, he took over, bragging about his remote-controlled cars, his computers, his TV.

"And he started in telling me all about one thing and the other and how he had this remote control and that remote control and he was showing me all this, and I was very nice. I said, 'Cool, okay, thanks, Josh,' but I was thinking: he's just like a five-year-old. Does he ever run down? The Eveready Bunny! It was as if maybe nobody ever pays attention to him. How did I know? And he went on and on and on."

After his extended toy demonstration, Josh suddenly became argumentative with Susan about plans for Thanksgiving. They were going to spend the day with some of Josh's relatives near Ogden, about an hour's drive away. The hostess had asked Susan to bake six pumpkin pies.

"I don't know why you can't just take one," said Josh, a notorious penny-pincher.

While JoVonna looked on, Susan shrugged it off a little. "Because that's what I was assigned to take."

Josh's winter pale complexion suddenly reddened.

"There are only four of us, so you shouldn't have to take six pies!" he shouted.

Susan didn't flinch. She simply pushed back. "Well, everybody else is taking enough of whatever they're bringing for everyone so I'll be making six pies."

JoVonna kept her mouth shut and took it all in. Every couple had disagreements, but Josh was acting like a big baby, as though making extra pies was somehow unfair.

It didn't take one of Mary Higgins Clark's detectives to figure it out. JoVonna put two and two together. JoVonna had lived with controlling husbands, and she knew one when she saw one.

Another time while visiting, JoVonna offered to give Susan a ride whenever she needed one and asked how to contact her. Sitting in view of the home telephone, JoVonna asked for the number.

Susan stiffened and shook her head. "No, that goes directly to Josh's business. You can't use that phone," she said, adding that it was something about charges on the line.

Susan concluded the discussion of the "Josh rule" by giving out her cell number. JoVonna thought it was all weird, but wrote down the cell number, unaware that it was Susan's father, Chuck, who had provided the phone—just in case Susan needed help, fast.

That week Susan had confided to JoVonna that she thought she had been pregnant and miscarried. She shared the news with Debbie, too. On November 24, Susan had received an angry e-mail from Debbie Caldwell, who was furious that Josh had made her miss her CPR class. After agreeing with Debbie that Josh had disrespected her, Susan responded in an e-mail:

Sometimes I seriously hate him. This am I got my period, so I might have been pregnant, barely and miscarried like a normal period. The dr today said 1 in 5 pregnancies miscarry and look like a normal period. I think it was a message from God to go ahead and get

*drugs! [the antibiotics] I've got a couple of hot items
to discuss for our next counseling session.*

Although Josh always discouraged Susan from visiting a
physician or taking the children to one, she had made the decision herself to wait on getting antibiotics for an ear infection, believing she was pregnant. A blood test at the doctor's
office determined that she wasn't. Susan told friends that she
had felt ill for weeks.

In the days after Thanksgiving, JoVonna would see Susan,
Josh, and the boys more than a half dozen times. Each time,
a small glimpse into their relationship emerged. It was like a
dripping faucet in the middle of the night—faint and concerning.

Something was off. JoVonna just couldn't put her finger
on it.

Josh did quite a bit of shopping Thanksgiving week. None
of it was to get a jump on the Christmas season.

On Wednesday, November 25, Josh visited Air Gas Company to ask about "steel-cutting equipment." He bought an
acetylene torch and other supplies for $383.89. The next eve-
ning, after Thanksgiving dinner and all those pies Susan had
made against his will, he went to Lowe's to ask about parts
for the metal-cutting torch and a paint sprayer. He left without making a purchase.

On Friday, he stopped by another store and bought a fifty-
foot roll of white tree wrap, described as "breathable fabric."
He ignored an employee's warning that it would not work to
repair the broken tree branch that Josh described.

He returned to Air Gas on November 30 and December 1
to pick up additional items. Employees described him as
"annoying" and said he asked questions about "technical
aspects" of the torch.

On Thursday, December 3, Susan talked to her father. It was
the kind of phone conversation between parents and children
that occurs as Christmas approaches—plans being made,

gifts to be mailed, cards to be sent. Susan seemed excited about the holidays and the things she'd be doing with Josh and her boys. Braden, almost three, was more aware that something special was coming and Charlie, soon to turn five and very active, was ready to start ripping open packages.

That evening, Susan put highlights in Debbie's hair. Susan had been a hairdresser in Washington but she wasn't licensed in Utah, so she often cut and colored the hair of friends for free. It was her way of thanking them for helping her. Josh wanted Susan to charge for her services, but she refused. Her friends usually reciprocated by bringing dinner for the Powells, often a pizza.

That's what Debbie did that Thursday. She knew to check to see what Josh wanted to eat. He alternated between passive and impulsive behavior. He had famously thrown a pot of spaghetti on the floor on an evening when he'd felt ignored.

On Saturday, December 5, the Powells joined other ward members at a church Christmas breakfast. Josh took pictures and Susan dished up plates of food from a buffet for Charlie and Braden. Josh liked to be behind the scenes, observing life through the camera lens. It was as if he could be there, in the moment, but not really be a part of it.

Susan wore a red satin blouse under a jean jacket and her favorite earrings, a dangly series of silver loops of different sizes that nearly reached her shoulders. Josh wore a black leather jacket, oatmeal-colored sweater, and jeans. Charlie gripped a candy cane. Braden rested in his mother's arms. The Powells posed with Kiirsi Hellewell's family in what would be the final photograph of a family headed toward disaster. All were smiling, all were unaware.

JoVonna and one of her sons spent the afternoon at the Powells while Susan was at work. Josh explained to police that he was showing the boy how to build things. But JoVonna knew exactly what was going on: Josh didn't want to have to babysit his own children himself.

That evening, Susan and Josh attended the trucking firm's Christmas party. JoVonna's teenage son babysat Charlie and Braden.

Josh won the raffle prize, another camera.

Everything seemed picture-perfect.

At 8:58 A.M., Sunday, December 6, Susan Cox Powell made her final Facebook posting:

> *My husband won a digital video camera called a "Flip" at his work party last night . . . what the heck good will it do for us?*

Several friends, knowing how tightly Josh controlled their spending, suggested that she regift it or, better yet, sell it on Craigslist or eBay.

After posting, Susan, Charlie, and Braden left for church at their neighborhood ward. Kiirsi, Susan, and their friends belonged to the Hunter 36th Ward of the Church of Jesus Christ of Latter-day Saints. Josh had pulled away from the church, but had recently attended once or twice. But that day was a stake conference and Josh decided to skip the meeting. Susan and her sons walked past streets with names that evoked a blissful 1950s version of family life: Patti Drive, S. Jodie Lane, and streets named Deann, Dixie, and Marsha.

After the service, Kiirsi joined Susan and her sons bound for home. Although she considered Susan to be her best friend, they hadn't had a long talk in a while. Kiirsi, a mother of three, had been contending with the drama of a sick mother and problems with her husband's employment. A resourceful woman, Kiirsi was up to the task of dealing with all that, but it left little time for her closest girlfriend.

Later, Kiirsi would get emotional, thinking of the lost connection with Susan.

"I was so caught up in the problems in my life. I'd ask her every couple of months, 'How are things going with Josh?' 'Oh, they're a little better,' she'd say, 'Maybe he's trying a little bit more.' She seemed pretty happy and her posts on Facebook seemed pretty upbeat so I didn't think things were bad."

On the walk home, Susan told Kiirsi how glad she was that

the boys were well-behaved so that she could listen to the sermon at church.

Everything—and everyone—seemed to be in a good place. Kiirsi, like JoVonna and the others in Susan's circle of friends, had no idea that in less than twelve hours Susan would vanish from the face of the earth.

Josh phoned his father, Steve, at 12:14 P.M., before Susan got home from church. Steve later told investigators that his son had asked for a pancake recipe, which he'd gladly provided.

It was the last call Josh would make for more than twenty-four hours.

4

I just hope obviously that this counseling will help
Josh and everyone else can see the guy I fell in love
with.

—SUSAN POWELL E-MAIL, JULY 29, 2008

At 2:29 P.M. on Sunday, Susan called JoVonna. She had finished crocheting a blanket for Charlie and was partway through one for Braden, when she found herself in a literal web of yarn.

"I've got the yarn horribly tangled up," she said. "Can you come and help me?"

JoVonna, who had a bit of a reputation for sorting out the most hopeless yarn tangles, happily agreed.

Before hanging up, JoVonna heard Josh in the background saying he would cook something and she could stay and eat with them.

"But I'm not making much," he added, which JoVonna took to be his way of his saying, "She can come over but her kids can't."

Fifteen minutes later, JoVonna arrived at the Powells'. Susan met her at the door, then the two women planted themselves on the love seat by the front window and proceeded to tackle the knotted yarn for more than two hours. JoVonna's goal was to unknot the orange, yellow, and turquoise strands without cutting a single piece of it.

She remarked on the color combination—not something she would select.

"Braden's favorite colors," Susan said.

JoVonna smiled at Braden; he and his brother were taking turns playing in the living room and going in and out of the kitchen, "helping" Josh make dinner—a meal of cream cheese pancakes and scrambled eggs.

There was an artificial Christmas tree in a corner, half decorated. Susan had asked Josh again and again to get the rest of the ornaments down from a high shelf in the garage. He hadn't done it yet and Susan would probably end up doing it herself. The presents her parents had mailed for Charlie and Braden were under the tree.

In a voice loud enough for her husband to hear over the din of his dinner preparation, Susan told JoVonna that she had recently been able to return to the temple. Josh was opposed to tithing, but Susan had started to keep some of the money she earned, and had resumed the practice, a requirement to enter the temple. She also said that she and Josh were having marriage counseling with an LDS Family Services counselor and had an appointment scheduled for the coming week. She was hopeful, but a little skeptical at the same time. Josh had stopped attending the sessions and wasn't reading their homework, a book on marriage by a Mormon author.

This was a pattern of Josh and Susan's that longtime friends knew *well*. JoVonna was just beginning to see it. Josh would publicly berate Susan and sometimes she would respond by being quiet or by standing up to him, as she had about the six Thanksgiving pies. She could get in her digs at Josh by making sure he overheard her complaining to friends.

"How are you feeling?" JoVonna asked. Susan had endured an ear infection for nearly three weeks, but there was something else there, too. Susan lowered her voice and talked about a miscarriage—but not so low that Josh couldn't hear her. It was also possible that Susan didn't want the children to overhear. JoVonna, who had suffered her own miscarriages, knew she would see Susan on Tuesday at a Relief Society dinner.

"I didn't want to go into it that night because I felt that this should be a private conversation where I could talk with her and not have him butt in," she recalled later. "He had a tendency to butt in."

At one point, Susan indicated that she was chilly. Josh stopped what he was doing and brought her a blanket.

No matter what she'd heard—from Susan or Susan's friends—JoVonna was charmed by the gesture.

Oh, how sweet that he would do that, she thought at the time.

Josh took forever making his special version of "breakfast for dinner"—a hit among kids in every American home, especially when a dad dons the cook's apron. It was true he had two little boys underfoot and little claim to knowing his way around a kitchen. The kitchen was small and tidy. The refrigerator was bare except for a couple of drawings Charlie had made for his mother and promotional magnets left over from Josh's brief career in real estate. Susan loved wolves, and frequently wore an old wolf T-shirt, and a wolf plaque hung on a wall. There was plenty of stopping and starting, the sound of the mixer interrupting the conversation across the living room on the floral printed love seat that Susan had saved her money to purchase. Susan let Josh struggle in the kitchen, something that JoVonna admired. A husband didn't need to cook every night, but he should be able to fill in when his wife was ill or too tired to make a meal. First the blanket, then the meal . . . Josh was really on his best behavior.

After a couple of hours of banging around in the kitchen, Josh served dinner. He put two pancakes on each plate and smothered them with canned apple pie filling. A spatula of scrambled eggs nested on top . . . and dinner was served. The women remained on the love seat to eat. Josh prepared the plates separately. He fixed one and took it to JoVonna, then returned to the kitchen to prepare Susan's. He and the boys took the three chairs at the table.

"It was nice because the last time I had been there he had to dominate the conversation. He had to be the center of everything," JoVonna said later. "When he came into a room it was all about Josh, what Josh had to say. This time it wasn't like that, and I thought, 'That's really nice.'"

Between 4:30 and 5:00 P.M. Susan said she was tired and retreated to the bedroom. JoVonna attributed Susan's fatigue to the miscarriage and recent ear infection. She stayed until about 5:30 P.M. working on the yarn. Josh busied himself cleaning the kitchen and washing the dishes. He instructed Charlie and Braden to go to the bathroom and get dressed for sledding in the freezing December air. When it became obvious that Josh and the boys were going outside, JoVonna knew it was her signal to leave.

When JoVonna left that evening the house was pristine.

Around 8:30 P.M. a neighbor saw Josh return home and pull into the garage. Three hours later, Marco Bastidas, who lived one house away from Josh and Susan's, was locking up his car when he heard an alarm sounding inside the closed garage at the Powell home. He couldn't see any lights on in the house. After listening to the alarm for at least two minutes, Marco's sister suggested he alert the neighbors. He was reluctant to bother Josh or Susan, and eventually the alarm stopped.

Another neighbor, ill in bed, later heard what sounded like a man and a woman arguing. She told the police her story, and regretted not getting up and looking out her window at the time to see who was yelling.

Was it Josh and Susan?

Sometime later, the Powells' garage door opened and the family's light blue minivan pulled out. There were no neighbors awake to see it.

5

He used to buckle me in and give me a kiss, hold
doors open, sincerely worry if I didn't put on a coat,
buy groceries and help me cook/clean and/or cook/
clean for himself. Hang out and talk together, watch
movies and relaxing tv just for entertainment. Care
and make time for being with friends/group dates etc.
GO TO CHURCH! NOT be all radical about the latest
huge world problems that all his rantings can't fix,
(although he thinks it can) But when we moved to
Utah...and then we had Charlie, his priorities
seemed to have changed.
—SUSAN POWELL E-MAIL, JULY 28, 2008

Susan Marie Cox, the third of four girls, was born on
October 16, 1981, to Chuck and Judy Cox in New Mexico,
where Chuck served as a staff sergeant working in the air
traffic control tower at Holloman Air Force Base. Those
early years had been good ones, living on the edge of the
desert with roadrunners and the occasional lizard as visitors to the backyard of the first house the family had ever
owned.

Chuck left the Air Force after six years. When it came
time to make a move, Chuck and family looked north. First,
way north to a job in Alaska. Next was a stint in Vancouver,
Washington, before the family finally settled in Puyallup, just

east of Tacoma. Chuck became an investigator for the FAA, visiting crash sites and asking questions to find out why things went wrong. There were always answers.

The Cox daughters all had their distinct personalities. As the oldest, Mary was the one who kept track of everyone and everything, a trait she would use later in life as a paralegal. Denise loved animals and called herself the black sheep of the family because she experimented with smoking and drinking and became pregnant at eighteen. Marie was the baby of the family—a role she played to her advantage. Susan, number three, was the dreamer, the girl who saw beauty in everything and everyone. All four played music and sang in the church or school choir.

Of the sisters, Denise and Susan shared a particular interest in and love of animals, especially birds. At one time, the girls had a menagerie of twenty-seven parakeets, finches, and a cockatoo in their room—much to their mother's dismay. Judy made the girls clean the cages twice a day, which Susan and Denise grudgingly did. At one time, the pair formed their own exclusive club, which they dubbed "The Bird Club."

As young teens, they dreamed of a business they could open together. It would be a combination hair salon—for people—and dog grooming business, for their customers' pets. They wanted to call it "Beauty and Your Beast."

Susan wanted to make a career out of making people beautiful. She loved to color hair and experiment with her own hairstyles—sometimes to less than desirable results. She gave her mom and her sisters pedicures whenever they wanted them—or whenever she insisted they needed a little filing and polish.

When Susan announced that she was going to beauty school neither Chuck nor Judy was surprised. Everyone had expected it. Susan had a veritable storage locker of makeup and hair supplies in her bedroom. When she started taking cosmetology classes, the back of her car was filled with smiling head models. It looked like someone had decapitated a team of cheerleaders. Years later, eldest sister Mary remembered the time she sat on a stool in the living room while Susan snipped and snipped away.

"When Susan was going to school for cosmetology she had to practice on other people, so I was her dummy. I let her cut and color my hair. She told me to lean my head back rather than sit straight up and she ended up taking a lot more than I wanted. Let's just say I told her she could never cut my hair again!"

Joshua Steven Powell was born on January 20, 1976, being one of five children born to Steve and Terri Powell in Spokane, Washington. Jennifer was the oldest, followed by Josh, Johnny, Mike, and finally, Alina. If Chuck and Judy's marriage and family were a reasonable example of a family who knew how to work out its problems with love and faith, the Powells were at the other end of the spectrum. The very farthest end. And while the Powells had gone through a bitter divorce when Josh was a teenager, their lives together weren't always acrimonious. At one time, Steve and Terri seemed very much in love. They loved the outdoors, reading, and spending time with others of their Mormon faith. Terri was eighteen and Steve was twenty-three and recently back from his mission service in Argentina when they were married in the Ogden, Utah, temple.

Times were tough. Terri had three children—and a miscarriage—all in two and a half years and wound up hospitalized. She described their life as "lower middle class," with Steve working nights at a grocery store before trying real estate. Many months they didn't have enough money to get by.

Over time, their love for each other, and Steve's faith in the church, began to fracture. The consequences of the seismic shift were noticed by everyone, including friends and family. Many worried about what the Powells' war with each other might do to their children.

Josh, unlike his father and most Mormon young men after high school, did not go on a mission. By the time he was nineteen, his parents had been divorced for three years and he continued to live under his father's roof, a man who by then was vehemently anti-Mormon and who made sure that his kids felt the same way. Josh, more than the others, seemed especially susceptible to the rants of his dad. He drank in, guzzled really, everything Steve said.

In contrast to the volatile Powell family, Chuck and Judy Cox had been married for thirty-five years when Susan went missing. Chuck hadn't been raised Mormon. He met Judy when they were sixteen and in high school in Medical Lake, Washington, just outside of Spokane. Judy was Mormon and Chuck was searching for a faith. Something clicked. Chuck discovered that the teenagers he saw who didn't do drugs and treated people well happened to be members of the LDS. Chuck joined the faith at seventeen and he and Judy were married after high school. Like any family, over the years there were good times and challenging times in the Cox household—but it was infinitely more stable than Josh's upbringing. The Coxes' daughter, Denise, the "misfit" in the family, was a divorced mother of four and was in a custody fight over two of her children. That was about as bad as it got in the Cox family.

Susan was nineteen when she met twenty-four-year-old Joshua Powell and his buddy Tim Marini at an LDS singles event in Tacoma in 2000. Josh no longer attended the Mormon church, but he hadn't turned against the faith yet. Plus, it was a good place to meet single young women. Tim wanted to date Susan but, unfortunately for him, she wasn't the least bit interested. Susan had the kind of sparkling personality and energy that drew other people to her. She was a magnet. When Josh showed interest, Tim made the introduction and Susan agreed to go out with him.

From the beginning the match was an odd one. Josh came from a troubled family. He talked so much that the room filled with his words. He could be annoying, but he could also be endearing.

Susan laughed at Josh's incessant ramblings, his preoccupation with everything from cameras to computers. He had big, grandiose plans for the future, a different plan every week.

Judy and Chuck had some reservations about their daughter's new boyfriend. They had met him before, when Josh tried asking out their oldest daughter, Mary. Josh had shown up at their house the night of Mary's prom. She had a date and was at the dance but it didn't matter to Josh. He planted himself in a living room chair intent on staying to chat with Judy about Mary, the weather, anything at all. Judy felt like she'd been caught in a steel-jawed leg trap. There was no getting rid of the kid.

Finally, Chuck came home. In his typical no-nonsense fashion, he was direct when he told Josh that the visit was over.

"You need to go now," he said.

Josh didn't get it. He just sat there, looking blank-eyed. And kept talking.

Chuck had never seen anything like it.

Despite his peculiar nature, Susan fell for Josh. In some ways it was inexplicable. She was stunning, vivacious. His personality swung between stiff and remote, and gregarious and overbearing.

Mary had tried to warn her sister when things turned serious. She thought Josh was just plain weird. So did their parents.

"I have a bad feeling about him," Judy said as she and Susan sat at the massive family table that filled nearly every square inch of the dining room.

Susan didn't want to hear a thing about it.

"You need to date lots of people," Judy said, choosing her words carefully, like she always did. "Kid, you got it made. You're a pretty girl. You're smart. You know what you want. You make friends easy. Just enjoy yourself. You can have so much fun."

Susan appeared to understand what her mother was saying.

"I'm *going* to have fun," she said. "I *am* making lots of friends. Josh just happens to be one of them."

Judy pondered that for a moment. "Well, that's fine," she said, seeing that Susan was not about to abandon her interest in Josh Powell. "You can date him. But date others, too. Don't get serious with Josh. There're more guys out there. Take a year and really discover that."

Judy could have said more. So could Chuck. It passed through Susan's father's mind to be straight up about the situation. Chuck wanted to tell his daughter to head for the hills when it came to her suitor, but as the father of four girls, he knew better.

"I knew if I said 'Stay away from him,' that's exactly who she would go for," Chuck said. "So you knew that wasn't going to work."

Even so, Chuck, the FAA investigator, grilled the young man about the kind of life he would offer Susan.

With Josh sitting across from him at the table, Chuck ticked off all the boxes. Yes, the boy had a job. Yes, he had an apartment where they could live. Yes, he was going to further his education by finishing college and getting a business degree.

Josh was alert, convincing, and solicitous. He said all the right things.

Chuck still wasn't completely convinced, but he gave his blessing.

"That looks pretty good," he said, a little halfheartedly. "Self-supporting and everything."

He later told Judy that his first impression of Josh might have been wrong. Maybe there was hope for the couple after all?

"She's marrying him," Judy said, "because she feels sorry for him. Susan thinks she can make him happy, she thinks she can help him to change."

In their engagement photo, which Chuck took in a rambling field near their Puyallup home, Susan sits on Josh's knee, her head tilted and resting on Josh's chest. They look very young and very happy, excited to begin their lives together.

Families of the bride and groom often meet before the wedding. They spend a little time together, if only for the sake of their children. Not so with the Powells and the Coxes. Chuck and Judy had met Josh a few times, but there had been no polite or celebratory get-acquainted parties or dinners between the families. Chuck sized up Josh's family quickly.

They knew Steve was anti-Mormon, wrote anti-Mormon treatises, and considered himself an expert on a lot of things. "He likes to talk, and Josh likes to talk, and I didn't really feel like being bombarded by somebody who thinks they know everything when they really don't know anything," Chuck said. "I didn't make an effort to talk with him, and they never made any effort to talk with us."

On that happy note, the families managed to tolerate each other over lunch at an Old Country Buffet restaurant in a Portland suburb a few hours before Josh and Susan were married. It had been decided in advance that Steve's contribution to the day was to pick up the tab, but he grumbled about it.

"I heard Steve complaining that he had to pay just a little over a hundred bucks, and how dare he have to pay!" Judy recalled. "And Josh said, 'Oh, come on Dad, just pay.' And I was so tempted to go up there and say, 'Maybe you'd like to help pay for the wedding and we'll split it. My part is thousands of dollars and yours is a hundred dollars and you're complaining?' But I thought, 'I don't want to embarrass my daughter,' and it's the only thing that stopped me."

On April 6, 2001, a couple of hours after the old Country Buffet lunch, Josh and Susan's marriage was sealed for eternity at the commanding LDS temple in Lake Oswego, a few miles outside Portland. Most of Josh's family couldn't attend the actual wedding, since Steve had renounced the LDS church and, except for his eldest daughter Jennifer, his children had stopped attending church.

After a one-night honeymoon in a beautiful and historic hotel overlooking the Columbia River Gorge, the newlyweds celebrated at a reception at the Coxes' ward in Puyallup. Josh spent most of it taking pictures. His sister, Alina, a heavyset young woman who acted like a servant to her brothers and father, shadowed the groom as he took photos. Chuck felt sorry for her.

"It's like she doesn't have a mind or a life of her own," he said.

The Coxes took photos, too, of Josh looking very young and gawky in a tuxedo and Susan pretty in her long white wedding dress. The gown was perfect for a temple wedding, with a modest, slightly rounded neck and long, lacey sleeves. Her parents bought the dress at a Tacoma bridal shop for $399 along with her pillbox hat with a trailing veil and the bouquet of white flowers she carried. The reception line included Susan's sisters as her bridesmaids. They wore long dresses in Susan's favorite color, purple. They stood with their parents to Susan's left. To Josh's right were his father and mother, his sister Alina, and his brother Mike. No one asked about Johnny, and Jennifer was absent; she had avoided her father since her parents' divorce.

Susan overheard a conversation on her wedding day between Josh and his father that she passed along to her mother.

"Steve said, 'Well, she's no lawyer or doctor but she'll do.'"

Judy looked confused. "What's he talking about?" she asked.

Susan knew exactly what her father-in-law meant and she spelled it out.

"In other words," she said, "I'm not going to make big money but I'll do well enough that Josh won't have to work."

Judy was appalled by the remark, but it was the next thing the new—and flabbergasted—bride said that really shocked her.

"Steve said, 'Josh, she's going to divorce you someday.'"

Judy wondered what kind of father would say that to his son on his wedding day.

Who bets against love and marriage while the commitment is being sealed forever?

Josh and Susan moved into an apartment near Susan's parents. Susan had earned a scholarship to Gene Juarez

Academy, the Pacific Northwest's premier cosmetology school. Later she worked at Regis Salon at a mall south of Seattle. She said she liked to help people look their best. But more than anything, Susan loved being an aunt to her older sisters' children and dreamed of the day she would be a mother.

When money was tight, they lived with Josh's father, Steve, an experience that would send Susan running.

Josh worked for Virco, the same manufacturing company as his father, selling and installing office furniture.

In the early days of their marriage, Josh and Susan seemed close, very much in love. Friends and family described them as happy, holding hands, and frequently kissing.

Susan was still giddy with love when, just before their second wedding anniversary, she handwrote a note to Josh on Valentine's Day titled "Reasons I Love You." On five pages of lined paper she listed 132 reasons. Within a couple of years some traits she found endearing would become irritating; others would be bittersweet reminders of the young couple they had been. Her "Reasons I Love You" included:

> *You want to talk about irrelevant topics until you've resolved the issues of the world*
> *You'll drive aimlessly*
> *You want children*
> *You pray for people*
> *You show affection in public*
> *You don't care what others think*
> *You love my family get-together occasions*
> *You watch "Friends" with me for hours*
> *You can be patient*
> *You let me wax you*
> *You hold me in the middle of the night*
> *You calculate everything*
> *You went to church when you didn't feel like it was worth it*
> *You pay tithing without question*
> *You double-check locks*

But while they didn't know the full extent of the trauma and drama in Josh's childhood, Susan's parents were worried about Josh's sometimes odd behavior. Occasionally, he seemed not to be all there. At other times, he'd be oddly evasive. He made a habit of arriving hours late to family functions, with no awareness that others were waiting for him. It appeared as if Josh either didn't care about others, or was unable to empathize with anyone else's problems. They didn't give voice to their greatest concern, because to do so would have been almost too scary to say out loud. Chuck and Judy began to wonder if Josh's aberrant behavior was an indicator that he might have a mental illness.

Earlier in the marriage, Josh had some ambitions though he was woefully bad at bringing them to fruition. Always chasing a better opportunity, a chance to make his mark in some grand scheme, Josh and Susan moved to Yakima and then Olympia to train to manage an assisted living facility. While their bosses always loved Susan, they couldn't tolerate Josh. When the assisted-living job fizzled in late 2003, the young couple pulled up stakes and headed nine hundred miles south to West Valley City in Utah—not far from where Josh's sister Jennifer and his mother Terri lived.

For Susan, the greater the distance from her father-in-law, the better. Steve had done and said inappropriate sexual things to Susan and she put her foot down: she told Josh they had to get away from his father. Nine hundred miles should do it.

They lived with Jennifer Graves and her family for the first three months. "Susan was rather short with Josh. Very snippy and somewhat nagging," she later wrote in a statement for police. "She would give Josh orders instead of asking in a loving spousal way when she wanted something. Josh was controlling. He didn't want her to go to Relief Society [the women's arm of the LDS church] activities while they were staying at my house, even though they had no children. Over the years, Josh got worse and I think Susan did too for a while. She was prone to yelling out of frustration. She said she hit him at least once and said he hit her back. . . . I talked it over with her during that time and encouraged her not to do that again because Josh is stronger than her and she'd lose that physical battle (not to mention it's simply not appropriate). . . . There was a night (maybe 2–3 years ago) that she called. . . . I know we talked about how it was very bad for the children to be witnesses to the severe verbal fights they were having."

Kiirsi and John Hellewell first met the new neighbors soon after Josh and Susan bought the house on W. Sarah Circle in 2004. John was an IT professional, and Kiirsi homeschooled their children. Josh and Susan were just starting out, and the couples became close. They spent a lot of time together playing board games, watching movies, and going on picnics and bike rides. Both families were active in the church. Josh and John were paired as "home teachers," visiting families in the ward once a month to give a short spiritual lesson, offer a blessing, and to see if there was anything needed.

Josh was different from anyone the Hellewells had ever met before. It was almost like he had a traveling soapbox and at any moment he would stand up on it and ramble on about something he was doing. It didn't matter if anyone else had any input, Josh didn't seem to care.

"When they first moved here it was all about their house, because they were fixing it up," Kiirsi later recalled. "They were putting in the world's most amazing drip sprinkler system, and the garden, and this and that, and on and on and on about the sprinkler system and the garden for probably two or three months. We got so sick of hearing about it. We came to find out later Susan did most of the work but he'd take the credit for it."

Early in their friendship Susan told Kiirsi the real reason behind the move to Utah.

"It was because of Josh's father," she said, gauging her friend's reaction. "We had to get away from him."

This time, Susan didn't use the same old line about needing a fresh start when explaining the move, as she had told others. She told Kiirsi that to save money for a house early in their marriage, she and Josh had moved in with Steve. They'd slept in a dining room with a curtain hung for privacy. Then something had happened with Steve.

"I don't know how to say this exactly," she continued, "but I started to feel uncomfortable. Steve was always there. Always watching me. One time I caught him trying to watch me get dressed."

"You didn't," Kiirsi said, her eyes widening.

Susan nodded. "There's more. One time Steve tried to kiss me. After that, I told Josh that we had to move out."

"No," Kiirsi said.

If Susan had dropped a bomb, this next one was a cruise missile. "Yes. One time after we moved here Steve sent me a package, an envelope with what I thought were pictures of my favorite actor, Mel Gibson. You know what he did?"

Kiirsi had no idea. How could she? She'd never heard of a father-in-law hitting on his son's wife. It was disgusting and vile. It was wrong in every way imaginable.

"Tucked into the photos were a bunch of other naked pictures," Susan said pausing a moment for emphasis. They weren't of Mel Gibson.

This was too much. Kiirsi found the whole idea of it crazy, revolting. As she listened to Susan, it was clear that Susan had slammed the door shut on any relationship with Josh's father. Susan thought Steve was a creepy, sleazy, nasty man.

The Coxes had also heard bits and pieces of the story about Steve and the reason behind the move.

"What do you mean he made advances at you?" Judy asked when Susan announced they were moving away.

"I don't want to go into it," Susan said. She didn't tell her parents, but in 2003, when Steve professed his love for her, he had tried to kiss her and touch her.

Judy pressed her daughter for details. "Susan, you should report it to the police."

Susan couldn't bring herself to do that. "This is my father-in-law we're talking about."

"I don't care," Judy said. She saw her daughter as the kind

of person who would stand up for herself, someone who would right the wrongs. Why was Susan protecting Steve?

"What if he's doing it to other people?" Judy asked. "You need to be one of those who step forward."

Her father had similar advice.

"Call the police," Chuck said. "Make a report. Do whatever you need to do. And certainly get away from him."

The truth was Susan and her parents didn't know the half of it. No one did. Since 2002, when Josh and Susan temporarily lived at his house, Steve Powell had been sexually obsessed with his daughter-in-law. At the time he was fifty-three and Susan was twenty-one. Over the years he wrote more than 2,330 pages in seventeen notebooks about how he was "crazy with desire" for her, and how falling in love with her was both his "greatest problem" and his "greatest pleasure." It could sound romantic—except it wasn't. Not only was it unrequited, even Steve called his actions "sociopathic." He chronicled what he admitted were his "sick" sexual urges about Susan, including secretly videotaping her and masturbating while he watched the tapes. According to his journals, he would masturbate every morning and every evening to pictures of Susan. It didn't take much to turn him on. He had taken hundreds of photos of Susan—many without her knowledge—partially dressed, putting on makeup, eating a bowl of cereal, inserting a tampon, shopping at Costco.

It was in 2003 that Steve finally confessed to Susan—and to his journal—that he was in love with her.

I am in so much pain right now. I don't know where to turn with it. I spoke to Alina, who has been very supportive of my infatuation or obsession. Her advice was to accept that Susan is a "player," and that is what players do. They lead guys on.

Susan refused to speak to Steve, She told Josh about his father's declaration of love and insisted he break off contact with his father.

Steve seemed heartbroken about the young couple's escape to Utah. He made mention of it in his journal several months later.

> *Today has been an emotionally sick day, knowing that*
> *Susan will not be coming here, maybe never again.*

Certainly in the beginning, living in Utah accomplished what it was meant to do: put nine hundred miles between Susan and her father-in-law. Josh had been briefly angry at his father for coming on to Susan back in Puyallup and, despite their close relationship, he retreated from him. That didn't mean that the pair didn't talk occasionally. Josh had idolized his father. Communication was only when needed.

Susan's pregnancy with Charlie in the summer of 2004 was a reason to make the obligatory call.

On July 5, Steve wrote in his journal that Josh had telephoned with the news. Steve was miffed because he'd likely been the last to be notified. He was also disappointed that Susan herself had not made the call.

> *I am not unhappy that she is pregnant. I am unhappy*
> *that she did not share it with me. . . . I kind of feel like*
> *an outsider.*

The move to Utah did little to stem Steve's obsession and lust for Susan. He turned to songwriting in order to express his feelings for her. At a keyboard in his bedroom, Steve wrote and recorded some fifty songs about his daughter-in-law, then put them on his Web site where he called himself Steve Chantrey. One was titled "I Said, I Love You":

> *I said, "I love you." Is that a crime?*
> *. . . I love you, so put me in jail.*

Some Mormons believe that no professional or personal success compensates for a failure in the home. When a couple is married in a holy temple, as Josh and Susan were, the marriage is sealed. They promise to stay together for eternity, on earth and in heaven after they die. As time went on and the mood darkened in the house on W. Sarah Circle, Susan began to tell friends that she was having trouble imagining eternity with Josh. He changed after his sons were born. Josh used to be affectionate, but now he was cold, distant, and found every way he could to control Susan, including cutting off access to the money she earned.

Susan spent the early years of their marriage trying to help Josh pay off his mid-six-figure school loans—loans that had never quite added up to a college degree, although he claimed to have completed one. But Josh's inability to keep a job more than a couple of weeks at a time caught up with them. Susan seemed stressed and friends suggested that she leave Josh, who they called "very, very controlling" and "emotionally abusive."

Josh and Susan began marriage counseling offered by their church and, after fasting and praying, Susan decided to keep working on the marriage. Early on, they had both embraced their religion and the expectations of family life and marriage. On the surface, they seemed to be succeeding. They met and married in the church. They started a family. Josh shared his interests in woodworking, radio-controlled cars, and gardening and landscaping with his boys. Susan was active in the Women's Relief Society at her ward and the family walked to church together. She learned to garden, can, bake, and crochet and made friends with other young wives and mothers. Susan loved being a mother. She was less happy being Josh's wife and often being the only steady income earner in the family.

Susan was disappointed when Josh stopped going to marriage counseling and refused medication. Josh often exhibited paranoia. He said he was worried that if psychological counseling and medication for manic-depression appeared on his employment records it could be used against him if, for example, they ever wanted to buy life insurance.

Despite a deep faith that put family first, Susan's friends

felt she should leave Josh. Susan told them that if her marriage didn't turn around by their wedding anniversary in the spring of 2008 she would file for divorce. She later gave Josh new deadlines: April 2009, then April 2010. She gave him a hundred second chances, not so much because she loved him—although she did—but because she didn't know what he'd do to her or her boys if she left him.

She was held captive by love, fear, and the church's promise that if she prayed harder, everything would get better.

6

Yesterday I helped him organize/clean his office and the loose papers (another one of his excuses/stalling tactics) and as I was soundlessly crying myself to sleep last night I told him kind of desperately, "now is the time you can say nice things to me" so he said in a tired/bored voice "thanks for helping me clean my office and stuff" and that was all . . . then he kind of bumped me and I said as a hopeful suggestion "are you trying to hold my hand?" and he muttered something not audible and then a little bit later I held his hand for a while until he pulled away.
— SUSAN POWELL E-MAIL, JULY 11, 2008

Being a Mormon in Utah is different from being a Mormon anywhere else. The faithful who live there are at the center of the universe. Temple Square in Salt Lake City is to Mormons what the Vatican is to Catholics, what Mecca is to Muslims. In Utah, the local church or ward is the focus of a couple's life. And while obligations to the ward are large and time-consuming, nothing is more crucial than maintaining a happy, peaceful home. Husbands are the breadwinners and heads of household. Women are the nurturers and homemakers and are generally submissive to their husbands, as indicated by scripture.

When the Powells joined the Hunter 36th Ward, everyone there immediately loved Susan. They put up with Josh for her sake. He seemed selfish and immature. Susan was the opposite. She never met a stranger. She never saw a baby that she didn't want to hold.

Josh, raised in a troubled family, with parents in a volatile marriage, had never had a positive role model. When they moved into the house on W. Sarah Circle, Josh seemed to do his best to emulate what others were doing. He talked about raising a family, about planting a large vegetable garden, about making sure that he could bring in a decent income.

For a brief time, the Powells were the embodiment of the ideal young Mormon couple—in a place where they needed to be.

In the first years after the couple's move, Chuck and Judy Cox felt more optimistic about Josh and Susan's marriage. The Coxes didn't like the idea of Susan being so far from home, but the incident involving Steve had made the departure necessary. Susan didn't tell her parents the details, how Steve had confessed that he loved her, had tried to kiss her and had spied on her.

Without knowing the particulars about why Susan wanted to leave Washington, Chuck reminded Judy that all couples need to build their own lives. In Utah, Susan and Josh had the support of the church, as well as Josh's sister Jennifer, and her husband, Kirk.

Both of them immediately got jobs with Fidelity Investments, Susan in the phone bank and Josh in the IT department. Then—at Josh's urging—Susan got her broker's license, required to climb the ladder at Fidelity.

After just two weeks on the job, Josh—who'd never had a job he thought was his equal—was being Josh.

"How is the job going?" Chuck asked his son-in-law.

Josh started to grumble and complain about Fidelity and his manager.

"Terrible. They've got some really old computers and they

have bad procedures and they really need to make some changes."

Chuck sighed. He'd heard that before. Josh always considered himself the smartest guy in the room. His over-the-top assessment of his value and abilities got him fired from the assisted living jobs in Yakima and Olympia.

"Josh, Josh, get along," Chuck said. "Do what you need to do to keep your job. They don't want to hear all that from you on your second week. Try and get along, you can't control everything."

Shortly after father and son-in-law spoke, Fidelity "phased out" Josh's job and he was let go. Josh always thought he knew more than his employer. His track record as a furniture installer, working in Internet sales for a car dealership, training to get a commercial driver's license, and managing assisted living facilities, was short and spotty. And then there were his grand plans, including becoming a lawyer—without bothering to attend law school—a real estate developer and builder, and a professional photographer.

Josh had a habit of making life messy. When he was fired, or laid off, or disgruntled, he routinely threatened lawsuits, made a beeline to the head of the human resources department, and never accepted that *he* might be the source of the trouble.

During the brief time Josh worked at Fidelity, the Powells qualified to buy a three-bedroom house that had been repossessed by a bank. They were able to close the deal on the home on W. Sarah Circle before the mortgage lender knew Josh had been fired.

Susan felt uncomfortable about the deception, but Josh explained away the ethics.

Susan gamely kept doing double duty. She was the breadwinner *and* ran the household. Josh was always too busy on his computers to lift a finger. When she returned home from working all day, Susan was expected to cook the meal. No matter that he'd been home all day doing whatever it was on one of his computers. Susan suspected Josh was looking at pornography and she and a friend examined his computer to find out. But he had put up all sorts of firewalls to prevent snooping.

Around that time, Steve Powell wrote in his journal that he thought Josh would leave Susan if there were not a financial incentive for him to stay in the marriage. It was almost as if he was wishing for the breakup so that Susan would be free—free to be with him. And he commented on their arguments.

> *Theirs is truly a marriage made in hell. It's hard to believe that two people could be so nasty to each other . . . in public they look like the loveliest couple, but in private they have no respect for each other, and little love.*

In time there were noticeable fractures in the perfect life they presented. As his sister Jennifer and others noticed, Josh appeared to be spiraling downward. When Tim and Rachel Marini visited Josh and Susan in West Valley City in the summer of 2005 the guys took the living room couch and floor, and Susan and Rachel took the bedroom. The women stayed up most of the night talking, while Charlie slept.

Susan was very concerned about Josh and the direction of their marriage.

"It's not the same," she confided to her friend.

"How?" Rachel asked, knowing that she'd seen marked changes in Josh's personality, too.

"He is so controlling," Susan said. "He controls everything I do. He won't let me spend money on meat. On anything. He has to have an accounting of every dime."

Rachel was glad her husband wasn't like that. Their marriage was a loving partnership. She felt bad for Susan living with that kind of situation. But Josh wasn't just a tightwad, with a control-freak personality. There was a side to Josh that only his wife could have known.

He used sex—or the lack of it—as a weapon.

"If I do anything he thinks is wrong, he punishes me. He

says, 'I can't believe you did that. No more sex for three months!'" Susan told her. Since the year before, when she'd been pregnant with Charlie, Josh acted as if she repulsed him.

Susan also told Rachel about Steve Powell sending her the photos of Mel Gibson, seemingly all a ruse to get her to open the envelope and find photos of other men. She added a detail she hadn't told anyone else: at least one of the pictures was of Steve, leering at the camera in a way that was presumably supposed to excite Susan. Instead, it made her skin crawl. It was so disgusting and embarrassing, she hadn't told Kiirsi.

On the car ride home, Rachel told Tim what Susan had said during the marathon conversation in the Powell's bedroom. Tim was blown away.

"That's not the Josh we knew in Washington," he said.

Rachel nodded. They were in complete agreement.

"Right. This is a very different Josh."

Later, Tim tried to talk to his best friend about his increasingly weird behavior. It was the kind of awkward conversation that close male friends seldom attempt. But Tim was fond of Josh. And he had long adored Susan, first as a would-be suitor and now as a good friend. He believed that Josh and Susan's marriage couldn't survive unless Josh made some changes.

"He didn't have any kind of answer," Tim remembered about confronting Josh that day. "It was a kind of a 'What do you mean? I'm fine.' I don't know if he *knew* he was different. It was very strange."

The rift between Josh and his father continued for most of 2005, but with the icy November wind change was in the air.

Steve wrote on November 10 that he and Josh had talked on the telephone for two hours.

That was the first time I have spoken with him since the baby was born, which was, I think, last February.

He was wrong on the date—it was January—but the entry made in his diary was important.

Steve had somehow managed to wriggle his way back into Josh's life. They patched up their toxic relationship. If Susan knew about it then, she never mentioned it to any of her Mormon sisters or her family in Washington.

7

... my bottom line is he WILL DO COUNSELING at
least. I expect by our anniversary next april (8 yrs)
we will both be in counseling and FINALLY FIXING
the marriage OR somewhere in mediation/divorce
court ... sad, but simple as that.
— SUSAN POWELL E-MAIL, JULY 28, 2008

It had been forty-eight hours since Susan was last seen when
Josh walked out of the police department. Charlie and Braden
were with his mother and his sister Jennifer, so he was free
to do whatever he needed to do.

He took a cab to the Salt Lake City International Airport
and at 10:26 P.M. on Tuesday, December 8, he paid $79.61 and
rented a 2009 Ford Focus from the Hertz counter. Over the
next forty-five hours he drove 807 miles, but most of the mile-
age occurred over a sixteen-hour period after he picked up
the car and before he got a new cell phone. The phone was
activated at 4:20 P.M. on Wednesday at Tremonton, about
seventy-four miles north of Salt Lake City and eighty-six
miles north of West Valley City.

The location of the phone activation gave Chuck Cox and
others pause when they learned of it. Why had Josh gone
there? Presumably, he was on a mission associated with

Susan's disappearance. But Tremonton is hundreds of miles from Simpson Springs, where Josh said he'd gone camping three days earlier. North of Tremonton, Interstate 84 crosses the Idaho border and leads to nearly two million acres of national forest and 50,000 acres of national grassland. I-84 cuts through Oregon and meets up with I-82—the route home to Puyallup, Washington.

At the same time that Josh rented the car, his father Steve called in sick for two days, December 8 and 9, from his job as a salesman delivering office furniture made by prison inmates. His daughter Alina explained later that her father was on "bereavement" leave from work because Susan was missing.

No one could pin down exactly where Steve had been during those two days, though many—Chuck Cox and the police among them—had a pretty good idea. They thought he was helping Josh move Susan's body. No one thought about where Josh's younger brother, Michael, might be. As Susan often said, he was the "sane" brother in the Powell family.

The West Valley City Police Department wouldn't learn of Michael's potential involvement in Susan's disappearance for a year and a half. Chuck and Judy Cox wouldn't know about it for more than three years.

Michael, Josh's younger brother, was an Army veteran and college graduate but like all his siblings—except for Jennifer—always seemed to make his way back to his father's house. The week Susan went missing, Michael and his 1997 Ford Taurus were, too. But from Friday, December 4, to Saturday, December 12, he wasn't seen or heard from by anyone outside the family.

Josh returned to the West Valley City area on Wednesday, December 9, but didn't return the rental car until the 10th. The only person to see Josh on the 9th was a neighbor, Tim Peterson. Tim was surprised that Josh had been out of town and wouldn't say where. Josh seemed to be missing the big picture, that his wife had vanished. Instead, he complained to his neighbor that the police had torn his house apart and taken his computer and a comforter.

"Now I'll have to go to Walmart and get a new blanket," he said, bitterly.

Josh appeared to be fretful about his hands—they were red and raw and he kept applying lotion to soothe them. When Tim asked about their condition, Josh said it was just from the cold weather.

Things had been a little tense between the men before that night. Josh thought that Tim had a crush on Susan. Tim looked at Susan as a friend. She had told him about her marital problems.

Later, when Tim's wife Crystal asked where Susan was, Josh snapped at her.

"It's not like I stabbed her," he said.

Josh had telephoned Jennifer to say he would pick up Charlie and Braden on the evening of the 9th, but he never showed up.

The next day, Thursday, the 10th, Josh drove the rented Ford Focus to Jennifer's house in West Jordan. He was picking up his mother so that she could help him return the car and retrieve his minivan from the police. Chris Jones, a reporter from KUTV, the Salt Lake City CBS affiliate, and a cameraman approached Josh the moment he pulled up. For six minutes Josh haltingly and politely answered questions.

About his boys:

"They're doing good . . . as far as I can tell."

How he was feeling:

"You know, people have been really helpful and supportive, so it's been really hard, but you know you just keep going."

How suspicion normally falls on the husband:

"I didn't do anything. I don't know where she's at. I don't even know where to start looking."

And then he excused himself and went into Jennifer's house. Josh told his mother and his sister that he had spent the previous two days just driving around, since he couldn't go home. He said he had driven by Jennifer's one night but the house was dark. Jennifer didn't buy it. As Jennifer's husband, Kirk, pointed out when they talked about it later, Josh was never considerate, so why hadn't he knocked on the door?

She begged Josh to leave Charlie and Braden with her, so they would have at least a little stability in their lives, but he refused.

Before he left to return the rental car he needed one more favor from his sister. He asked to borrow a candle and some matches. He planned on attending a vigil for Susan that evening.

When Josh went to the police department to get his van, he was told to return Monday for another interview and a polygraph test.

While Josh had been absent—the police didn't know yet that he had rented a car and left the area—they had gone over his van more thoroughly. They found a trash bag stuffed with burned metal, wires, and sheetrock. It wasn't there on December 7. Josh must have burned the stuff that night, when neighbors saw him coming and going from the garage. He had left it in his car, not knowing police would take the keys on the 8th. Investigators concluded the burned items indicated an "attempt to destroy something using high heat."

Kiirsi Hellewell knew she had to do something. There weren't the organized massive searches for Susan that some communities held for missing women. The West Valley City police wanted to handle things themselves and Susan's family and friends accepted that—for now. So Susan's best friend turned to Facebook, the tool that had helped her and Susan and their friends keep in touch while they juggled their family and church responsibilities.

Her first post on Facebook about Susan was at 12:02 A.M. on December 8:

> For some of you who may be out of the loop (coworkers, etc.) . . . Josh and his kids returned home Monday night. Police talked to him. Susan is nowhere to be found. . . . We are all praying for her like crazy.

Next, she created a Facebook group she named Friends and Family of Susan Powell. Within a couple of days 1,200 people had joined. Kiirsi didn't stop there. Over the next few days and weeks with the help of an army of volunteers, Kiirsi helped create a major social media blitz. Kiirsi also started Service for Susan, a blog focused on a national "week of service" in Susan's name, encouraging people in the arts and crafts community to make projects for organizations that benefit women and children. The donations supported shelters for women escaping domestic violence.

8

Josh reiterated this week that he refuses to touch her.
She has told Alina that she doesn't love him anymore.
—STEVE POWELL'S JOURNAL, JUNE 26, 2008

Josh might have underestimated Susan's tight circle of friends.
They were young Mormon couples, neighbors who saw one
another a few times each week. In private, the women sometimes addressed each other, as Mormon women sometimes
do, as "Sister." They worshipped at the same ward every
Sunday morning, they visited while doing craft activities a
couple of times a month, and they talked at church choir practice. They were at the ward for Christmas breakfasts and for
family Halloween parties.

Susan and some of her friends shared the same day-care
provider, Debbie Caldwell. JoVonna Owings, the last person
to see Susan, was related by marriage to Barbara Anderson.
Susan went to Barbara's house to do her hair and give her
pedicures since Barbara had muscular dystrophy and was
confined to a wheelchair. JoVonna's landlord was Mike
Khalaji, a real estate agent who had worked with the Powells.

Michele Oreno was older and a mature voice of reason who could speak bluntly to Josh. Kiirsi lived down the street and her husband spent many hours teaching Josh computer programming. Rachel Marini was married to Josh's best friend, Tim, and their friendship predated all the others.

Josh could not have predicted their fierce determination to find out what had happened to his wife.

On Thursday night, Kiirsi organized a candlelight vigil at a local park. More than two dozen friends and church members braved the ten-degree weather to pray for Susan.

About halfway through the vigil, Josh and the boys arrived. It was the first time Kiirsi had seen him since Susan went missing.

"He was very standoffish, acted like he didn't trust us," Kiirsi remembered later. "We tried to be really friendly, because my thought was, if I turned on Josh and refused to have anything to do with him, I'd have zero chance of getting him to tell me anything."

The vigil was also the first time that Debbie Caldwell had seen Josh since Susan disappeared.

She was consoling Charlie when Josh came over and picked him up and started to walk away.

"Wait, Josh. I was just talking with Charlie," Debbie said.

Josh cut her off. "We have to go."

"You haven't called me, Josh."

"We're not going to be coming back to day care," he said curtly, edging away. He was angry at Debbie for bringing the family's absence to the attention of the police three days before.

"Why not?"

Josh shrugged it away. "With everything going on . . ."

"But you have to work, you have to make a living, and the boys will need a place to go," she said, trying to persuade him.

"We won't have any money to pay you," Josh said.

Debbie didn't care about that. The boys needed looking after.

"We can figure something out," she said.

Josh wouldn't budge. "No, no, no. I'm just going to have my family take care of them," he said.

Before she could say anything else, he turned and walked away with Charlie. It had been just two days since Charlie told police that his mommy went camping with them but did not come back home.

Kiirsi had invited Josh and the boys to come over after the vigil. The boys were freezing and hungry and literally scrounging the floor of Josh's minivan for any cookie crumbs, so she made hot chocolate and toast.

Like Chuck and Judy Cox, she decided to pretend to be sympathetic to Josh. Maybe he'd let down his guard. Maybe he'd open up. But he didn't. He sat glumly in the living room.

Kiirsi kept Charlie company as he played quietly in a downstairs room with some building blocks scattered on the carpet. The boy suddenly blurted out, "I hate my dad!"

Kiirsi saw a crack, a chance to probe and ask the little boy why he hated his father. Did he hate him because he'd seen him hurt his mommy?

But Kiirsi didn't ask. She was fearful that a confrontation like that might set Josh off. Since Kiirsi and her husband John had broken the ice with Josh, he came to their house a few more times the week Susan vanished.

"He said the police had taken all his computers and he wanted to use our computer to put up a Web site for Susan. And I thought, 'Finally, he is showing some desire to do something to help her.' So my husband let him use his laptop and he sat on the couch for a couple of hours."

Later, Josh and friends stood outside the Jazz basketball game in downtown Salt Lake City and handed out missing person's flyers to fans arriving for the game.

But that was it. The Web site he had claimed to be working on became an anti-Mormon, anti-Cox, anti–Jennifer Graves, anti–Utah police manifesto. He never lifted another finger to help find his missing wife.

9

Biking is good, no more accidents. We are going to
look into getting a better bike—you know, with actual
working gears!!!, it takes only 40 minutes in the morning, about 50+ on the way home b/c its hot, I'm tired,
and there is a mile long hill at the very end, so I'm told
I look like I'm dying when I get near the top.
—SUSAN POWELL E-MAIL, JUNE 30, 2008

On the day of the vigil, West Valley City Police Department
(WVCPD) search teams went out to the desert where Josh
said he and Charlie and Braden had spent the night in their
minivan. Even in summertime Simpson Springs is a solitary
place to camp, with spotty cell phone service and only a few
picnic tables and fire rings. No matter the season, campers
are advised to carry spare tires, food, and extra water. Authorities encourage Simpson Spring campers to let someone
know where they're going, when they plan to return, and to
be prepared for severe weather.

A marker near Simpson Springs indicates that the road
was part of the Pony Express Trail across the western Utah
desert in 1860 and 1861. The site adjoins the U.S. Army's
Dugway Proving Ground, an area where the military tested
chemicals and biological agents and where hazardous conditions may still exist, according to the military.

In winter, it is especially bleak, with thousands of acres of flat terrain, brush, and snow, the horizon broken only by the occasional tracks—or skeleton—of an antelope or coyote.

As for the allure of camping there in the coldest time of the year, a Web site promoting winter sports sponsored by a Provo newspaper put it this way:

> *Have you ever wondered what it would be like to be the only person on the Earth? Some people may ask what it would be like if only a handful of people were left on the planet. You can get close to that answer by going camping during the winter.*

As Josh explained to investigators working Susan's case, people don't go camping at a place like Simpson Springs in the hot summer. People go there in winter.

When asked if he could remember seeing or talking to anyone who could back up his story, Josh shook his head. He and the boys were there alone. Then Josh remembered they had seen a sheepherder early on the morning of December 7.

Police could never corroborate the actual camping trip, complete with s'mores, but they did find two sheepherders who remembered a silver van on the lonely road early that morning.

After the search, West Valley City police captain Tom McLachlan told reporters that fresh snow hid any potential evidence. They couldn't prove or disprove that Josh had been there. Josh was "cooperative and not a suspect, nor a person of interest," he reiterated.

"It could take years, if ever, to identify his campsite," Assistant Police Chief Craig Black said. "We would really like to go on a two-hour road trip with Josh."

It wasn't exactly the trip they imagined, but the next day, Friday, December 11, the police put a tracking device on Josh's car. They followed him as he drove from West Valley City to the parking lot of a strip club in Nevada. The name of the club was American Bush. It's closed now, but in 2009 it was a storefront in West Wendover, a town of about 4,000 just across the Nevada border from Utah. It's a straight shot west from Salt Lake City on I-80, which continues to California. Other roads out of West Wendover lead to Las Vegas, 366 miles south.

American Bush offered topless dancers and private lap dance rooms. Someone who worked in the casino end of the business told police Josh visited a few times, would lose money, and get angry.

Josh had his two sons with him on December 11 and he knew he was being followed. He tried to evade police surveillance by driving in circles, repeatedly taking on-ramps and off-ramps and sometimes going east and then cutting back and heading west. In response, police called in aerial surveillance to follow the van.

Was Josh playing with the police? Probably.

On the way back to West Valley City they followed him to a gravel pit where he stayed for two hours. Police searched it after he left but found nothing.

The WVCPD still wanted to take Josh on a road trip, one where they would share a police car and he would take them to the exact spot he and the boys had camped.

Wasn't it time he helped search for Susan?

10

... Fast for me this Sunday. I've got family and friends doing that for me. My parents are ready to help pay any lawyer fees/mediator (since I think its required) and if I am supposed to divorce him, I will know with assurance and somehow the divorce won't be as ugly as I fear (like him kidnapping the kids and taking me for broke . . .).

—SUSAN POWELL E-MAIL,
NOVEMBER 31, 2008

Chuck Cox wiped tears from his eyes as he spoke to more than a hundred of Susan's friends and neighbors at the Hunter 36th Ward. It was Saturday, December 12, six days since his daughter had gone missing. Chuck had flown in from Seattle the day before to meet with police investigators and to attend this special gathering of people who knew and loved Susan. He was running on adrenaline and the hope that things wouldn't end up with the worst possible conclusion. He hadn't wanted to leave Judy, who was terribly worried about their missing daughter, but he made sure there was a friend or family member with her night and day. Judy had turned fifty-five years old the day Susan was reported missing—there was no celebration.

There would be no celebrating anything until Susan came home.

Chuck thanked everybody for their help. Josh and Charlie and Braden were there, but the boys didn't sit with their grandpa. In fact, they didn't sit at all. Josh seemed not to have control of his young sons. They were running loose, almost as if they were at a party.

Afterward, Josh and Chuck hugged. It was an awkward, stiff embrace. In an instant, Chuck let go in order to stifle a nearly overwhelming urge to wrap his hands around Josh's neck and scream out "What have you done with my daughter?"

But he didn't, of course. The impulse surprised him, *stunned* him. Chuck knew better. He knew that he had to keep his cool, keep his distance.

Josh, he was sure, would be arrested soon.

After the ward meeting, a coworker of Susan's told Chuck that Susan had kept a journal at work, and Chuck alerted the police. As he talked to the media outside the church, Chuck commented that Josh's midnight camping trip might sound weird, but the important thing was to not stop looking for Susan. As photographers and television cameramen captured Josh's every move, Chuck suggested that the police stop focusing solely on Josh as a suspect and said that he didn't think Josh was capable of hurting his daughter.

Chuck was being careful. He wanted to find his daughter, and to do that, he believed he had to keep his enemy close.

One by one, however, Josh and Susan's friends were turning away from Josh. As many saw it, he simply didn't behave like a husband desperate to find his wife. He wasn't prodding the police to let him help or turning to his friends and family in his anguish. He appeared depressed about something, but didn't seem worried about Susan. He hung his head and avoided making eye contact with the reporters. His brother-in-law, Kirk Graves, stood by him. At a news conference on that same Saturday, Kirk stated that portraying Josh in a negative light was harmful to the case.

"I can tell you that the pain he feels is real. I could feel it," he said.

The Powell family hoped to find Susan alive, he said. Josh

was letting Kirk do the talking. When reporters persisted in asking Josh where Susan was, Kirk cut short the interview. It was the last time Kirk gave Josh the benefit of the doubt.

During his visit to Utah, Chuck Cox had dinner with Ed Smart, fellow Mormon and the father of Elizabeth Smart, who at age fourteen was abducted from her Salt Lake City bedroom and found nine months later. Ed had reached out to Chuck earlier that week when Susan first went missing. Although Ed's daughter had been found, the Salt Lake City police and the FBI were criticized for ignoring information that could have led them to find the girl earlier. Like the West Valley City Police Department, Salt Lake City police discouraged family members from seeking public help in finding her abductors and encouraged them to leave the search to the pros. Chuck Cox asked Ed how his family had made it through the ordeal. He also wanted advice on what the Cox family could do to help find their daughter.

Ed Smart had been there. He didn't hesitate to tell Chuck that it was family and faith that sheltered them. He also said something that Chuck would put into practice.

"Keep her name and face in front of the public," he said.

That same weekend, Josh hired Salt Lake City defense attorney Scott Williams. That way he could stave off more meetings with the police by saying his attorney had advised him not to speak to them. One of Williams's previous high-profile defendants was Wanda Eileen Barzee, who had been convicted, with her husband Brian David Mitchell, of kidnapping Elizabeth Smart.

The long horrible first week of Susan's disappearance ended at the same place as her last day, at church. On Sunday, December 13, the ward invited LDS grief counselors in to help both the congregation and Josh. Cornell Porter, president of Salt Lake Hunter Central Stake, said that the ward was supportive of the family and not speculating about Josh's role in Susan's disappearance. Josh skipped the normal three-hour Sunday service, but he made an appearance and accepted the prayers of his neighbors, and talked to an LDS counselor.

Kiirsi Hellewell watched as Josh cried on and off throughout the day, while he muttered over and over, "I can't believe this is happening."

About that time, Josh called his brother, Mike, and his sister, Alina, and asked them to come to West Valley City.

Not to help search for Susan.

Not to comfort him.

Not even to comfort Charlie and Braden.

He wanted Alina there to cook, change diapers, do the laundry, and think up ways to distract his sons.

Mike and Alina would later share different memories of their week in West Valley City. Mike said he saw Josh in tears, and that the boys had asked "Where's Mommy?" more than once.

Alina said that the boys didn't seem too concerned about Susan's absence. Mike and Alina claimed they never asked their brother about his possible involvement in Susan's disappearance.

Their most important task was to help Josh get out of town without the media or the police knowing.

In a ruse, Alina and Mike stayed behind while Josh and the boys slipped away and drove north to Washington.

Mike and Alina's own road trip back would be eventful.

11

I came home from work on Sat and felt so depressed
I couldn't make decent dinner for my boys. (the only
protein we have is hot dogs, me making eggs or planning ahead and soaking beans and doing the beans
and rice thing) so I just kept trying to disguise their
food with sour cream and ketchup etc. and finally laid
down in my bed and went to sleep (around 7 pm) . . .
—SUSAN POWELL E-MAIL, JULY 7, 2008

Josh insisted that Susan's paychecks go into their joint account via direct deposit, and because he was continually
changing the password on the account, she often didn't have
money to buy groceries or diapers. Josh closely monitored
Susan and required her to make a record of every penny she
spent.

She explained it this way in an e-mail to a friend in July
2008:

> . . . he said I lied b/c I bought $90 instead of $30 worth
> of groceries, one of his examples was $0.25/lbs.
> for watermelon was too expensive. I looked at the re-
> ceipt, it came to $3.35 and just yesterday he bought a
> watermelon for a flat price of $4 (I remember the one
> I purchased as larger than his).

Money, sex, and food were ways through which Josh controlled Susan. The other ways included not letting her drive the family vehicle and, most hurtful, chipping away at her relationship with their boys.

Susan didn't know how to handle her husband's streak of passive-aggressive games, and his overt attacks against her role as a mother.

"Do you want to go to boring, boring church with Mommy, or do you want to stay home and have cake with Daddy?" he asked one time.

Charlie and Braden loved their mother, but the lure of cake with Daddy was too much. Josh would win his little battle and grin ear to ear when he did so. Susan would be reduced to tears. And once again she would wrestle with her doubts about their marriage and its survival.

Not long after moving to West Valley City, Josh and Susan had dinner at the home of Michele and Brent Oreno. The Orenos were parents to six children ages thirteen to thirty-one. Like John Hellewell, Brent was a computer programmer.

During dinner, Josh proudly told Michele and Brent about a spreadsheet he had made to track household expenses.

"Susan had to research what was on sale at what store. Then she had to come home and put it into the computer, what she spent on every single item," Michele recalled years later. "And he was really ticked off because the week before she had spent two cents more on a can of peas than he found it for at another store. He was serious. And it got so he wouldn't give her money for food or anything."

When Susan complained about the budget, Josh told her she needed to be more resourceful.

"We've got a garden," he said. "You figure something out."

So in the beginning, Susan did. She learned to bake bread, and to puree her own baby food when the time came for that. If Josh's game playing and unreasonable edicts were meant to crush her, he had failed.

It was during that dinner, when both couples were forming their first impressions of the other, that Michele and Brent heard all about Susan's father-in-law.

Susan asked her new friend if her father-in-law had ever made advances on her.

Michele was shocked by the question, by the very idea that any father-in-law would do that.

Josh, on the other hand, dismissed the specifics of Susan's charges and supported his father.

"Susan, he's not all that bad. He's got some good points," he said.

Michele wondered what kind of good points a man might have if he's trying to seduce or molest his son's wife.

Josh tried to pooh-pooh the incident that sent them down to West Valley City in the first place, when Steve came on to Susan and proclaimed his love for her. "Susan," Josh said, "that's just the way my dad is. You know how he is."

"I know he's an evil man," she countered.

Finally, at one o'clock in the morning, Brent stopped the discussion and everyone said good night. It had been a long evening for all.

As soon as the Powells moved to Utah, Susan began working on finishing their basement so that she could have a hair salon in the house. She already knew her plans would always take second place when it came to the dreams and ambitions of her husband—no matter how ill conceived.

During the hot summer of 2004, Susan was pregnant, studying hard for the stockbroker exam called a Series 7, and answering the phones at Fidelity Investments. She wanted to make more money. In reality, she had little choice. Josh's résumé was a catalog of short-lived positions.

She found refuge during the Utah scorcher at Kiirsi's air-conditioned house, a few doors down. Not only was the temperature more comfortable, it gave her a little distance from Josh, who "worked" at home. He was trying to get a business going creating Web sites and marketing materials.

In the middle of one study session, Susan looked up and shook her head.

"Do you believe this?" she asked, letting out a sigh. "I never wanted to go to college. I never cared about that stuff. I just wanted to do hair and make people look pretty."

Kiirsi turned the subject away from school to the baby and how Susan thought it would affect their marriage.

"I'm not worried," Susan said. "I think he'll be a good dad."

Kiirsi wasn't convinced. "Why do you think that?" Kiirsi asked.

"Because of the way he acts with our bird."

The bird.

Josh had a parrot that went everywhere with him. On his shoulder. In the car. Everywhere that Josh went, the bird went, too, even to a New Year's Eve party. The hostess couldn't believe that anyone would bring an uninvited parrot to a party.

Josh nuzzled the bird. He talked baby talk to the bird. If a prospective father could be judged by the way he treated a pet—as Susan was suggesting—then Josh was in line for a Father of the Year award.

Charlie—named after his grandfather, Chuck Cox—was born January 19, 2005. Chuck and Judy went to Utah to be there when the baby was born. When the morning arrived and Susan knew she was in labor, Josh was too busy on his computer to drive her to the hospital, so Chuck and Judy did. When Josh finally showed up at the delivery room hours later, he had his laptop in tow. Whatever he was doing was much more important than comforting his wife while she had his first baby. When Susan called out for him, Josh barely glanced up from the screen. Annoyed and exasperated, Chuck took Josh by the sleeve and pulled him over to Susan's bed and told him to hold her hand as Charlie was born.

"See, Dad," Susan said later, looking up with a weary smile. "He does care."

In 2006 Susan became pregnant for the second time. She had expected her parents to be overjoyed when she called them in Puyallup with the news; instead she was met by disappointment. It had nothing to do with a new baby, and everything to do with the fact that the bond between their daughter and Josh Powell would be that much harder to break.

Chuck was especially disenchanted.

"Why would you want to do that twice?" he asked.

Susan kept the cheer in her voice, though she knew what he meant. "Oh, Dad. Don't say that," she said.

Yet Chuck couldn't be stopped, no matter how much he loved his daughter. She needed to hear it. "You have to get rid of Josh and get a real person for a husband," he said.

Susan sounded hopeful in her last word on the subject during that call.

"Everything will get better," she said.

Chuck was skeptical. He'd never forgotten how he had to drive Susan to the hospital when Josh was too busy.

Braden was born January 2, 2007.

Josh and Susan had a second car until Josh decided the gas and maintenance were too expensive. He didn't factor in all the extra trips they would have to make in the van and how inconvenient it would make Susan's life.

Or maybe he did.

"He bought Susan a bike," Michele Oreno recalled later. "So she had to bike back and forth to work, which isn't a short distance—about seven miles each way."

It took Debbie Caldwell's husband, Ken, to tell Josh just how crazy it was to have Susan ride a bike to and from work. It was too far. It was dark in the morning. It was an all-around bad idea. So Josh decided he would show them all that it was no big deal. He tried riding a bike to work—and quickly realized how arduous the task was. He spent $1,500 to motorize it. Josh's experiment at bicycling ended after just a week or two, as soon as it got cold.

Next, Josh decided that driving Susan to work, then taking the Town & Country minivan on to his workplace was the answer. He was off work earlier in the afternoon than she was and was supposed to pick up the boys, and later, Susan. He usually left them stuck without rides. For some reason, Josh didn't like Susan to be alone with the boys in the van. Her friends speculated it was because Josh was afraid she'd leave.

For Susan, dealing with Josh's restrictions on spending was toughest around the holidays. She sent Rachel Marini an e-mail one year saying that Josh wouldn't let her buy Christmas presents for their sons. It broke Rachel's heart.

One thing Josh didn't seem to skimp on, however, was life insurance. In the first few years of their marriage he and Susan held a million-dollar policy—$500,000 on each of them—from Beneficial Life. Two years later, they took out another policy, this one with New York Life. That policy's payout was for $2.5 million—a quarter-million dollars on each boy, and a million each on Josh and Susan.

Susan's friends remember another day when she needed a babysitter for just an hour or two. But the meeting Josh took her to stretched into the night. Josh had apparently arranged for some legal work to be conducted that day, including the signing of a power of attorney. That way he would have written authorization to represent or act on her behalf in private affairs, business, or other legal matters should she become incapacitated. Or worse.

About three months after Josh and Susan took out the second life insurance policy, they made a trip to Puyallup. On September 6 and 7, 2007, Steve Powell wrote in his journal about a visit Josh and Charlie had made to his home. Braden, just eight months old, was at the Coxes with Susan because Susan didn't like the boys around Steve. Steve wrote that Susan wanted another child, a daughter, but Josh didn't want to have sex with her and wished he had ended their marriage years ago, before they had Charlie and Braden. Matter-of-factly Steve noted:

> *Josh talked on and on, very openly, about how he would love to get rid of her. He is not attracted to her. He said he daydreams about having someone come to his door to report that she was killed by a drunk driver . . .*

While Susan prayed for a baby girl and tried out possible names she liked—Adeline, Jadeline, and Aubrey were a few—Josh was wishing her dead.

As far as anyone knew, Josh had never been physically abusive, although Susan told some friends she had once shoved him and he had threatened to hurt her if it ever happened again. Another friend recalled that Susan said Josh had shoved her, slapped her, and tried to lock her out of the house. If there was a physical altercation, there was no record of any police report or evidence that Susan sought medical attention. She did, however, call her sister. It was in the spring of 2007 when Denise picked up the phone to find Susan in tears. Between Susan's sobs, Denise tried to make out what she was saying.

"What's wrong? What's happened?"

Susan took breath. "Josh pushed me."

Denise had been there—she'd made some bad choices in men. "Oh, no. Are you okay?"

Susan said she was all right, but she was frightened.

"I don't know what to do," she said.

"You need to get away from him," Denise said. "I'll get in my car and come and get you and the boys."

Susan turned down the offer. "No, no, Denise. It's such a long drive. And he'll get custody of the boys if we try and leave. He told me it would be kidnapping."

And there was something else that Josh had told Susan.

"He said I'd get the boys over his—or *my*—dead body."

Susan was not a coward. She often stood up for herself and she *always* stood up for Charlie and Braden. She tolerated Josh's unpredictability and tirades because she was hoping that with counseling he would change. Susan was a pretty woman, maybe the prettiest in her ward. She wasn't particularly vain, but she did pay attention to her looks. She played with her hair, did her nails, and carefully applied just enough makeup to look pretty but not draw attention to herself. When her husband ignored her, she tried even harder to win him over.

Although there were years when she carried some extra weight after the boys were born, Susan was very fit. She had exercise equipment in their basement, and according to Michele Oreno, Susan could "whip Josh's butt anytime, any day. She was strong. She worked out and she was buff. Josh was a wimp," she recalled.

None of Susan's efforts to be attractive meant anything to Josh. After attending a sister's wedding in Puyallup, Susan wrote in an e-mail that her sister wanted five children, and her new brother-in-law wanted twelve.

I'd be good with three but I'm not sure how that would come about.

Yet, just when Susan despaired of living the rest of her life without sexual intimacy or even casual affection, Josh would surprise her with some attention.

In an e-mail in July 2008, when their relationship was particularly rocky, she wrote:

. . . He even initiated some intimate time Wed night, shocker, I know. Funny, it's been so long it feels like a dream or surreal. And yes, I still love him/care about him and think we can have a happy, loving, functional marriage and be a good example to our kids . . .

12

My 3 yr old told me for the first time yesterday, "mommy I can't I'm too busy working" which is verbatim what his father tells me, and he was stomping around the house acting angry (which we both do) and gives scowls to me and others at church when being told no (which is I think another thing from his dad) . . .

—SUSAN POWELL E-MAIL, JULY 11, 2008

There is always help for Mormons who are struggling. Susan and Josh got help at least once by going to the "bishop's storehouse," one of many LDS food storage buildings around the country stocked with mostly nonperishables meant to support the faithful if the need arises.

In April 2005 Susan wrote in her journal that the church was paying for their groceries and utilities. Josh and Susan were given some meat in addition to vegetables and canned food. In return for the food, they agreed to perform a service for the church. Susan did, but Josh, who had been asked to do some gardening for his ward, never did. None of the Powells' friends had ever heard of anyone reneging on such a commitment.

In good times and bad—including when they earned a decent income together—controlling the finances was a way for Josh to exert authority over Susan.

Things became even more serious after Charlie and Braden were born. When he was about a year old, a doctor diagnosed Charlie as malnourished. The backyard garden that Josh thought could feed the family was not enough for a baby. Susan bought some supplements to feed the boy.

One time Rachel Marini overheard Josh say something about Charlie's dietary needs that nearly knocked her off her chair.

"He gets one meal a day at day care. That's all he needs. You can give him formula and that is it. You are not wasting my food on him because he's just going to poop it out!"

Who in the world talks like that about their own kids? Rachel wondered.

When Susan and Josh were helping Rachel and Tim move into their home in American Fork—the first and one of only a handful of houses Josh sold as a Realtor—Susan began to cry as she helped unpack groceries and kitchen items. She told Rachel that she had never seen so much food.

"He'd take her to the grocery store and give her $20 and say 'Buy the food for the week for the family,'" Rachel said later. "And then he'd go buy whatever he wanted. So he was allowed to spend money on whatever he wanted, but she wasn't." Josh also forbade Susan spending money on makeup or yarn, what he called her "crap."

And despite his constant Ebenezer Scrooge routine, at the time of Susan's disappearance thousands of dollars' worth of chairs and desks filled the couple's garage on W. Sarah Circle. It was office furnishings that Josh had grabbed when he had worked as an installer for Virco, an office furniture company his father was a salesman for at one time. The garage was also crammed with remote-controlled cars, box after box of batteries, and expensive tools. Anyone who knew their money woes would have understood right away: money—whatever they had—had been spent on Josh.

Susan scrimped for almost a year to get a washer and dryer, and later, a love seat for the living room.

"She gave up so much stuff to finally get her love seat," Rachel said. "That was a big deal to her."

It was the same love seat where Susan and JoVonna sat and crocheted on December 6. The same love seat confiscated by police. The love seat near where the blood was recovered after Susan vanished.

Before Susan could begin work as a stockbroker, Josh got the brainstorm to get a license to sell real estate and he wanted her to help him, so she studied and got her license, too. He suggested they work together, which was code for his real plan—that Susan would do the difficult work.

Josh first sold homes through Prudential, then switched to HOMEnet Real Estate, which took a smaller percentage of his profit. When Rachel and Tim Marini moved to Utah, Josh sold them their house in American Fork. It seemed like a good start, but despite Josh's hopes, it wasn't the harbinger of great sales to come. He didn't have the upbeat, can-do personality that is the hallmark of most successful agents.

"He was a pain," Rachel recalled later. "He was very inattentive. We would call him and say, 'Hey, we're really interested in this house.' He'd say, 'Okay, we'll go look tomorrow.'" They had to prod him to get him to move more quickly.

Chuck Cox thought just *maybe* Josh would do well in real estate. No employer could stand him for more than two weeks, and that's about all the time a client would have to spend with him.

Mike Khalaji worked for HOMEnet. Since Josh worked out of W. Sarah Circle, he went into the broker's office only on occasion, which suited Mike and others in the office just fine. As Mike saw it, Josh was a compete braggart, the kind of guy who wouldn't shut up about all of the amazing things he was doing.

Josh's career selling houses turned out to be very expensive. He was more interested in promoting himself than in finding clients and selling houses. He asked his father to create a radio jingle for him, and Steve did.

> *Come home to your castle*
> *Call Josh Powell Realtor!*

Rachel and Tim—the best friends Josh ever had—saw two distinct Josh Powells. They even named them: Washington Josh and Utah Josh. Washington Josh was quirky and a lot of fun. Utah Josh was controlling and selfish. As close as the couples had been, the Marinis cut off contact with their best friends after an awkward road trip to Puyallup in the spring of 2006.

The weirdness started before they left and escalated every mile of the journey.

As they packed the Marinis' van, Susan quietly hid an extra bag under a seat.

"What's that for?" Rachel asked.

Susan wore a grim expression. "If things don't improve, Charlie and I will stay with my parents. I'm not coming back with him."

Rachel didn't know what to make of the remark, but Susan didn't need prompting to clarify.

"I've done everything I can think of to do. Even, at this point, my bishop, my parents, everyone is telling me I've done everything and it's time. I've done my due diligence and can leave with a good conscience."

Susan told Rachel that Josh was talking to his father for hours at a time, several times a week. After every conversation with his dad, Josh was more controlling and more insulting to her.

During the trip they put up for hours at a time with Josh, his pet bird, his berating Susan, his ignoring one-year-old Charlie, his lateness, his disrespect, and his completely annoying cheapness.

"We had to eat out along the way, and he would let Susan order one thing from the dollar menu," Rachel recalled. "He'd get a tray full of stuff for himself but she was allowed to order just one thing on the dollar menu. And we were buying extra stuff and slipping it to her."

Rachel felt sick about the changes she'd seen in the couple. Susan was angry and fearful. Josh seemed bitter and cruel. Something terrible had happened between them.

"They were happy as newlyweds. Josh was a very different person when they lived in Washington. He was still annoying, and talked your ear off. He never shut up. He was obsessive about things, but he wasn't controlling. I loved hanging out with them. They were our best friends. I remember going home after that trip and talking about it: Love, love, love, love, love 'Washington Josh' and Susan; do not like 'Utah Josh,'" Rachel said. "It was like he was possessed or something. It was like he was a completely different person."

Rachel noticed that Josh and Susan's bickering seemed to be contagious; she and Tim argued more after being around their friends. That's when they knew they had to make a break.

Like other Realtors, Josh wanted the exposure that came with an ad in the Yellow Pages. A big ad meant big success. The Yellow Pages publisher required a deposit and then a monthly payment for the promotion. Josh agreed to an $83,000 contract and also bought ads on city bus benches and thousands of refrigerator magnets. In a photograph duplicated on the magnets, Josh is wearing a smart leather jacket and smiling. All in all, it was going to cost him nearly six figures. The commitment was huge for even a veteran agent, let alone a newbie like Josh.

Not long after the ads started appearing and magnets were stuck all over friends' refrigerators—and reality set in—Josh had a change of heart. He told Chuck and Judy that a phone number on the magnets had been incorrect and that a Yellow Pages employee had written a letter absolving Josh of any responsibility for the cost of the marketing. In reality, Yellow Pages sued Josh for the debt, so Josh sued Yellow Pages. He shrugged off the incident and decided the way out of debt was to declare bankruptcy. Josh planned for it, deliberately maxing out credit cards and buying clothes and expensive tools at Sears and JCPenney. Susan begged him not to, saying it wasn't honest, but he did it anyway. In April 2007 the Powells filed for Chapter 7, listing more than $200,000 in credit card, furniture, student loans, and other debts, not including their mortgage and car.

When Josh's real estate career completely dissolved, Josh wanted John Hellewell to teach him computer programming. John said no, that he had better things to do than spend the day programming at work, then spend the evening with Josh Powell instead of his wife and children. It was Kiirsi who made it happen. She made a deal with Josh.

"I've got a proposition for you, Josh," she said, when he refused to let up on his latest plan of action.

Josh looked at her suspiciously. "What is that?"

"I'll tell John it's okay to work with you in the evening . . . *if* you go to church once a month and spend ten minutes a week with Susan. Just ten minutes!"

"I dunno," Josh said.

"And it's not ten minutes on your laptop, or computer. Just sitting by Susan, holding her hand. Maybe watching a movie together."

"No," Josh said. "I can't do that. I'm busy."

"No, you're not, Josh. That's the deal. John teaches you programming . . . for *free*. All you have to do is go to church once a month and pay Susan some attention."

Josh, not without reluctance, finally agreed.

He didn't stick to the agreement for long. He stopped going to church. He stopped paying Susan even the few minutes of attention Kiirsi had mandated. Instead, his sole focus became his new career—computer programming. As John continued evening training sessions, Josh got an IT job at Aspen Distribution, a trucking and warehousing company.

At the time, Susan wrote to a friend:

They gave him a work issued laptop and an identity badge so I know he feels special. I pray and hope that

*his skills will keep his company satisfied and he can
stay long term.*

Despite Josh's new career and Susan's hope that her husband would find his way in the world and some stability in a
new career, she was taking concrete steps to formulate an escape plan. The day he was at his job interview, Susan was
home on the phone calling around to divorce attorneys,
setting up phone consultations. She wrote in another e-mail:

*I did manage to get ahold of one and feel a lot better
about my rights.*

On the advice of a divorce attorney, Susan made a videotape of their belongings. Looking into the camera, with Charlie underfoot, Susan narrated the tour of their home:

*This is me. July 29, 2008. It is 12:33 Mountain Time.
I'm covering all my bases making sure that if something happens to me or my family or all of us that our
assets are documented. Hope everything works out and
we're all happy and live happily ever after, as much
as that's possible.*

On the last sentence she smiled slightly and rolled her eyes
while sounding skeptical.

During the forty-four-minute video she pointed out Josh's
elaborate computer setup in the basement, with multiple
screens and five hard drives; his locked filing cabinets; 3,000
pounds of wheat stored in huge buckets and bags; thousands
of dollars' worth of tools, cameras and bikes; an unused
treadmill; a $300 meat grinder; Josh's remote-controlled cars;
every type of saw made; a motorcycle; welding machine;
strollers; and old VCRs. In the garage is what Susan calls the
"chemical cabinet," multiple shelves of lawn and plant chemicals, and carton after carton of new, unopened furniture,
window blinds, and water purification systems.

The video shows a family in chaos. The contents of the

house, garage, yard, and storage shed aren't just the everyday young family's belongings. It's a picture of both obsessive spending and hoarding. The clutter, the stacks of stuff, are overwhelming to see. Josh never met a tool or gadget he didn't covet.

Susan was afraid Josh would find the video, so she gave it to Kiirsi for safekeeping, in case anything happened to her.

13

I don't know how you can help except talk with me and be another individual that would know about the situation if questioned b/c things went crazy later. Sad that I'm this paranoid.
—SUSAN POWELL E-MAIL, JULY 7, 2008

On Monday, December 14, the day after his church opened its arms to him, Josh failed to show up for a police interview—and for the polygraph the police wanted to administer. When word got out, people were saddened and suspicious that he wouldn't meet with the police or move heaven and earth to find Susan.

His Salt Lake City attorney, Scott Williams, said Josh had cancelled the Monday meeting because the lawyer needed time to "advise and consult." Josh also contacted a media consultant so he would "look and sound more sympathetic when questioned about Susan Marie Powell's disappearance."

The police did see Josh briefly on Tuesday, December 15, when they obtained a warrant to collect a DNA sample. The detective trained to draw blood repeatedly asked Josh if he was anxious or nervous. He was so tense it was difficult to draw the blood sample.

It was the last time Josh would ever talk to the West Valley City police.

He answered general questions about Susan, although his attorney answered most of the questions and spoke for Josh. The police asked about Susan's shoe size, any scars she had, what kind of jewelry she wore, and how recently she had highlighted her hair. Josh refused to take a polygraph and wouldn't pinpoint exactly where he and the boys had gone camping. He was still vague about naming Simpson Springs.

West Valley City police had already flown state helicopters over the Simpson Springs area and within a few days they would be on the ground, inspecting dozens of mines along the Pony Express Trail.

The police said they still had questions about the camping trip and Susan's state of mind on the Sunday she vanished.

"We're not marriage counselors," Assistant Police Chief Craig Black told the media. "If she wants to be away, that's her business. We just would like to have information that helps us find her."

On Wednesday, December 16, police named Josh a "person of interest." They said that he had information and details that could help locate Susan and described an "unusual lack of cooperation" on his part. They said that the case was suspicious and stopped short of calling it a criminal investigation, but were busy preparing warrants for Josh's work computer, telephones, mobile records, USB drives, and the family's bank accounts.

That same week, the Coxes held a news conference in Puyallup. Sitting at a long table with his wife, his daughters, and his parents John and Anne, Chuck said that Susan had never said anything about being afraid or wanting to leave the marriage. With a Christmas tree behind him and tears in his eyes, Chuck called Josh "a super father" to the boys and said he didn't think the marriage was ever abusive.

Like he'd done when he hugged him at church, Susan's father tried to keep his true fears from being known. He didn't want to scare or push Josh into doing something that could harm Susan . . . if she was still alive. Chuck was holding out hope that Josh had locked Susan up somewhere, and if the police put pressure on him, Josh would cave and say where she was.

Inside, Chuck never believed that camping trip story for one minute.

Who would?

By the end of the first week of Susan's disappearance everyone, especially local and national media, were well into the familiar routine that follows the disappearance of a missing young woman, especially a pretty one. First, hundreds of people gather in groups to help search the areas in which the missing woman was last seen. Next, suspicion falls on the husband or boyfriend. Then as pressure mounts, candlelight vigils and colored ribbons mark the woman's disappearance. While there was no massive search—there was no place *to* search—there was a vigil, and there were remembrance ribbons for Susan in purple, her favorite color.

Susan Powell's disappearance, however, was different from that of other women who go missing or are murdered. Police had never been called to the Powell home on a domestic disturbance. Josh didn't appear to have a secret life. There was no other woman, or man, with whom he was sneaking around.

Utahans know a thing or two about missing people. Thousands turned out to help search for Elizabeth Smart when the fourteen-year-old was kidnapped from her bedroom in her house in Salt Lake City in 2002. In 2004, they helped again, that time searching for Lori Kay Soares Hacking. Her husband said she didn't return from a morning jog.

Chuck Cox was a quick study. He'd picked up on the media's fascination with a missing girl, a news hook that even had a name: "missing white woman syndrome." Television in particular devoted a disproportionate amount of air time to crimes involving a young, attractive, white, middle-class woman or girl. Susan's father took advantage of this to give the media everything they wanted, all in an effort to find his daughter. By the end of the first week, Chuck had given at least forty interviews, including to *Larry King Live*, *Good Morning America*, *The Today Show*, and *Geraldo*.

Susan's friends—and most of Josh's friends—began to suspect Josh. Although their marriage had been sealed for eternity in the temple, Susan had contemplated divorce. She had started to stand up for herself. Friends said she would never, ever have walked away from her boys and that she would not have permitted the midnight camping trip. Some knew that she had found a way to set some money aside, just in case.

They reflected on Josh's odd personality and offbeat sense of humor and were reminded of bizarre comments he had made, which took on a sinister light in retrospect.

They remembered how Josh, in casual conversations, seemed obsessed with how one could get away with murder. He talked about the mistakes Mark Hacking had made when the Salt Lake City man reported his wife, twenty-seven-year-old Lori, missing July 19, 2004. According to family members, Lori Hacking was five weeks' pregnant at the time. Mark Hacking eventually confessed to shooting his wife and disposing of her body in a Dumpster. Josh said Hacking "screwed up disposing of his wife's body" and that it was best to "stick close to the truth" when talking to the police and "don't tell too many lies."

The husband of a coworker remembered a Christmas party in 2008 when Josh talked about his fascination with TV crime investigation shows. He discussed "how to kill someone, dispose of the body, and not get caught," and told the partygoer that Utah's thousands of mine shafts and tunnels were the perfect place to "dispose of someone and no one would ever search for the body."

14

My friend came over b/c he was at her house getting
help from her hubby for his business and my friend
knows short hand so she wrote down the crazy stuff
he said so I'll let you see it once she gets it to me via
e-mail. I've also written a sort of will in my desk b/c
at this point, I don't know what to think anymore.
—SUSAN POWELL E-MAIL, JUNE 30, 2008

Susan told a surprisingly wide circle of friends that she had
an escape plan. When she got a raise at Wells Fargo, her
mother urged her to put some money in a separate account.
Judy said that Josh would never know the difference. So
Susan did it. Josh found out and was upset about her having
money that he didn't have access to, so it was one more thing
they argued about. She had started the process of finding an
attorney and had sent an e-mail to a friend saying she and
the boys might need a temporary place to stay. Even her
father told her to get out if she had to, even if she had to
leave the boys. They'd hire an attorney and get custody.

Susan had written a journal since childhood and she kept
the most recent one at work. Up to her last entry written a
few weeks before she vanished, she wrote about the issues
in her marriage. On June 28, 2008, Susan even wrote out an
informal will stating:

>*I want it <u>documented somewhere</u> that there is extreme turmoil in our marriage.*
>
>*If something happens to me, please talk to my sister in law Jenny Graves, my friend Kiirsi Hellewell, check my blogs on MySpace, check my work desk, talk to my friends, co-workers, and family.*
>
>*If I die, it may not be an accident, even if it looks like one. Take care of my boys.*
>
>*I want my parents Judy and Chuck Cox <u>very</u> involved and in charge of [Charlie and Braden]. I love you Charlie and Braden and I'm sorry you've seen how wrong/messed up our marriage is. I would never leave you!*

She also wrote that the night before, Josh had threatened her, saying he would "destroy" her and her life "would be over" if she filed for divorce. She put the will in her safe deposit box.

More than once Susan had used her wedding anniversary in April as a goal and as an ultimatum to Josh—if things weren't better by April 6, she would leave him. Whenever she and Josh talked about divorce he threatened to take the boys and leave her with nothing, as his father had done to his mother. As the fall of 2009 approached, Susan seemed to have made a decision. She lost some weight, maybe to prepare herself for her new life apart from Josh, maybe over stress, maybe just losing the weight she had gained during her last pregnancy.

For years Susan had begged Josh to have individual counseling and to go with her to marital counseling. He'd go once and stop.

"She tried to get him to see a psychiatrist, because she thought maybe he was bipolar, but he refused," Kiirsi recalled. "He'd say, 'No, my real estate clients might find out I was on medication.' He'd say, 'You're probably the crazy one, you need to go get checked out.' She did see a psychiatrist and asked him if she was crazy. He told her, 'No, you're fine.'"

Susan also knew that prayer, like counseling, wasn't going to save her marriage, either. She wrote to a friend:

I recognize now that me praying or reading scripture and hoping is not going to cut it anymore. I need help and so does he. I'm thinking he will be a lot more receptive to my suggestions of counseling for himself once he sees my own improvements.

Susan had even gone to talk to her ward's lay bishop. In an e-mail she wrote:

The bishop talked with me for an hour, opened with a prayer, and I was already almost in tears. Managed to ramble out my story, he agreed with me on all points (josh has mental issues and/or has lost touch with reality = I'm a stressed, overworked, neglected/abused single mother down to her last straw) he repeatedly asked "what can I do to help?"

The Powells' LDS marriage counselor had suggested they read the book *Bonds That Make Us Free: Healing Our Relationships, Coming to Ourselves,* by C. Terry Warner, the same book Ken and Debbie Caldwell had read when they went to counseling. A professor of philosophy at Brigham Young University, Warner based his approach on what he called "the problem of self-deception," or how we create and perpetuate problems, blame others, and resist solutions.

Since Josh stopped going to counseling and refused to read the book, Susan would read occasional pages to him. She seemed to be applying what she was reading, writing to a friend in the weeks before she went missing:

I'm only on chapter 2 of bonds that make us free, and I'm already realizing that I view him as the "enemy" often. Counseling should be interesting, I've got to keep my mouth shut and let his side come out. It's a female [counselor] so I don't know how he'll handle that.

15

Spoke with RS president @ friend Kiirsi's house and
they both have experiences with mental illness/bi
polar family members. It seems that overall, if someone is bi polar, you don't want them to feel boxed into
a corner or threatened or stressed (or else they'll
"swing manic" etc)
   —SUSAN POWELL E-MAIL, JULY 18, 2008

In early 2009 Susan, Josh, and the boys made the trek from
Utah to Washington to visit with their families. The drive was
a long one, with Susan gamely trying to hold the marriage
together for the sake of Charlie and Braden, and Josh oblivious to his role in its meltdown. Shortly after they arrived,
Josh told Susan that he wanted to take her on a special overnight camping trip. He wanted to leave their sons with his father, instead of her parents.

Susan talked it over with her folks.

"I don't feel comfortable about this," she said.

Chuck didn't either. "It's suspicious."

"He wants us to leave the boys with Steve," Susan said.

Chuck, who could be the calmest person in the midst of a
crisis, bristled at that suggestion. "No. Don't do that. Possession is nine-tenths of the law. If anything happened to you
and Josh, Steve would have the boys," he said.

She had asked Josh why they didn't make it a family trip and take Charlie and Braden. Josh, who had never cared about "alone time" with Susan, was adamant that it be just them.

When Susan finally told Josh she'd go, but only if Charlie and Braden stayed with the Coxes, Josh told her to forget it.

By then the distrust between father and son-in-law was insurmountable. Later, long after she went missing, Chuck Cox wondered if the "alone time" camping trip had been a foiled plan to get rid of Susan in some kind of accident.

"I think he was planning to get rid of her then and it didn't work out because she wouldn't let the kids stay with Steve. She dodged the bullet then," Chuck said later.

During that trip Susan's parents overheard a yelling match between Josh and Susan. The couple and their two boys were staying downstairs at the Coxes. The fight had to do with Susan not wanting to go to Steve's house. Chuck heard Josh call Susan a bitch and a Goody Two-shoes, and heard her respond that she might be a bitch, but at least she wasn't a child molester. There was some kind of scuffle, as if Josh was trying to get the kids out of bed, but Susan stopped him. Josh screamed and slammed the door on his way out. It seemed that Susan had held her own, so Chuck didn't interfere.

It was Susan's last visit home.

In October 2009, Susan's friend Amber Hardman spent the day taking photographs of Susan, Josh, Charlie, and Braden at the International Peace Gardens, a botanical garden in Salt Lake City. She posed Charlie and Braden in the trunk of a tree and their parents beside them. The family looked incredibly happy. But she remembers some awkward moments when she attempted to take pictures of Josh and Susan alone near a gate. She suggested the couple pose with their arms around each other and even asked Josh to kiss Susan. That's when things turned weird. Josh was stilted, uncomfortable, and didn't want to kiss his wife, Amber said. He looked far more comfortable and was more animated when he didn't have to pretend an intimacy with Susan.

Amber and Susan had been friends since 2004, when they had worked together at Fidelity Investments. Now they worked together at Wells Fargo. Amber was no longer attending the Mormon church, but the women were close. Several weeks after the photo shoot, Susan told Amber that she thought she was pregnant. The women bought several home pregnancy tests for Susan to take into the bathroom at work. The results were always negative. But Susan continued to feel nauseous. "She went and got a blood test at the doctor's office, and it was negative, too. But she still thought she was pregnant," Amber said. Susan told her that Josh was hoping she wasn't pregnant, but that after a while he had softened his stance a little.

Amber, like others, now wonders if Josh was poisoning Susan. "He made a lot of organic products for her to drink, a lot of thick yogurt stuff and fermented drinks with kefir."

At about that time, Josh was "leading her on, making her think that their marriage was better," Amber said. Until a huge fight in November. It was a Sunday, the family was home, and Susan overheard Josh telling Charlie and Braden that "Mommy is evil" and "church is evil." Susan didn't hold back and told him she didn't want him saying those things to her sons.

She was furious, and phoned and asked Amber what *she* would do. Amber suggested she go for a drive with the boys, but Susan said Josh would call the police and accuse her of kidnapping.

16

I just miss her and . . . I love her, my boys love her, I
mean a lot of people love her. And she is just . . . just
wonderful. And all I ask is that anyone who can just
help us try to find her.
—JOSH POWELL TO KTVX-TV,
DECEMBER 14, 2009

It was the week before Christmas, but the ringing of the doorbell at the Powell residence in Puyallup was not the UPS
man or FedEx lady with a package. Far from it. In fact, the
sound at the door, and the ringing of the phone, were becoming a major irritant to Steve Powell. Steve liked control. He
didn't like to be questioned about anything.

He opened the front door, but only a sliver. *So much for
living in a gated community.* Steve's face reddened. Outside was yet another reporter. If Josh had believed that
leaving Utah would mean ending the questions about Susan,
he was dead wrong. Steve told the reporter that his son was
being "vilified" and made a scapegoat over Susan's disappearance.

Then he shut the door.

Josh's father would be his best, and nearly only, defender,
leading the charge against Susan's friends, her parents, the

Mormon church, the West Valley City Police Department and, sadly, Susan.

Josh was in Puyallup to spend Christmas and celebrate Steve's sixtieth birthday, but he almost certainly needed help with Charlie and Braden. After all, Josh didn't cook, clean, grocery shop, change diapers, or have any patience with his sons. While home he told his father and sister Alina that Susan might have been having an affair and might be pregnant.

Back in Utah, Kiirsi and John Hellewell were getting their children ready for church the next day when the phone rang. It was Josh.

"John, I need a phone number for Barbara," Josh said. "I need for her to get the bird and take care of it."

"Why can't you take her the bird?" John asked.

"I'm in Washington. The boys and I are here for Christmas," Josh said.

"What?" John was flabbergasted. He had assumed that Josh was staying in the area for the holidays—and for the hunt for Susan. "Why didn't you tell us you were gone?"

Josh skirted the question a little.

"I was fired from my job and I need to get away from the media," he said. Josh hadn't contacted his manager at Aspen Distribution about missing work. Steve Powell had called the company soon after Susan disappeared to find out if they'd heard from Josh. But, as usual, Josh avoided taking responsibility and received a termination letter in the mail.

The two men talked a little longer, Josh telling John that he was unsure if he'd be able to keep the house.

John was disappointed and angry, but he provided the phone number for the bird sitter, Susan's friend Barbara. He hung up and told Kiirsi that Josh and the boys were in Washington.

Kiirsi was stunned. She felt that the circling of the Powell siblings had been a purposeful distraction to allow Josh to sneak away. A man who loved his wife, even just a little bit, would never have left town.

"Let's call the police," she said.

The West Valley City police didn't hide their feelings. The officer on the phone sounded surprised that Josh had left town. It was true that Josh was free to come and go, but they still wanted to talk to him about exactly where he had gone camping the night of December 6 and where he had driven when he rented the car two days later. They were also waiting for results from the state crime lab, which was testing DNA evidence collected from the couple's home.

They were busy getting warrants, which allowed them to track Josh's van for a few days and eventually monitor the phone calls of Josh, his father, and his sister Alina, and the Internet use by Josh and his brother Mike.

Josh would return twice in January and February, to pack up the house and then to get it ready to be rented. But before he left for Christmas—in fact, just ten days after his wife's disappearance—he cancelled Susan's upcoming appointments, including one with her chiropractor. With his power of attorney, he withdrew all the money in Susan's IRA account, about ten thousand dollars.

Although many would later question what the West Valley City police were doing to put pressure on the case, investigators were going where their gut instincts and evidence took them.

It took them to Puyallup, Washington, to see Steve Powell.

Detectives from West Valley City, Utah, and the Pierce County, Washington, sheriff's departments all wanted to meet with Steve. Finally, he agreed to an interview at a neutral place, a library branch in South Hill, near Puyallup, on December 17. The two-hour interview was conducted by Detective Gavin Cook of West Valley City, and two detectives from the Pierce County Sheriff's Office. Steve arrived with his own tape recorder.

The police expected to hear a routine expression of worry and dismay over a missing daughter-in-law. What they heard instead, they wrote later, was "disturbing."

From the beginning, Steve made it clear that he and Susan had had a special relationship.

SP: I mean, she talked to me about her problems and even a little bit about their sex life . . . I mean, she tended to be a little bit open about stuff like that, you know.

Steve said he hadn't seen Susan since February of 2009.

SP: When she and Josh and I were together with the boys it was perfect . . . She was always nice to me, she, she seemed to like me a lot.

He explained, however, that he wasn't welcome at the Coxes, where Susan and the boys spent most of the last visit to Puyallup.

SP: These people are, are very good Latter-day Saints and I'm not.
GC: Okay.
SP: I'm a dropout.
GC: Okay.
SP: I'm, I'm, I'm a bad influence on Josh. I could be a bad influence on their kids.

The conversation quickly went to Steve's favorite topic: his sexual obsession with Susan.

SP: When she was living with me she was very open sexually . . . and she liked to, um, she, she liked to do things.
GC: Okay.
SP: Let's just put it that way.
GC: And, and that would be or what? What did you pick up on or notice in that, that way?
SP: You couldn't possibly miss it. I mean, she, she would, ah, she would, ah, wax her legs and, ah, you know, take a shower and then she would come into my office and say you know, "Feel how smooth they are." You know what I'm saying?

GC: Ah-huh.

SP: I mean, that's kind of a titillating thing, you know.

GC: Was there any sexual contact or any sexual relationship between you and Susan? I'm sorry to be blunt, but you know, what other way to ask?

SP: We never had any actual, you know, like vaginal sex or . . .

GC: Okay. Any kissing or touching or . . .

SP: Oh, yeah.

GC: Okay.

SP: One night she wanted me to um, um, massage her feet and legs and so on because she was kind . . . she had been standing up a lot that day and I, I, I you know I did it and, ah, you know I of course moved her feet to my crotch so she could feel, you know, what she was doing to me and that went on for about an hour.

Steve told the police that he had finally confided his love to Susan.

SP: I didn't want her to move to Utah and I hoped that there was enough feeling there that she would stay and, and she got really upset at me. She would not talk to me for months. It was, it was, it was the worst thing I ever did and it was so troubling . . .

They asked Steve if he thought she might have gone away with another man.

SP: I don't, I can't, I like not to think that she had any kind of relationship with anybody. I mean, she just seemed very happy to be around me to—and among other things, um, which always pleased me because I mean she's the mother of my grandchildren. She's um, she's, she's a beautiful young lady, you know, um.

Steve said Susan's disappearance had hit him hard.

SP: I was in shock when I found out she was missing and I, I kind of was just literally sick for a few days. I couldn't, you know, I couldn't even function.

The detectives, who tried to build a rapport with Steve by being sympathetic about his "deep feelings" toward Susan, asked to walk through his house with him—so they can go back and tell their bosses in the WVCPD that he isn't hiding Susan. Steve is in tears at this point. "I was actually wishing she was there. I wish she was there."

They carpooled back to Steve's house and found no trace of Susan.

The police report notes that Steve was "aroused" and nostalgic while recounting his sexual encounters with Susan. There's no indication if they meant sexually aroused or emotionally aroused. Or both.

Steve told the police that early on he found Josh's alibi "fishy" but that he later changed his mind after talking to Josh.

Soon after Alina and Mike covered for Josh so he could sneak out of West Valley City, they started their own trip back to Puyallup in Mike's 1997 Ford Taurus.

It wouldn't be known for a long time, but at the corner of Elm and Indiana in Baker City, Oregon, the car reportedly broke down. Rather than have it repaired—there are definitely garages in the county seat that could have worked on it—Mike used Alina's AAA membership to have it towed. But he didn't want it fixed. He had it towed to Lindell's Auto and Truck Parts in Pendleton, Oregon, ninety-six miles north. The receipt, dated December 22, indicates Mike sold the car for $100. There are mistakes on the receipt. It refers to the car as a 1997 Ford Escort (it was a Taurus), and it noted that the mileage from Lindell's to Baker City is forty-five miles one way, half the actual distance.

A relative went to Pendleton to pick up Mike and Alina and drive them home to Puyallup.

Sooner or later, Mike would have had to do something with the car anyway. Better to have it picked apart, door handle by door handle, and sold for scrap metal. Now he could stop worrying about the police searching it.

On December 20, two weeks to the day after Susan was last seen, friends, family members, and strangers touched by the story of the missing mother gathered for two candlelight vigils. One was at the Coxes' LDS ward in Puyallup and the other was at Susan's ward in West Valley City.

Friends and neighbors at the West Valley City vigil couldn't believe that Josh would leave the state while they were searching and praying for Susan. Kiirsi was still trying to keep Josh in her life, in hopes that he might reveal information about Susan.

"I know we are all praying for Josh," she told a reporter, amending her words with a quick: "At least, some of us."

The vigil concluded with the singing of Susan's favorite Christmas song, "Silent Night." Kiirsi, Debbie, JoVonna, and others wept as they sang, the lyrics now a prayer for Susan.

Sleep in heavenly peace,
Sleep in heavenly peace.

Few outside his family knew that Josh was back in Washington, so many were surprised when he and four-year-old Charlie attended the Puyallup vigil. When they arrived it was concluding, and for a few minutes he stood silently under an umbrella in the pelting rain. His face carried that same miserable, haunted look that he'd had in front of the TV cameras back in Utah. He made sure that Susan's parents didn't speak to Charlie, although Chuck caught a glimpse of his grandson holding a candle.

Susan's father wrote on Facebook that night:

I just hope being [at the vigil] will encourage Josh to help with the search.

* * *

There were blood spatters everywhere. On the love seat where Susan sat and crocheted December 6. On the tile floor between the sofa and the front door. Near the winter boots she always wore.

In late December, the WVCPD received its first serology results on items from the W. Sarah Circle house. Furniture, the contents of Josh's van, and boxes of items from the house had been hauled to the state's crime laboratory. Luminal testing found widespread traces of blood. There were sixteen drops on the tile, but only a few were substantial enough to test. It was Susan's blood. The lab also tested the rags Josh had used to clean his car the night of December 7, a latex glove, the attachments to the Rug Doctor, the backseat of the van, including a seat belt, and the charred debris found in a bag. There was either no other blood or not enough to test. They tested the couch for other substances, on the theory that if Josh had strangled Susan, she might have urinated. It was negative. They also tested a pancake and "crepe-like" food found in the kitchen garbage, but there was no sign of poison. Of course, Susan had eaten the pancakes Josh had made individually for her.

Tests of the 2009 Ford Focus Josh had rented turned up none of Susan's DNA.

The police kept all the findings to themselves, including that they had found Susan's blood in the house.

17

Susan, I love you SO much! I wish you could know how hard we are looking for you. My heart has a huge hole in it. Your dad is being so strong and so awesome. We've mobilized the internet and the West Valley PD is using everything they can to find you.... We will not give up until we find you! Don't give up! I pray all day that angels will guide you and watch over you.

—JANUARY 8, 2010, NOTE FROM
KIIRSI HELLEWELL TO SUSAN,
HIDDEN IN SUSAN'S SLIPPER

Chuck and Judy Cox went through the motions during the days around Christmas. Despite the presence of their other daughters and grandchildren, there was a profound emptiness in the house where Susan had grown up.

Chuck wrote on the Facebook page dedicated to Susan:

It has been a very difficult few days. We were able to see Charlie and Braden on Christmas Eve and Christmas day for several hours. Both are in good health and spirits and seemed to be unaffected by the current situation . . . We are comforted by all your prayers and support.

Neighbors left candles and notes outside the Cox home, which had a nativity scene in the yard.

The Coxes did not hear from Josh or see him. A family friend drove the boys back and forth between their residence and Steve's. Chuck planned to return to Utah the next week to meet with police, who would tell him that there were no new developments in the case.

But there were.

Police and prosecutors had made a decision that wouldn't come to light for more than two years. Although they continued to call Susan's disappearance a missing-person case, police had concluded by December 8—one day after Josh returned from the camping trip—that they had a criminal case on their hands.

The Salt Lake City prosecutor's office filed paperwork and received court approval to conduct an investigation into what they now believed was kidnapping and murder. It meant they could keep all evidence, facts, and testimony related to Susan's disappearance secret, including search warrants of the Powell home and the minivan. Based on what they'd heard from West Valley City detectives, the prosecutor's office believed that disclosing information about the case could impede the investigation.

Then Josh caught them by surprise, again. Police didn't know where Josh had gone when he was camping on December 6. They didn't know where he had gone when he rented a car December 8–10 and drove 800 miles. They hadn't known he'd left West Valley City to spend Christmas in Puyallup until Kiirsi and John phoned with the news.

They were about to learn that he was leaving West Valley City for good.

It is rare for the family of a missing person to move. Sometimes families hang on to the same address and telephone number for decades in the event that their loved one tries to contact them one day. The exception to the rule is men who kill their wives. They often begin purging all traces of their spouses within days of their vanishings, so eager are they to start new lives.

Josh Powell appeared to be that kind of husband.

To Susan's closest Utah friends—her Mormon sisters Kiirsi, JoVonna, Debbie, Rachel, Amber, Michele, and Barbara—it was inconceivable that Josh was moving away from West Valley City.

Kiirsi talked to Debbie and the others about it.

"How could he leave Susan, wherever she is?" Debbie asked.

"You know the answer," Kiirsi said.

Debbie still wanted to believe that the worst possible thing hadn't occurred right under their noses.

"Why didn't he stay and help look for her?" she asked.

This time Kiirsi didn't reply. Her doubts had deepened, but she still believed there was a slim chance that Susan was alive somewhere.

When Josh returned to W. Sarah Circle in early January to pack up his house, members of the ward and even suspicious friends pitched in. Kiirsi, for one, sought to stay in Josh's good graces, though it sickened her. She did so to see if Josh would confide in her about what he'd done.

With John at work, Kiirsi sat her three children down in their cozy house not far from the Powells'. Charlie and Braden had been a part of their lives since birth, and Kiirsi wanted her children to understand what was going on. Ciara was ten, Bran was barely nine, and Nia had just turned seven.

Kiirsi spoke in that gentle but clear way of hers. She didn't mince words. She just couldn't find a way to sugarcoat the awful reality of what she needed to say.

She took a breath. "You know that Josh may have killed Susan," she said.

The kids looked up at her, their eyes widening.

"I think if we stay his friends," she went on, "and he feels he can trust us, he'll tell us something about where she is. Is it okay with you, knowing he may be a murderer, for him to come into our house? Daddy and I will be here the whole time."

The children looked worried, but said nothing.

Kiirsi prodded them a little. "If you don't want him to, he will not set foot in the house."

"It's okay, Mama," Ciara finally said. "We understand. We really want to help find Susan."

"I promise you that when you go to bed at night we will make sure he leaves, we will lock the door, and we will turn the alarm on. He will not go upstairs. I promise he will not hurt you. He will not come near you."

The kids nodded and said they understood. In turn, each one gave Kiirsi a hug.

Josh came to John and Kiirsi's house a couple of times, to eat something, to take a break, to ask for something he needed in order to pack. He was still working on *his* Web site for Susan. Josh planted himself on the couch with the borrowed laptop and created SusanPowell.org, a site that soon had Susan's friends questioning Josh's motives.

It was a bizarre mix of self-aggrandizement and hate. As time passed, Josh or Steve or Alina added subject headings such as "Mormons Mobilize Against Susan Powell and Family," and "False Claims About Josh *and* Susan Powell." It was tantamount to a smear campaign targeted at a missing mom. Instead of the lovely photos of Susan that had circulated in the local and national press, the team behind SusanPowell .org seemed to use the most unflattering images they could find. Josh said it was to show that Susan wasn't "perfect."

There was more that made Kiirsi's blood boil. The site was more about Josh than Susan. It read like a dating profile.

Josh . . . enjoys gardening, woodworking, and building construction projects. He knows a few songs on the piano and guitar. And he has been known to sing a song when the mood hits. . . . Josh is very involved in his children's lives and every day he includes the children in many hobbies, educational events, and outdoor activities.

While Josh continued to drop in at the Hellewells, Kiirsi didn't ask many questions.

"I was afraid he would run and not come talk to us again," she said later. "And I was hoping and hoping that he would tell us something. I even asked the police, 'Should I put on a hysterical crying show?' And they said, 'Well, if you think it will help. I really don't think he's gonna tell you anything.' So I did. And it wasn't hard to work up real tears—the anguish of missing Susan was always there, just under the surface. I was crying really hard and I said to Josh, 'I miss her so much. I just don't know what could have happened to her.' And he was just kind of looking down and not saying anything and he started crying, too. And I said, 'Josh, when Elizabeth Smart went missing her dad was accused, and he hated it, but he cooperated with the police in every possible way because he knew that the faster his name was cleared, the faster they could find out who took his daughter.' I said, 'If you're innocent and have nothing to hide, what do you have against cooperating with the police? Why won't you go talk to them and fill them in?' He wouldn't answer me. He just stared at the ground.

"It was a huge change from how he used to be, bragging and talking at the top of his voice, talking over you and arguing. He did break down and cry several times at my house but wouldn't say why. And to me, it wasn't like 'My wife is gone. I'm so sad, help me find her.' It was kind of like, 'I've done a horrible thing and now I'm feeling . . . whatever.'"

As they stood in the kitchen of the half-empty house on W. Sarah Circle, Josh surveyed the scene and asked Kiirsi to pack the kitchen things for the move to Puyallup.

"Could I pack her clothes instead?" she asked, adding that she wanted to do something more personal for her friend than boxing up dishes and utensils. There were others who didn't know Susan all that well helping out, too.

"They can do the kitchen stuff," Kiirsi said. "I don't want strangers touching her personal things."

Josh looked around and shrugged. It didn't seem to matter

to him what anyone did, as long as everything got done and he could leave town. Kiirsi started to retreat down the hall to the bedroom, stepping past the half-filled boxes that were a sad reminder that Susan was absent.

Kiirsi wanted to gauge Josh's reaction to Susan's personal belongings. Did he care about them? Did he have something to hide?

She turned and caught his eye. "You know, we can store her things at my house so you don't have to haul them to Washington."

Josh hesitated. "No, I'll take them with me," he said. "She might come back . . . or something."

Josh busied himself with the Christmas tree which had not been fully decorated that season. He packed up the tree lights and the ornaments Susan loved, and eight years of married life, while Kiirsi sorted Susan's belongings in the master bedroom.

In a very real way, it was like packing up after someone's death. Things of little value carry great importance, reminders of the person missing from the scene. Kiirsi could remember when she had last seen Susan in a favorite top, or wearing special earrings that now rested in her jewelry box, or even one of those old wolf T-shirts she loved so much. Each item was more than just a garment or an adornment, they were bits and pieces of Susan. The bags of yarn in particular flooded Kiirsi with emotion. She could visualize Susan sitting in the living room laughing and crocheting, making a blanket for one of her boys or for a new baby at church.

Lost in these memories for only a moment, Kiirsi picked up Susan's favorite blue slippers. They were in sad shape from constant wear, but Susan loved them so much that she refused to throw them out.

As Kiirsi started to put them in the box, it suddenly occurred to her that Josh and his father might have stashed Susan somewhere and were in the midst of brainwashing her or beating her down by telling her that no one was ever going to find her or come for her. Telling her over and over that she was nothing and she had to submit to their will. Making her believe that her family, her friends, and her boys no longer loved or cared about her.

Kiirsi thought that if Josh had hidden Susan, he might need to bring her some clothes. She knew that he was too cheap to buy her anything new.

She set down the slippers and took a breath to listen. Josh was somewhere else in the house.

She would write Susan a note. It would give Susan some hope. And since she had only one pair of slippers, that might be a good place to hide it.

Kiirsi took a notepad and pen from Susan's bedside table. She found some paper with crayon scribbles on one side. Susan had identified that little masterpiece as Braden's artwork and written his name beside it. It was perfect. Not only could Kiirsi use the paper to send a message to Susan, the flipside would be a reminder of one of her babies.

She wrote Susan that everyone loved her, was missing her, and was searching for her. She ended her note with something she needed Susan to know.

> *I've remembered everything you told me and have told it all to the police.*

She hurried because she was afraid Josh would walk in on her.

She folded the note as small as she could and wedged it up inside the toe of a slipper. Josh and Steve wouldn't think to look for a note, but Susan would find it when—and if—she put her foot in there and felt something.

"I knew it was a huge long shot and she was probably dead," Kiirsi said years later. "But I couldn't pass up this opportunity, just on the million-to-one chance she might be alive somewhere, demoralized, scared, and alone."

In addition to Josh's brother Mike, some members of the ward helped Josh pack up both a U-Haul truck and a U-Haul trailer. There was also a small contingent of pro-Josh friends. One, a young woman, in a show of solidarity with Josh, dropped her pants and mooned a TV news camera. She made the evening news.

One friend who helped with the packing later told the police of an incident that had horrified him. After making a trip out to the U-Haul, Josh laughingly called out, "I just loaded Susan's head into the truck!" as if pieces of her had been in his garage all along. He said Josh also joked that ordinary floor stains were blood and seemed secretive about a cellar.

One friend who didn't help with the move was Tim Peterson. Although he had seen Josh a couple of times since Susan's disappearance, he became suspicious when Josh decided to move away. Tim wanted a swing set back that he had given Susan and the boys. After a scuffle between Tim and Mike, the police were called. Josh wisely stayed in the house and the police never saw him. The dispute ended with Tim taking the swing set. His last words to Mike that night were colder than a hurled snowball.

"Susan is gone . . . did you happen to notice Susan is gone? Because I don't see you guys doing anything about it."

18

> If Josh did something to Susan or not I've always said this: his soul was in mega-agony, because if he did something he knew his damnation. He had been to the temple, and we get a lot of instruction in the temple, and it is a lot about the eternities and what is to come.
> —MICHELE ORENO, MARCH 20, 2012

Josh's out-and-out battle with the Coxes began the week he packed up his things in Utah to move to Washington. Josh could be stubborn and defiant, especially when backed up against a wall. He would not be pushed around. The first salvo of the war came innocently enough, however, from Chuck Cox. Susan's father had asked Josh's sister, Jennifer, and her husband, Kirk, to go to W. Sarah Circle to retrieve the photo albums that Judy had painstakingly made to document her daughter's life, her babies, and her marriage to Josh. When Josh, who had promised to return the albums—in his own time—found out about the plan, he blew up.

"They will *never* get those photo albums, not *ever*, and that I'll make sure of it," he told Michele Oreno, who'd never really seen that type of personal outrage coming from her friend and neighbor.

"From that point on," Michele said, "he was against Chuck."

While few had managed to do so, somehow Michele had forged a bond with Josh. It had started at their first dinner when he and Susan argued about Steve for hours at Michele's home, and she may have talked to Josh more than anyone else during the first weeks after Susan disappeared. Michele saw Josh just after he returned from his 800-mile trip in the rental car—although she had no idea he'd been gone for nearly twenty-four hours. Like Tim Peterson, she noticed the chapped and red appearance of Josh's hands.

Michele asked him about this. "What did you do with your hands?"

Josh, who had been applying gobs of lotion, shrugged.

"I don't know," he finally said. "Just being out in the weather."

Michelle had lived through many Utah winters and she'd never seen anything as bad as those red, raw hands just from being outside.

What had Josh been doing? she wondered.

Another time, before he left town for good, Josh went over to return some of Brent Oreno's tools. Brent wasn't home. Michele was never afraid of confronting Josh Powell—or anyone else—whenever the circumstances required a direct approach. She decided it was now or never. She was going to use her encounter with Josh to laser in on what had happened to Susan. She was conflicted, however. There was no denying that part of her cared about Josh. Twenty years older than he, it was partly the mother in her. And yet it went beyond that. It was also Michele's deep belief that everyone is worthy of forgiveness and redemption.

Inside, Michele also hoped that maybe, just maybe, he'd blurt out the truth.

She hurled question after question as they sat in her comfortable kitchen. For his part, Josh, his eyes downcast, seldom met Michele's gaze.

"Why are you moving, Josh?"

"I can't take care of the boys on my own," he said.

She knew that was true.

"Who's going to watch them?" she asked.

"Alina will."

Michele knew that solution wasn't ideal. She thought Steve Powell was a class-A creep. Alina *lived* with Steve. In fact, as far as Michele knew all the grown Powell kids, with the exception of Jennifer, lived with their father.

"Why are you moving in with your dad?" she asked. "You know as well as I do Susan's feelings about him. There is no way on this earth that she would want her babies to be in that house."

Josh defended his father.

"My dad's changed," he said. "He's really a good guy. He's doing things differently."

"Josh, don't lie to me."

"He's changed. He has."

Michele went in for the kill. She felt that she had nothing to lose. She loved Josh, but she was increasingly feeling that Josh had done something so evil, so despicable with Susan that soft-pedaling was not the way to deal with him.

"Josh, what is this you're telling people about how you lost track of time? You don't lose track of time. You knew darn well it was Sunday. Give me a break."

"That's what happened," he repeated a couple of times.

Michele evoked Susan's name, carefully so.

"Josh, what happened to Susan?" she asked, searching his face for some glimpse of something behind his facade.

He bowed his head. "I can't say. I can't say."

"Do you honestly, in your heart of hearts, believe she is still alive?"

"I don't know," he said. "I don't know. I want to, I really want to."

They talked for at least two hours, with Michele desperately trying to find out something about Susan's whereabouts, hoping to trip up Josh, but she got nowhere. It was as if she were talking to a cardboard cutout of a human being.

Josh Powell seemed to have absolutely nothing inside. No sorrow for his missing wife. No concern about where she might be.

Or if she was even alive.

"You need help, Josh," Michele finally said, taking a different tack when it became clear that the ambush interrogation was getting her nowhere. "You need counseling. The boys need it, too."

Josh, his eyes landing anywhere but on Michele's, appeared to acknowledge that he knew he was in trouble.

"I feel empty inside," he said.

Michele wasn't sure what to think. She was sympathetic, but only to a point.

"I always thought he knew what happened to Susan," she said later. "I didn't know if he *did* it, but I knew he knew."

Michele wasn't done with her quest for the truth. She tried to reach out to Josh and e-mailed him three times after he moved away.

He never answered.

And she never forgot his answer to her most important question: What happened to Susan?

I can't say.

Not "I don't know."

I can't say.

Just before the new year, the still-smoldering body of a woman was found under a freeway overpass in Box Elder County, northwest of Salt Lake City. The remains were too badly burned to identify right away, but the police in Utah notified Chuck and Judy Cox. They didn't want the Coxes blindsided by the media. Later, the Coxes would learn that it was not their daughter, but a fifty-five-year-old woman who had committed suicide by dousing herself with a flammable liquid and igniting it with a cigarette lighter.

This was just the first of many false alarms.

On January 7, a body wrapped in plastic and duct tape was discovered in a remote desert valley near West Wendover,

Nevada, about 150 miles from where Josh claimed he'd gone camping.

That, too, brought phone calls to Susan's parents in Puyallup. The deceased was described as five-feet-four—about Susan's height. It turned out that this particular victim was a forty-six-year-old male. Before Susan's disappearance, Chuck and Judy could only vaguely imagine the hurt that consumed a family with a missing child. It was a wrenching ache that just didn't go away. They grieved for the family of the man.

That night they sent out a tweet of condolence to the family. By then Chuck and Judy understood that the world was full of missing people. Some, like that man, who'd never come home again. And even fewer, like Elizabeth Smart, who did.

19

He said he was innocent and we took him at his word.
We thought that's for the police. He had not been
charged. He had not been arrested. So our job as a
Christian neighbor, we felt, is to pray for that, for the
truth to be revealed, and let God handle those things
with the authorities. Let the Lord handle that.
   —PASTOR TIMOTHY ATKINS, MARCH 9, 2012

As bunkerlike as Steve Powell must have wanted his Country Hollow neighborhood residence to be, Josh Powell couldn't dodge the police—from Utah *or* Washington—or the reporters, the purple ribbons, and even Susan's picture, which would soon loom over Puyallup.

Finally, however, Josh caught a break. He met a peer who didn't rush to judgment and assume he had murdered his wife.

Introducing Josh to Timothy Atkins might have been the best thing Steve Powell ever did for his son. Steve had no use for any religion. Tim Atkins knew that, of course, but when his neighbor called to suggest that he meet his son and grandsons who were moving up from Utah, Tim and his wife Brenda agreed. Tim was the pastor at Faith Bible Church, an independent church with about forty members in the nearby South Hill area of Puyallup. The two men had a few things in common. Tim was thirty-five; Josh turned thirty-four in January. Each had clipped dark hair and a goa-tee. And both men were fathers to young children. Three of Tim's four children attended Carson Elementary School where Charlie would attend kindergarten.

The Atkins family had Josh and his sons over for dinner, and Josh and Charlie often stopped by after school. "He didn't have a job at the time, so he'd come by the house," Tim re-membered. "We'd sit and talk and I'd open the Bible. I'd talk to him about putting his faith in the Lord Jesus, and share the gospel. He'd always thought of Christianity from the standpoint of Mormonism, and he was really against Mor-monism so we were talking to him and trying to help him, even emotionally."

Josh had lost a lot of weight, wasn't sleeping, and appeared to be grief-stricken. Tim and Brenda had questions about Susan's disappearance, and sometimes they asked about it. Like Kiirsi back in Utah, however, they didn't want to frighten Josh away.

Tim refused to give in to media reports and neighborhood gossip. He and Brenda made a pact that they'd treat the young father as an innocent man. They weren't there to judge him, but to help him and his two little boys. Tim had his suspi-cions, but he didn't press Josh for answers right away.

"I told him that maybe there would be a time that he would be willing to open up and talk with us. And there was. On a number of occasions he would begin to explain what he thought happened," Tim later said. "He said he thought she had taken off."

Tim encouraged Josh to talk to the police, and take them to where he said he'd gone camping. And he made another point repeatedly: that Josh should reconcile with the Coxes.

"It's the right thing to do," he said.

After doing his own reading and research, Tim created a list in his head of ten things about Susan's disappearance that he thought were suspicious:

There was new snowfall overnight, but no car tracks or footprints leaving the house the next day.

Why would Susan leave her keys and purse in the house?

Who had locked up the house? Susan couldn't have without her keys.

Josh was unwilling to meet again with the police.

Josh wouldn't tell the police exactly where he had camped.

It seems strange to go camping in the middle of the night with two little boys.

Josh took their only vehicle. How would Susan get to work?

Josh said he lost track of what day it was.

Josh delayed contact with the Coxes while Susan was missing.

Josh wouldn't say where he drove in the rental car.

Josh gave some short answers to some of the questions, and mumbled his way through others, but he never changed his story. He looked Tim and Brenda in the eye and said he didn't know what had happened to his wife.

Although he had been vehemently critical of the Mormon church long before he left West Valley City, Josh surprised Tim and Brenda when he took Charlie and Braden to attend Sunday school at a Puyallup ward. That lasted only a couple of weeks.

A disappointed and angry Josh told Tim the reason why.

"Everyone thinks I'm guilty," he said. "They are treating me like I killed Susan. I didn't kill her. I don't know what happened to her."

There was, likely, another reason why Josh stopped taking the boys to church.

Rachel Marini, despite living in Utah, had kept her finger on the pulse of what was happening in Puyallup. She talked to a friend who was a member of the ward.

"Charlie was being a pain in the Sunday school class," the friend said. "And the teacher said, 'Look, if you don't stop, I'm going to go get your mom and dad.'"

Charlie, who'd taken to acting out in the weeks following his mother's disappearance, looked at the teacher.

"My mom's dead," he said.

The Coxes weren't blind when it came to Josh and his need to control every moment of his disintegrating life. But they might have been a little naïve about the lengths to which Josh would go to maintain a toehold on his old life.

It was a damp, cold January afternoon when Chuck and Judy bundled up and drove over to Steve's house to see their grandsons. They were concerned about the boys and, of course, they were missing Susan.

Country Hollow's gates were wide open as usual, and the Coxes drove right in. Near the entrance, they quickly spotted Josh and the boys at a park. Chuck parked and he and Judy walked over. Almost immediately the smiles on their faces from seeing the boys melted away.

Josh stood and faced them while Charlie and Braden hung back.

He was stone-faced. "This is not acceptable," he said.

"We were nearby," Chuck said, although that wasn't true. Their hearts ached for the boys and they just wanted to see them. It was strange that they'd have to lie about that kind of thing, but Josh was acting like they were there to do the boys harm or something else completely absurd.

"You can't just drop by. From now on you're going to have to e-mail me to make arrangements."

Both Chuck and Judy were taken aback. *E-mail? Is it really getting to that?*

In fact, it was, and it was about to get worse.

Even after they knew the rules, Josh made it difficult for the Coxes to see their grandsons. Both boys had birthdays in January and Chuck and Judy asked if they could have a party for Charlie at their house.

"No," he said flatly. "We're having a party at my dad's. You can come to that."

It wasn't ideal. After all, Steve Powell would be there.

Chuck decided to spend the day helping a friend and he and Judy didn't attend the party.

Rachel heard through the grapevine that Josh had contacted the ward for help with the party. Specifically, Josh wanted the ward to invite some other kids to attend Charlie's fifth birthday party. Braden's third had recently occurred, too, but at that age it wasn't as crucial to have a bunch of other kids around.

As every parent knows, a fifth birthday is one of the biggies.

Ordinarily it would have been no big deal for the ward to help out. On the surface, the circumstances warranted it. The dad was new in town. His wife was absent. His little boy was having a birthday party.

But word had circulated that Josh was *that* Josh Powell and some members were reluctant to have their children around him.

"I feel badly, but I have to think of my family first, right?" one member asked Rachel.

Rachel could see the conflict. She didn't know what she'd do if she had a little one invited to a possible killer's home.

When Josh got the word, he dumped the ward and stopped going to church. He and his boys threw themselves deeper into his father's world. Steve Powell, who despised the Mormon Church, must have felt victorious.

Josh was not above doling out favors—for reasons of his own. Out of the blue, he called the boys' great-grandparents, Anne and John Cox, and invited them over for a visit. Chuck's sister, Pam, was visiting her folks at the time, so she came along. While Anne and John talked awkwardly with Josh and Steve, Pam curled up on Steve's sofa with Braden on her lap and read from the only book with photos and illustrations on hand, *World Psychology*.

"The police have cleared me," Josh said. "I'm no longer a person of interest in Susan's case."

Steve nodded and smirked in that manner that made Anne

Cox sick to her stomach. She and her husband knew that was not the case at all.

Josh hadn't been cleared of anything. And why would the police tell him that?

After a while, Charlie moved over to the dining table where he'd begun to assemble some kind of an art project—paper and glue were taking shape in that way that five-year-olds can do. In one moment it's a bird, in another, a dinosaur. Whatever it was, the boy was quite pleased with his creation and was happy that his great-grandparents were there.

When Pam flipped to a page showing an illustration of a woman, Braden pointed at the figure's chest and looked up at her.

"Mommy has an owie," he said.

Alarmed, Pam glanced over at the others, but no one else had heard him.

Mommy has an owie?

When it came time to leave, Braden grabbed his aunt's arm and refused to let go. Charlie begged them to stay longer, but it was clear that Steve and Josh hadn't intended a longer visit and they needed to leave.

Charlie started to cry and ripped up his art project.

It didn't matter that he put his heart and his soul into that project; it was clear to the Coxes that he was hurting, and tearing that up was a way to deal with the pain.

They left Country Hollow stunned by the bizarre household, the creepy vibe that Steve gave them, and Josh's insistence that he'd been absolved of any suspicion by the West Valley City police. But more than anything, it was what Braden had said to Pam that had them reeling.

When the trio told Chuck and Judy their story, Chuck went for his phone to notify the West Valley City police and emphasized the need for another interview with Charlie and Braden.

"They know something about what happened to their mother," Chuck said. "You need to talk to them."

Interviewing children and keeping the interviews admissible to the courts is no easy endeavor. The annals of crime are littered with cases in which coaching young witnesses has been alleged, and proven. The West Valley City police knew all of that, and followed rigorous protocol when investigators interviewed the boys in Puyallup in early 2010. There was no leading, no pushing, just a gently probing conversation with Charlie and Braden while a child psychologist and investigators from Pierce County looked on.

A conspiracy of silence appeared to be reigning over the Powell household.

"Do you know what happened to Mommy?" an investigator asked.

"It's the big secret," Charlie said.

20

Josh's sister, Jennifer, knew that she had to face her father.
No matter that she'd had a zillion reasons to avoid him since
she was a teenager. He had mistreated her mother, introduced
her brothers to pornography, and she thought—as the police
did—that he probably had a hand in her sister-in-law's disappearance.

It was an icy Friday night in January when Jennifer and
Kirk Graves made the surprise visit to Country Hollow. It was
a first for Kirk, too. In fact, in their sixteen years of marriage,
Kirk had managed to avoid his father-in-law when they found
themselves in the same state. Although the Graves had been
friendly with Josh and Susan, Josh had distanced himself
from Jennifer since Susan's disappearance. But now she had
driven 900 miles to ask Josh face-to-face the question she felt
only he could answer: What had he done to Susan?

According to a page Josh added to SusanPowell.org titled

"Jennifer and Kirk Graves ousted from family because of her hysterical behavior," Steve and Josh "tried to be hospitable," even inviting Jennifer and Kirk to stay for dinner. Jennifer had arrived with "a preconceived notion of Josh's guilt" and hid her "true reason" for visiting: she wanted to confront Josh. After dinner, Josh and Jennifer went into another room in the house to talk. While Mike lurked and listened in so that he could back up his older brother's version of events, Jennifer asked Josh where he had hidden Susan's body and if he had ever loved Susan.

What no one knew except for her husband was that Jennifer was wearing a wire. She had gone to the police to offer to tape a conversation with Josh. The police got a court order allowing the secret taping. They called it "Operation Puyallup." While Jennifer was in her father's house, detectives in nearby unmarked police cars listened in.

Jennifer was scared. She didn't know what Josh and her father might do if they figured out she was wearing a wire. She told Josh that there were rumors that he was about to be arrested and encouraged him to turn himself in to the police.

"I haven't done anything and I don't know what rumors you're talking about," Josh said. "I sat down with the cops and I told them everything."

"You didn't tell *me* anything. I've asked but you haven't said anything to me," Jennifer said. "Why don't you put my mind at ease and tell me what happened? I'm your sister. Think about your children. She's your wife, for crying out loud. What happened?"

Josh stuck to his story. He didn't know what had happened to Susan. Jennifer continued to press him.

"Really? Really?" she asked. "Can you look me in the eye, and tell me you really did not have anything to do with it?"

Josh's denials continued.

"You haven't put any effort into helping find her," Jennifer said.

"That's not true," Josh said.

Josh was late picking up a birthday cake for a party for

Charlie and Braden the next day and was trying to leave the house. Jennifer persisted with her questioning.

"Where did you put her?"

Josh was incredulous. "I can't believe you're saying that."

"I was there the day after, when you were cleaning up the house. What the heck is that about? Who does that right after their wife goes missing? Why weren't you out looking? Why were you going around the house cleaning? I don't get it. Were you trying to cover it up? Where is she, Josh? Where is Susan? Where's the body? Did you dump it somewhere?"

Amazingly, Josh didn't lose his temper, and invited Jennifer and Kirk to hang out, and even return the next day for a birthday party for Charlie and Braden. But like a lot of family arguments, it got ugly when old family history was replayed. Alina and Jennifer began to argue about who was at fault in their parents' divorce, taking the same sides they took when they were young. Kirk and Steve argued about Steve's treatment of Jennifer. Jennifer and Steve fought over Jennifer's accusations that Josh had done something to Susan.

"I don't think he's going to be able to escape this," Jennifer said.

"Escape what?" Steve asked.

Jennifer put it as plainly as she could. "Let's see. Joshua's camping in the middle of the night and Susan's gone now. It's pretty obvious."

"Excuse me?" Steve said. "It's not obvious to me."

Her father told her she had worn out her welcome, and his next words were the cruelest he had ever said to her. They were also the last words he would ever say to her. "You are a goddamn fucking bitch is what you are, to talk about your brother and my son that way and make things up."

And that wasn't all. "Get off my porch, just get off my porch!" he yelled at his firstborn. "I'm ejecting you out of my family. I've just given up on you, Jenny."

"That's fine," Jennifer said.

"So, please don't even bother coming back," Steve said.

And she never did.

After that night, Alina, who continued to circle the

wagons with her father and Josh, began to refer to Jennifer as her "former" sister. So did Josh. Mike would describe her as *biologically* his sister.

Like a novel with its most crucial pages ripped out, the most dramatic moments in Steve Powell's life are missing from his journals. In his last entry for 2009 he relates a dream that woke him early on November 10. In the dream, he was at an LDS church attending a party with one of his children. A woman, apparently a teacher, slaps the child. Steve goes to a phone to call the police. A man stops him by placing a hand under Steve's shirt. When Steve tells him to take his hand away, the man says, "I just wanted to see if you had a heart." Steve wrote that he woke "humiliated" but didn't explain whether he was embarrassed over the crack about having no heart, or not defending his child, or something else altogether. There is nothing about Susan's disappearance.

Back in Utah, Kiirsi staged her three-day social media blitz to keep the focus on finding Susan. By the end of the blitz, the Friends and Family of Susan Powell Facebook page had grown to 43,000 members.

With no searches to take part in, the campaign gave Susan's friends something to do. It also gave Kiirsi and the other administrators of the Facebook page more than a few headaches. A few postings veered toward the negative when it came to Josh Powell, outright blaming him for Susan's disappearance. Someone posted sexually explicit comments about Susan and pornographic pictures on the site. Some posters claimed to *be* Susan.

As Susan's best friend—and because Josh refused to—Kiirsi gave a lot of newspaper and television interviews. She tried to keep it positive, refusing to call out Josh as Susan's suspected killer.

Soon, Steve and all his other children, except Jennifer, would create or contribute to Web sites that defended Josh and blamed the Mormon church, the Coxes, Kiirsi, Jennifer, Debbie, and the police for harassing Josh. They would claim that Susan was emotionally abused as a child and mentally unbalanced, had come on to Steve sexually, had renounced her Mormon faith, and had run away with another man.

At about the same time that the Powells began to turn on Susan, Chuck Cox went to his home computer to update followers on the Friends and Family Facebook page. He wrote that the West Valley City police had received results of some of the forensic evidence in the case. Police wouldn't comment, because it could impact the ongoing investigation. They wouldn't even tell the Coxes what they had found. Chuck asked people to continue to pray for his daughter.

> *We are still confident that Susan will be found, and very hopeful that she will be found alive. Make sure that people know she is still missing and make sure no one gives up hope.*

The war between the Coxes and the Powells raged on. The Powells had only the Internet in their arsenal. The Coxes had that and much more. They had national television, "honk and waves," vigils, purple ribbons, and photographs of a young, pretty mother and her two little boys. Most of all, they had America's interest in missing women.

In mid-February, Chuck and Judy Cox, Jennifer and Kirk Graves, and Cox family friend Shelby Gifford went on TV's *Dr. Phil.* The entire hour was dedicated to families coping with missing relatives. In addition to Susan's family, John Green and Ed Smart, both fathers of young women who were abducted, appeared.

Jennifer criticized Josh for not providing information to police or family members.

"I'm kind of caught in the middle. My brother is a person of interest, but my sister-in-law, my good friend, is missing," she said.

She also indicated that Josh completely avoided any questions about Susan's disappearance.

"I asked him if he was involved and he wouldn't

respond . . . he literally doesn't say anything, or he says his attorney told him not to talk to anyone," she said.

On television, Chuck and Judy Cox looked stunned and somber. They were not glamorous people, only parents trying desperately to understand why their daughter had disappeared. They never tried to be anything but who they were.

Host Phil McGraw joined them by wearing a purple ribbon in remembrance of Susan. His grief barely contained, Chuck spoke quietly about how he had been supportive of Josh in the beginning, believing that there must have been a reasonable explanation for Susan's disappearance.

"It's frustrating, he won't cooperate with the police and that's impeding the investigation and it's stopping us from finding my daughter," Chuck said.

The TV host seemed to speak for many when he asked Chuck rhetorically, "How have you kept from grabbing him by the shoulders and saying, 'Tell me what you know about my daughter'?"

Chuck nodded in silence. He knew that feeling, that *need*, to shake the truth out of Josh all too well.

After the Coxes appeared on *Dr. Phil*, a Country Hollow neighbor went door to door, asking if she could tie purple ribbons to trees in their yards in honor of the missing mother Susan Powell, whose children lived down the block. The neighbor with the ribbons didn't think Josh should be able to move to a different state and just forget about his wife. Nearly everybody on the street agreed to the purple ribbons wrapped around their slender-trunked trees.

It might have been an act of remembrance for Susan, or a big F-U to Josh and Steve Powell. In any case the ribbons could not be missed by anyone—especially the Powells. Several posters with Susan's photograph were placed at the gated entrance, and purple streamers and ribbons hung from signs, light poles, and trees.

Tim Atkins, the pastor who was Josh's friend and neighbor, tried to reason with the purple ribbon brigade. He knew another side of Josh and he wanted truth to prevail. A bunch of ribbons hung in an attempt to hurt and shame him was cruel, Tim thought.

"We're not going to let him forget," a neighbor said.

"You haven't talked to him," Tim said. "He's not trying to forget anything. He's trying to survive."

The residents who put up the remembrances of Susan didn't have the permission of the Homeowners Association, and Tim helped the HOA president take the ribbons and posters off light poles. The ones on private property, however, remained for weeks, outlining a path straight to Steve's door.

Steve complained that his grandsons, who had turned five and three years old a few weeks after their mother disappeared, were confused by the photos of Susan in the neighborhood and indicated that he would continue to try to shield the children from emotional trauma. Toward that end, Steve constructed a veritable fortress. He had a tall fence built to enclose the backyard and installed more than a half dozen video cameras, pointed in every direction.

No one coming to the door would arrive unseen.

21

It was ridiculous. How would HE know? He never went to church! I knew it wasn't true. I'd been going to church with her every week.
—JOVONNA OWINGS, ON JOSH'S CLAIM SUSAN HAD RENOUNCED HER FAITH, MARCH 21, 2012

Fifty-three days after Susan disappeared, Josh returned to W. Sarah Circle to get the house ready to rent. He would have preferred to sell it and pocket the money, of course, but couldn't with Susan missing. Instead, from his new home base in Puyallup, he had found some neighbors in Utah whose lease was ending and he struck a deal with them. They planned to make some repairs before moving in, and wanted to work on the basement space where Susan had dreamed of having her hair salon.

If Josh had expected to slip in and out with little fanfare or, even worse, media attention, he was mistaken. Much like in his dad's neighborhood in Puyallup, he faced another sea of purple. Kiirsi, Jennifer, and other friends had decided that if Josh was going to act as though Susan's disappearance was only an inconvenient occurrence, they were going to show him that he stood alone in that regard. Purple ribbons hung everywhere. The front door. The trees. The shrubbery under the windows. Everywhere anyone looked, all they could see was the gentle blowing of streamers made of Susan's favorite color.

Signs were hung outside that literally spelled out what Susan's friends were praying for—and served to send a reminder to Josh.

WE WILL FIND YOU!
WE WILL BRING YOU HOME.

Josh said that he appreciated the decorations. But late one night he snuck out and took everything down, telling Kiirsi that he didn't want the renters to have to do it.

The next day, Josh spent four hours at Kiirsi and John Hellewell's house, using a computer to prepare a lease agreement. He was worried about the media, so he parked his minivan at a Walgreens a few blocks away and John gave him a ride to their house. Later, when John drove him back to the van, the police and FBI were there. They had recognized the vehicle and waited for him to return so that they could serve him with a search warrant and tow it away.

A little while later, Kiirsi met Josh and John at the door.

"What are you guys doing back?" she asked.

Josh stood there, looking pale and shaking. For the first time, Kiirsi detected fear in his eyes.

"Josh was as white as a sheet. I've never seen him look so pale and terrified," Kiirsi later said.

John filled his wife in on what had happened and Josh excused himself. He needed a moment alone. Kiirsi watched as he embarked on a long walk to calm himself.

Three hours later, the West Valley City police returned the van.

Josh didn't know it at the time, but the FBI and West Valley City police had two court orders allowing them to secretly attach a GPS tracking device to the van.

Josh Powell had slipped away more than once. They didn't want him to again.

* * *

Josh saw as few people as possible during that visit. He picked up his beloved bird, which had been with Susan's friend Barbara Anderson since before Christmas. Josh had visited the bird when he was back to pack up the house, but now it would travel home to Washington with him.

Josh quit trusting the Hellewells after the trip. Not because Kiirsi had decorated the house, but because a friend of Josh's from his computer club told him that Kiirsi and John were not his friends, often called the police to share information about him, and liked the media attention too much.

Josh didn't say good-bye when he left. In fact, he never spoke to either of them again.

In mid-February, Chuck and Judy Cox started the Susan Cox Powell Foundation, a nonprofit registered in Washington State to help families of missing people and raise awareness of domestic violence. Josh was furious that Susan's maiden name was in the title, and called it a "pseudonym."

Josh also took issue with the implication that Susan was the victim of abuse.

"They are trying to solicit donations on the bullshit idea I am an abuser," he said.

Steve and Josh began a campaign to discredit Susan. It got ugly. Very ugly. They cast her as a harlot who'd leave her husband and children for a casual fling with a stranger. They made it sound like she'd hit on every man she ever met—and had been doing so for a long, long time.

Susan was flirtatious, but that was different from what Steve and Josh were implying. She even questioned herself after a man at work "had grabbed her butt." The man, interviewed by the police after Susan disappeared, said Susan asked him directly if she was sending out "wrong signals." He told her yes, she was, that she shouldn't tell him things only a wife should share with a husband. She had, for example, told him her "shaving schedule." The man went on to say that Susan was a flirt, but she was incapable of cheating on Josh and would never leave her children.

Steve and Josh next attacked Susan's Mormon faith.

Josh added a page titled Mormons Mobilize to his site of hate and misinformation. There, he criticized what he called "The Susan Cox Powell Movement" and said "the tone and rhetoric is led by Mormons . . . too many supporters are openly parroting the Mormons' hostility toward Josh and his father Steve, because Steve is an ex-Mormon."

Most shocking to Susan's friends, Josh claimed that just before she disappeared, Susan renounced the church by standing up in front of her Mormon ward and saying, "I cannot bring myself to believe in Mormonism, but I can lean on other people's testimonies."

That had never happened.

In fact, regular church attendees like JoVonna felt that the opposite was true.

"I always was uplifted and strengthened by Susan's testimony," JoVonna said later. "She made sure to encourage and always testified to her understanding of Christ's love. She never denied her faith."

Kiirsi said that it was Susan's strong faith that kept her in a loveless marriage with Josh for years.

"If Susan did not have this deep testimony she would have left him long ago and would most likely still be with us today."

Among the tips that continued to pour into the West Valley City police about Josh's whereabouts on December 6–7 was one from a strip club, Duces Wild, which calls itself "the best strip club in Salt Lake City." Three people there—a bartender, a bouncer, and a customer—claimed they had seen Josh drinking and talking too much on Monday, the day he returned from the camping trip.

"He just kept saying over and over, 'I've had a really bad day, and I've got a story to tell,' " one reported to the police. They said they had never seen him before and that he was hard to forget because he was so annoying. The bartender, who later picked Josh out of a photo lineup for the West Valley City police, said that Josh was rude and vulgar to her when she refused to bend down so he could see her breasts. The tip was interesting, but like so many, it didn't go anywhere. There was every chance that the bartender had seen Josh's picture over and over in the newspapers and on TV.

But the next time Chuck was in Utah, he drove by the club, just to see for himself. He didn't go inside.

Even Susan's friends said that, as much as the annoying part sounded like Josh, they couldn't imagine him visiting a strip club.

And where would he have left the boys, anyway?

A woman called the police just days after Susan disappeared to say that she had been having an affair with Josh. Several months passed before police could check out her story. Referred to as "Kourtney" by the police, she told them that she met Josh—who told her his name was "John Staley"—through an on-line dating service several months before Susan disappeared. He said his wife had died. They had sex five to six times in his van and he paid her $800 over the months. It wasn't until she saw news coverage of the case that she knew his true identity.

The police drove around with "Kourtney" to sites where she said she met with Josh, but concluded she was "not credible" and was "playing games."

A prison inmate contacted police to say that a woman he knew only by the name of "Summer" had been seen with Josh, drinking beer and kissing at a FatCats, one of a chain of bowling alleys in Utah. The inmate said "Summer" would tell the police where Susan's body was in exchange for $500,000 and immunity. He added that he thought "Summer" had once worked at American Bush.

Again, no credibility.

But if Josh had been having an affair or meeting someone for sex, did Susan find out and plan to leave him? It would give Josh a motive to harm Susan. In the past he had threatened her when she talked about divorce.

The police received hundreds of tips from Susan's family and friends, work colleagues, store clerks, and from psychics from as far away as Connecticut. A man who described himself as an "audio analyst" claimed he detected Josh state "I lied" and "I buried her" in a video posted on YouTube. The same caller told a detective that he owned a cat that could talk.

Although the police skipped over it the first time it was reported in 2009, they eventually took more seriously another tip from a waitress who had worked at a Comfort Inn in Sandy, Utah, south of West Valley City.

At about 6:30 A.M. on Monday, December 7, Robin Leanne Snyder said she greeted a young man and two small boys in the hotel's breakfast room.

"Do you know what happened to my mom?" the older of the two boys asked her.

"No, what happened to your mom?"

The waitress said that before the boy answered, she was called away to pour coffee for other guests. When she turned around, the trio had vanished.

"He didn't even give the kids time to eat their sweet rolls. Each had a small bite on them," Robin said.

Such tips were interesting, and though they were sometimes the product of media coverage, they also showed the genuine desire people had to help find out what had happened to Susan.

In time, Chuck Cox and the WVCPD created a kind of shorthand, a code for stories like Robin's that were followed up and filed away.

If the police told Susan's father, "There's nothing there," it meant that they had checked out a lead and followed it to its "nothing there" conclusion. If they said, "We're investigating," it meant they were uncertain and looking at the lead.

And, finally, the magic words, "It's a part of our case." That was the indicator to Chuck and Judy that the lead was credible and that an arrest was imminent.

They got used to hearing "nothing there."

Initially, Steve Powell had been suspicious of his son and his alibi. But, as he told police, he changed his mind. By March, his journals indicate he believed Josh was innocent of harming Susan.

Her disappearance nearly killed me, because I thought she was dead . . . Susan Powell's disappearance was quickly blamed on my son Josh. I even had my doubts. By the time 30 days had passed, and Josh had spent time at my house, I became 100% sure of his innocence.

Curiously, the journal entries made after Susan's disappearance read as if Steve expected them to be seized or published one day. He explains that Josh is *his son,* and Susan is referred to as *Susan Powell.*

22

It would be irrational to ignore the parallels between Susan Powell and Steven Koecher in time, place, and circumstance.
— AUTHOR UNKNOWN, FROM THE SUSANPOWELL.ORG SITE

Steve and Josh had only one tool in what had become a media onslaught: their Web site. When they went looking for a plausible reason why Susan might have disappeared, they linked her to a thirty-year-old Utah man who'd gone missing around the same time.

Steven Koecher was living in St. George, in the farthest southwestern corner of Utah, about five hours from West Valley City. He vanished from Henderson, Nevada, on December 13, 2009—a week to the day after Susan disappeared.

The Koecher and Powell disappearances were "cloaked in mystery," Steve wrote on his Web site. He claimed that Susan had been living a double life, with "secret plans to divorce Josh."

Using the slimmest of coincidences, Steve laid out how much Susan and Koecher had in common. Both liked the out-of-doors, were Mormons, enjoyed music, and had worked in downtown Salt Lake City. He was an intern in the Utah governor's office and Susan worked at Fidelity Investments.

Father and son seized on the young man's disappearance to account for Susan's absence. They theorized that maybe the two of them went to Brazil, where Koecher had done his Mormon mission? Maybe they started a new life?

Kiirsi found any connection between Susan and Koecher laughable. Susan would never, ever have had an affair, never have left her children, and as for keeping a secret—Susan never could. She blabbed everything to her friends.

Relatives of Koecher's said the theory that he and Susan had run off together was "nonsense" and that Steve Powell's assertions had "opened up wounds that were healing."

Naturally, Steve was already contemplating how Susan's possible return would affect him. He wrote:

I am not really sure what position to take when she comes back . . . will she return and own up to her affair with Steven Koecher? Will she want to stay with him, or will she realize it was just a fling she needed to bring hope to what must have become, for her, a meaningless life? I still fantasize and masturbate about her nearly every day.

There were two winters in Utah in 2009–2010. Southern Utah had storm after storm, creating twice the average snowpack. But only sporadic snow fell in northern Utah, including at the five-thousand-foot-elevation camping area known as Simpson Springs. By early April, the snow had melted where Josh Powell said he'd gone camping on December 6, 2009.

The search for Susan in the desert began.

23

It's kind of like looking for a needle in a haystack when you're not sure if the needle is in this particular haystack.

—SEARCHER MARIA DEDOMINICIS,
TO KSL-TV, APRIL 10, 2010

Finally, after months of waiting to reenact Josh's midnight camping trip, Susan's friends could finally search Simpson Springs for themselves, the spot where Josh had possibly done the unthinkable.

It was a long drive out to the middle of nowhere, but that was of no consequence to Jennifer Graves and Kiirsi Hellewell, who wouldn't have missed the opportunity to participate in a physical search for Susan. Susan's sister-in-law and best friend rode together out to the desert, talking about Susan and how the ordeal had changed their lives. Just months prior neither would have thought it possible that they'd be out in the Utah desert looking for a trace of Susan. Kiirsi had been sure that whatever had happened to Susan they would have learned before springtime. But truth is funny that way. Sometimes it is exceedingly slow in coming.

It was just after 8:00 A.M. when Kiirsi and Jennifer arrived to join the searchers. The air was bone chilling and the two of them huddled together. Kiirsi tugged at her coat, bracing herself against the elements. "You know she's not going to be there," she said.

Jennifer kept her gaze on the landscape.

Kiirsi thought the desert was lovely, possessing a kind of bleakness that she usually saw as quite beautiful. But not here and not now. Spring hadn't yet awakened the desert. It looked cold, empty. Sad.

"If Josh really left her here," Kiirsi went on, "he'd never have told reporters this is where he went."

Jennifer nodded. Josh was devious, to be sure, but he wasn't stupid.

They watched as a group of about seventy trained searchers composed of former military, law enforcement, EMTs, and others strategized and prepared for canvassing the region where Josh had stated he and the boys had camped.

"There are twenty thousand mines in Utah alone," Kiirsi said, again thinking of the worst possible outcome. "More if you include abandoned mines in Nevada and Arizona. If he killed her, he'd have dumped her in one of those."

Jennifer looked at her. "Or somewhere else. Somewhere we haven't even thought of."

The volunteers—many from the Bridgerland Fire Company in Logan, and Strategic Tactical Group—had formed their teams, divided up the area on a map, and began their work using dogs, one-man powered parachutes fitted with small engines and steered by the pilot's feet, and ATVs. They explained to Kiirsi and Jennifer, who were there to lend moral support, that they would look for bunches of sagebrush or large rocks that might have been moved and used to hide a body.

Just hearing those words was hard, but Kiirsi held it together.

Tooele County sheriff Frank Park was present with a crime scene investigative unit, just in case.

One person missing, who would have been there no

matter the outcome, was Chuck Cox. After preventing Chuck and Judy from seeing their grandchildren for months, Josh had finally agreed that the Coxes could see the boys—but only on that day. They spent the afternoon with Braden and Charlie at Bradley Park, a wildlife preserve with a small lake. It's behind a Walmart, but people who live in Puyallup and the South Hill area say it seems miles from civilization. A one-mile path winds around the lake, which is stocked with trout. There is a fishing area, but swimming is not allowed.

Josh told Chuck and Judy to come alone, not to bring any other family members or grandchildren. They had a warm greeting from Charlie and Braden and then— surprise!—Steve and Mike arrived. They said that they just happened to be in the area and they had their cameras with them. Despite Josh's restrictions, Chuck and Judy had a nice visit with Charlie and Braden, and the boys played on the swings.

Years later, Mike would say that he heard Chuck Cox threaten Josh, saying, "I have every reason to kill you but I have decided not to because of my religion."

The searchers couldn't go into the abandoned mines because of the danger of poisonous gases and drop-offs. The only item discovered during the search in the desert was a pair of women's underwear found by a search dog. It was bagged for the crime lab. Kiirsi and Jennifer thanked the searchers for their help.

Two weeks later, a motorist near Idaho Falls got his truck stuck in the mud. As he walked uphill in search of a better cell phone signal he stumbled on the remains of a woman.

Once more Susan's friends and family felt that sickening pang of fear, an emotion that stabbed at their hearts. They knew that other families felt the same way. Since Susan's disappearance they had followed the cases of several women missing from Utah and Idaho.

The media was quick to speculate Susan might finally have been found.

Eventually, dental records ruled out the possibility that the remains might be Susan's.

Although they lived three miles apart near Puyallup's main drag, the Coxes and the Powells were bound to run into one another once in a while.

Chuck made sure of it.

He wanted to know what Steve and Josh were up to and, most important, how his grandsons were coping. And he knew that the West Valley City police needed help to keep the pressure on Josh.

On a Saturday in late May, Chuck and Judy stopped at the Lowe's not far from their home—and not far from Steve's—on a hunt for strawberry plants. The store was so noisy that Chuck missed a text from friends alerting him that they had spotted Josh and his sons in the store. He knew that Josh liked to take the boys to Lowe's on Saturday mornings when the home improvement chain had its "Build and Grow Clinics." The free classes were designed to teach kids how to build a wooden toy, birdhouse, picture frame, or other small item.

Chuck turned a corner and there he was about thirty feet from Josh. Braden was in a shopping cart and Charlie was at his father's side.

The boys spotted Judy first and Charlie ran excitedly over to her.

"Charlie! Charlie! *Charlie!*" Josh yelled. "Get back here!"

Chuck watched Josh as he dealt with the dilemma. How to regain control of the situation? To do that Josh had to keep Braden in the cart, push it the other way from Judy, and still get Charlie to obey him.

"Charlie!" he shouted. "Get over here right now!"

Charlie walked slowly back to his father and as the cart passed just inches from Chuck, the grandfather reached out and patted Braden. Josh's head snapped toward Chuck. The Coxes watched as their son-in-law hurriedly picked up the unfinished project he and the boys had been working on and left the store like he was exiting a burning building.

Chuck and Judy decided that they would drop in to

When Chuck and Judy Cox and their four daughters, Mary, Denise, Susan, and Marie, posed for a family portrait in 1997, they were unaware that a tragedy would shatter their lives a decade later. *(Denise Cox Olsen)*

A month before their 2001 wedding, Susan Cox and Josh Powell were a happy young couple. Her father-in-law, Steve Powell, soon became sexually obsessed with Susan. *(Denise Cox Olsen)*

Susan Powell and Kiirsi Hellewell just "clicked" when they met after Josh and Susan moved to Utah in 2004. Kiirsi never gave up searching for her best friend. *(Kiirsi Hellewell)*

Although Josh, Susan, Charlie, and Braden appeared to be a happy family in the fall of 2009, Susan had started to put some money aside so she could leave Josh. She also wrote a note, implicating him should anything happen to her. *(Amber Hardman)*

On the day before Susan disappeared, the Powells attended a Christmas breakfast at their ward. In the last photo taken of Susan, they pose with their close friends, the Hellewells. *(Kiirsi Hellewell)*

LEFT: When Josh Powell returned from a mysterious two-day trip in a rental car December 9, 2009, he was met by reporter Chris Jones of KUTV. Josh and his brother, Michael, had probably been moving Susan's body. The extraordinary six-minute TV interview was the first time Josh had to publicly stammer through an explanation of where he was the night of December 6. *(KUTV-TV)*

RIGHT: Josh Powell, sullen and cornered, being interviewed by detectives on December 8, 2009, the day after Susan was reported missing. Josh had spent the previous night thoroughly cleaning his van. *(West Valley City Police Department)*

Judy Cox comforts her husband December 17, 2009, as they discuss a second search of the Powell home in West Valley City. By now, Josh had been named a person of interest in the disappearance of their daughter. *(KSL-TV)*

Although Michael Powell said he wasn't close to Josh, they talked for hours at a time on the phone. He helped his brother pack up and move back to their father's house, fought the Coxes for the right to inherit Josh and Susan's life insurance, and committed suicide when suspicion fell on him. *(KSL-TV)*

On January 4, 2010, JoVonna Owings and Kiirsi Hellewell kicked off a seventy-two hour media blitz to call attention to Susan's disappearance. Owings, who spent part of December 6, 2009, with Susan crocheting, is the last person to have seen her alive. *(KSL-TV)*

The West Valley City Police Department invited the media to tag along on a search of the desert near Ely, Nevada, in August 2011. Reporters decided they were used to put pressure on Josh and Steve Powell. The Coxes, Susan's friends, and law enforcement in Washington State still don't understand why Josh was never arrested. *(KSL-TV)*

With the encouragement of the West Valley City police, Chuck Cox staged a "honk and wave" on August 20, 2011, at a street corner near Steve Powell's house to remind people that Susan was missing. Steve showed up to argue with Chuck. *(KOMO-TV)*

After Steve and Josh Powell threatened to publish Susan's teenage diaries, police felt they had enough cause to enter Steve's house to look for evidence related to her disappearance. Even they were shocked by what they found during the daylong raid. *(KOMO-TV)*

Finally, there was an arrest, although it wasn't the one the Coxes and Susan's friends had expected. Steve Powell was arrested September 22, 2011, for voyeurism and pornography. He was convicted of voyeurism in May 2012. *(Pierce County Sheriff's Department)*

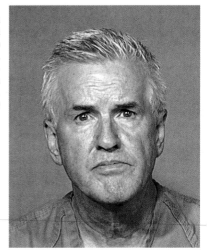

After the media caravan to Nevada that seemed to be a wild-goose chase, a search for Susan in the Utah desert near Topaz Mountain in September 2011, was more productive. Investigators found a site where something bloody had been burned. *(NBC News)*

When Steve Powell was arrested, Charlie and Braden were taken into custody and temporarily placed with Chuck and Judy Cox. The couple admitted life with the boys was exhausting. *(Laurie Nielsen)*

Chuck and Josh faced off often during a bitter legal battle for custody of the boys. *(CBS News)*

Debbie Caldwell missed Charlie and Braden desperately after they moved to Washington. She visited them in Puyallup on Thanksgiving weekend, 2011. *(Laurie Nielsen)*

A disturbing drawing Charlie made during a therapy session in the fall of 2011 shows what appears to be a child and an adult. Charlie drew a big X through the picture and in large letters wrote "Don't play with me!" Chuck Cox took a photo of it with his cell phone. *(Gregg Olsen)*

Josh was captured on a bank surveillance camera as he withdrew $7,000 from his account on Saturday, February 4, 2012, the day before he killed his sons and himself. He left the money with instructions about bills that needed to be paid. He did other errands that day, including donating books and toys. *(Pierce County Sheriff's Department)*

The fire blew the roof off Josh's rental house and burned it down to a few timbers. It was a crime scene for months and later demolished. *(Rebecca Morris)*

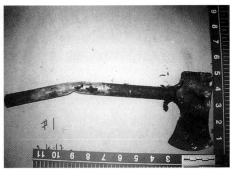

Investigators say Josh struck both boys in the neck or head with this hatchet before he poured gasoline on them. The hatchet was found in the rubble of the fire, along with the three charred bodies, Josh's cell phone, melted gas cans, and a bird cage. *(Pierce County Sheriff's Department)*

A few days after the fire that killed Charlie, Braden, and Josh, Alina Powell told ABC News her brother was trying to protect his children when he killed them. *(ABC News)*

Charlie and Braden were buried together in a single blue casket. Chuck Cox rests his hand on the casket as he and Judy walk to the stage to speak to the thousands who attended a public memorial service for the boys on February 11, 2012. *(KIRO-TV)*

Denise Cox and Anne Bremner appeared on *Anderson Live* on April 19, 2012. "So much attention has been on Josh," Denise told the TV host. "I want the focus back on my sister." (Anderson Live)

If Susan is found, there is room for her remains in Charlie and Braden's grave. The marker says the boys and their mother are already united in heaven. *(Gregg Olsen)*

Last Will & testament for Susan,
Susan McPowell - written sound a 2008

Saturday June 28, 2008

I am at work @ WF Env I bike to work daily &, have been having extreme marital diss for about 3 or 4 yrs now. For mine & my children's safety I feel the need to have a paper-trail @ work which would not be accessible to my husband. We've been to a church class about wills & I know he can override me w/ the legal paperwork but I want it documented somewhere that there is extreme turmoil in our marriage. He has threatened to "skip the country" and told me straight out " if we divorce, there will be no lawyers, only a mediator, and I will ruin you. I (also) would be ruined too, but you would be destroyed and your life would be over and the boys will not grow up with a mom and dad."

If something happens to me, please talk to my sister-in-law Jenny Graves, my friend Kiirsi Hellewell, check my blogs on myspace - ███████████ check my work desk, talk to my friendly co-workers →

Susan's handwritten last will and testament, which she locked in a bank's safe deposit box in 2008, implicating Josh should anything happen to her. *(West Valley City Police Department)*

Lowe's every once in a while, just coincidentally on a Saturday morning.

"We thought about showing up every Saturday," Chuck said later.

"But we decided not to push things. We didn't want Josh to feel we were stalking him," Judy said.

About a month after that encounter, Chuck and Judy happened to be at Lowe's on another Saturday morning getting more plants for their garden. They heard an announcement over the intercom that it was time for the crafts clinic.

"Heck, it worked last time," Chuck said, looking at Judy. "Maybe we will see them again."

Suddenly Chuck realized that he was about a foot behind Josh, practically breathing down his neck. Chuck immediately backed away. Judy regretted not giving Charlie a hug the last time they had seen him, and she wanted to now.

"Ask him if I can hug Charlie and Braden," Judy said.

So that he didn't startle Josh, Chuck said Josh's name and he turned around. His eyes were filled with suspicion.

"Hi, Josh," Chuck said. "Is it okay if Judy gives the boys a hug?"

Josh paused and looked around. "No," he finally answered.

"Why not?" Chuck asked.

Josh shook his head. "Just no," he said.

Chuck wanted an answer. "What can it hurt?"

"I have made my decision and now you need to go," Josh said.

Chuck was hurt, but he was angry, too. Josh was acting like a control freak, a selfish jerk. Those boys were his and Judy's link to their missing daughter. Where in the world could he get off with shutting down an offer of affection by their grandmother?

"You have no legal right to tell me I can't see the boys in public," Chuck said.

Josh gave him a nasty look and turned away, and Chuck decided to back down. He didn't want to cause a scene and traumatize the boys. Chuck and Judy started to leave, but before they exited through the huge automatic doors at the front of the store, Chuck changed his mind. He was utterly ticked off. He and Judy turned around and went back to their original position, about thirty feet from Josh.

Josh saw them and moved the boys around to the other side of a nearby stack of plywood so that he could watch the Coxes and text on his phone at the same time. The Coxes were all but certain he was trying to reach his father. Maybe Steve and Mike could swoop in with their cameras?

"I think we've done everything we can do. Let's go," Chuck said.

Judy, heartsick over being so close to the boys but not allowed to give them a hug, agreed.

But in a last dig, Chuck got Josh's attention and gave him a smile and a friendly wave good-bye.

Two weeks later, Chuck was served with a restraining order. Josh told a judge that Chuck had mouthed the words "You're dead" at him, which Chuck adamantly denied. The judge issued a mutual-harassment order. That night Chuck explained to Judy how he was not about to let a little restraining order give Josh the upper hand.

"I have to stay five hundred feet away from his work, and he has to stay five hundred feet away from my work, and seeing as how he isn't working that is not a problem," Chuck told his wife.

"Well, it's not like we want to hang around him," Judy said.

"I have no desire to go near him. But he wants this so I can't talk to the kids, ever," Chuck said. "I may not be able to approach Josh, but I can still approach the kids. I can talk to the kids, you can talk to the kids, and my parents can talk to the kids."

Their longing to hug the boys, however, would have to wait.

Josh flatly refused to talk to or cooperate with the police. By spring 2010, investigators knew that what little Josh told them had been lies.

They knew on Monday, December 7, after listening to voice messages left on his cell phone by police concerned about Susan's whereabouts, that Josh had called *Susan*'s phone—which was in the car with him—and left a message asking if she needed a ride home. They knew that Josh had removed the SIM card from both his phone and his missing wife's phone. They knew that a day later, Josh had rented a car and driven an astounding 800 miles. They knew it was Susan's blood on the tile floor in the house. They had seen the note Susan had written and locked in a safe deposit box implicating Josh, should something happen to her. They knew that a day after his mother went missing, Charlie told the police that his mother had gone camping with them but hadn't come home.

"Mommy stayed where the crystals are," he had said.

And, even more heartbreaking, they knew three weeks after Susan disappeared that the four-year-old had told a Sunday school teacher, "My mommy is dead."

Even though they knew all that, and more, they did not share their findings with Susan's parents. Chuck and Judy Cox continued to publicly support the police department's efforts to solve Susan's mysterious disappearance. In private, however, they believed that the police had adequate cause to arrest Josh. The police *had* to put pressure on him.

Chuck Cox understood police procedure. He was, after all, an investigator, too.

"The only way you can break him," Chuck told the West Valley City cops on several occasions, "is to arrest him. Put him in jail."

"We're building a case. Trust us," the detectives repeated.

Chuck wasn't convinced. "You're letting him get away with this," he said.

"We're doing our job," the police said, over and over. "We know this is frustrating, but we'll get there."

To the Coxes it seemed like a sad, broken record. Chuck and Judy didn't see any reason to lambast the police in public, but at home they had to wonder.

"What are they waiting for?" Judy asked.

Chuck put his arms around her shoulders. Judy was in a world of hurt. They all were. The pain would never, ever go away. But letting Josh run free and keep their grandchildren away from them was nearly unbearable.

"We will get through this, Judy," Chuck said.

Deep down, however, he really didn't know just *how* they would get through any of it.

"I warned the police over and over, 'He'll kill himself and the kids,'" Chuck said later.

24

There was some physical contact over the few days
she was here. A couple of times she was taking Braden from me and pressed her soft breasts against the
backside of my hands as she wrapped her arms
around him to take him. I didn't make any effort to
move my hands.
—STEVE POWELL'S JOURNAL, JUNE 26, 2008

Steve Powell's second meeting with the West Valley City
police, the FBI, and this time the U.S. Marshals Service, too,
was in May 2010. He let them into his house, again, without
the benefit of a search warrant. As if he were proudly showing off a stamp or coin collection, the investigators couldn't
help but see the pornography out in the open. What was just
a fraction of Steve's pornography collection was visible on a
table. In Steve's trove they saw photos of a woman they in-
stantly recognized as Susan. She had been photographed,
unaware, in her underwear. The photos appeared to have
been taken through a crack in a bathroom door. There were
also pictures that appeared to be composites—images of
Susan's face Photoshopped onto nude female bodies. While
there, the police removed the tracking device they had put on
Josh's van four months before when he was in West Valley
City to rent out the house. They no longer needed to track

him. They seemed more interested in his father. They should have been interested in his brother, Michael.

From Susan's friends the police learned that Steve had wanted Susan to act as a wife to both Josh and himself. Steve told police that he and his daughter-in-law were in love and claimed she was "very sexual" toward him. Steve told them that Susan had said their "flirtatious relationship could never be in the open due to her Mormon religion."

They knew that the way Steve described his relationship with Susan was different from what she wrote in her private journal, the one found in her desk at Wells Fargo. Susan repeatedly described Steve as a terrible influence on Josh. She thought he was creepy.

Steve told a former girlfriend that the investigators in May had missed his self-dubbed "porn cabinet," which contained more photos of Susan, her teenage diaries, and her Mormon temple garment underwear he'd stolen from a pile of laundry back when she and Josh had lived at his house in 2002. The former girlfriend had told the police as early as January 2010 that Steve was obsessed with his daughter-in-law. The West Valley City PD contacted her more than a year later, asking the woman to explain once more what she knew about Steve. She even had a map Steve had sketched of roads around where Susan might have disappeared.

The department admitted that they'd lost the notes she had sent.

Steve Powell's fascination with pornography went back to the early years of his marriage, if not further. Back then, Steve had to sneak around to the back door entrance of an adult bookstore on the seediest side of Spokane to satisfy his lust. That was long before he could just go online and view whatever he wanted—or create pornography of his own.

When Terri Powell was eight months pregnant with Alina, she discovered a diary her husband had kept, that detailed explicit sexual fantasies about women they knew. Steve wrote about one particular woman and indicated that if her husband died, he'd step in and marry her. He even wrote a song about her.

Did Steve want them to be one big polygamous family? Terri burned the diary. But she explained her fears during their divorce proceedings.

> *I was concerned sometimes that he might even have it in his mind to harm her husband to put himself in the position that he desired.*

Another time, Terri found a hard-core magazine in eight-year-old Mike's bedroom and confronted Steve about his lapse in good parenting.

Steve tried to dismiss her concerns.

"People are just animals anyway," he said. "We ought to be able to have sex with anyone, any time we please."

25

You're to blame!
That's why I never sleep at night.
—A LYRIC BY STEVE POWELL

Steve Powell wrote dozens of love songs about Susan and over ten years filled seventeen spiral notebooks with his sexual obsessions. In her father's defense, and to show that relations between Steve and Susan were not as weird as Susan described, Alina Powell made a point of noting on her Web site West Valley and Pierce County Malfeasance that the soprano heard backing up Steve on some songs was, indeed, Susan.

"Susan and Steve made beautiful music together," Alina wrote without irony.

Alina, whose employment history included only brief stints as a dog groomer, video clerk, and fast-food worker, was quite comfortable behind her computer screen. She created an avatar named Misty for games she played. Sometimes Misty was a blonde, and sometimes she had dark hair.

All in all, "I guess she would probably be considered prettier than I am," Alina confessed. Misty could also float above the fray, something that might come in handy at Steve's house. Alina posted regularly to Web sites and once guessed the number of her e-mail accounts at around two dozen.

On Mother's Day 2010, Josh or someone purporting to be him, posted a message to Susan on his Web site, SusanPowell.org. It included photos of Charlie and Braden, and talked about how they planted flowers for their missing mother.

> *Happy Mother's Day Susan. You are the beloved mother of two beautiful boys who remember you and miss you. We all hope you will come home soon. The boys love plants and gardening just like you so they planted flowers for your honor on Mother's Day. We hope you like the pictures, and are thinking about us as much as we are thinking about you.*

Chuck Cox nearly blew his top when he saw the posting.

"If Susan *could* come home, she *would*," he said to Judy, while they huddled over the computer screen looking at the latest insult to their daughter's reputation.

"She loved those little boys more than anything."

"Nothing would keep her from being with them," Judy said.

Chuck knew differently. "Just Josh," he said.

Susan's father was well aware that Steve and Josh were starting to spin their theory that Susan had chosen to abandon her husband and young sons. The idea that she would then check in via the Internet to see how her family was faring was ludicrous.

In his journal Steve continued writing of his obsession with Susan—*never* about fears that she was injured or dead. Or what it could mean for his son to be pursued by police. Or about his grandsons' confusion caused by their mother's lengthening absence.

Instead, Steve was trying to figure out how and when she

would return and what that would mean to him, especially if she had had an affair or was pregnant by the man she ran off with:

> *. . . I want to be a family with her and the boys, with Josh an important part of their lives. I even accept the possibility that she is soon to have another child, by an interloper . . . I am still convinced she loves me and is sexually attracted to me.*

In addition, he worried if there would be room for her at his increasingly crowded house. Josh, Charlie, and Braden were always underfoot with their toys, the bird, and all the stuff Josh had collected over the years. Steve, who had created the noxious environment that fostered his adult children's seemingly perpetual dependence, now lamented the fact.

> *How in hell do I unload this baggage? Alina and Johnny seem to be permanent fixtures in this house. Josh has no compunction about taking over as much of the house as he needs for him and the boys.*

The YMCA day camp in Puyallup really isn't much of a camp. It's more of a day care for busy parents than anything else. Certainly, there are crafts and activities for the older kids and story time for the younger set. In the summer after Susan went missing, Josh brought his sons to the cluster of modular buildings for what he'd promised would be a fun break from Grandpa Steve's house. Alina had been watching the boys and told people that she didn't mind. But Josh thought better of it. He thought they could use some other activities. Sitting at home all summer wasn't ideal in a household not really set up for little ones—a household with an uncle on meds, a caregiver aunt who'd been thrust into the role without any training, and a grandfather who was obsessed with pornography.

Josh probably had no idea that his fatherly gesture of sending Charlie, age five, and Braden, three, to camp would potentially provide strangers with a glimpse of what had happened on the snowy December night Susan disappeared.

Braden drew a picture of a car with figures inside, an image that left the women who were supervising the art project breathless from what they saw—or what they thought they saw in the little boy's drawing.

"Tell me about your picture, Braden," one woman said, gently prodding him.

"That's us going camping," he said, looking down at the drawing.

Another woman touched an index finger to a crude stick figure seated in the car.

"Who's that?" she asked.

"That's Daddy." He indicated the other figures in quick succession. "That's Charlie, and that's me."

But that wasn't everybody he'd drawn. There was another figure there, too.

He pointed. "Mommy's in the trunk," he said.

The women stayed calm. They thought they understood the meaning of what Braden was telling them, but they wanted to make sure.

"Why was she in the trunk, Braden?"

Braden looked a little confused for a moment. He didn't really have an answer. He stammered a little and stumbled over his words, trying to make sense of his recollections.

He couldn't articulate why she was in the trunk but he said they had stopped somewhere.

"Mommy and Daddy got out," he said. "And Mommy never came back."

The women would never forget that. They told their supervisor and eventually Chuck heard the story and told the police. A detective from West Valley City police met with the staff at the YMCA, listened, and told them that there wasn't much they could do. Charlie had told a similar version of the story. It was interesting, even sad, but it wasn't irrefutable evidence against Josh.

Braden took his drawing home to show his daddy.

When he enrolled Charlie in elementary school a few weeks later, Josh once more tried to cast himself as the misunderstood good guy, a devoted father who wanted only the best for his sons. He made it known that he was very interested in Charlie's school life—so much so, that he wanted to join the school's PTA. That was met with the same resistance as that of the members of the LDS ward, which he'd contacted for help with Charlie's birthday party. Some parents vowed to start a petition prohibiting Josh's participation. Others were thinking twice about joining. One said that Josh gave her "the creeps." Finally, the PTA president issued a statement about Josh's application:

> *Our PTA membership is open to anyone who would like to join and is interested in helping the children of Carson Elementary reach their full potential. All our volunteers are required to complete the background check through the School District before volunteering.*

Josh's friend and neighbor, Pastor Tim Atkins, might have been the only parent with children at Carson who was sympathetic to Josh. He tried to convince the others that Josh was trying to make his life better, trying to get back to something normal.

"Nobody would let him do that," Tim later said.

By then everything Josh did became fodder for the tabloids and TV news shows. On CNN's *Issues with Jane Velez-Mitchell,* the host skewered both Josh *and* the PTA—Josh for thinking he would be welcomed with open arms, and the PTA for protecting his civil rights.

When one of the show's guests, a family law attorney, speculated that the state's child services division could request psychological testing of Josh, the TV host asked:

"Maybe they'll find out he's cuckoo for Cocoa Puffs?" The panel chuckled.

Josh wasn't blind to how he was portrayed in the media. He joked that he "was a Marvel Comics super-villain."

By November, Josh had attended a few PTA meetings, despite the objections of other parents. But like a lot of things—best intentions, passing fancy—the routine ended. Josh just wasn't able to stick with anything for very long.

26

At one point Josh was being his usually rude, yelling and barking commands at me, old self and his dad was helping me take pictures and video of the blanket I was giving my mom that I made. After Josh left the room I told his dad, "the winds are going to change, I can't take this crap from him anymore." I told him that when Josh starts whining that I'm being unreasonable it's b/c he's so rude and never helps with the boys/house, etc. His dad told me that the entire family KNOWS how much I put up with.

—SUSAN POWELL E-MAIL, JUNE 30, 2008

The Coxes returned to Utah in September at the invitation of Ed Smart. Smart was bicycling across the country to raise awareness for kidnapped children and to promote legislation that would require DNA samples to be taken from anyone arrested on suspicion of a felony. Chuck and Judy stayed with Debbie and Ken Caldwell. The families had much in common. The Caldwells also had four daughters.

One night they were up late talking about those early hours after Susan had vanished. Something that had happened during that first week had been gnawing at Debbie. She recounted how she'd seen Josh at the December 10, 2009 vigil.

"I was talking to Charlie, and Josh walked over and just

kind of picked up Charlie and took him away from me and said, 'Oh, hi, we're not going to be coming back to day care.' I asked him why not."

"What did he say?" Chuck asked.

"He said, 'With everything going on . . .'"

"What kind of answer was that?"

"Right. So, I said, 'You know you have to work, you still have to make a living.'"

Either Chuck or Judy could have said something about Josh not being used to working—something he usually left to Susan—but there was no need for that because Debbie knew Josh all too well.

Plus Debbie was on a roll anyway.

"And then he said, 'Yeah, but we won't have any money to pay you.'"

Debbie continued. "I said, 'There are programs, we could figure something out.' And then Josh looked at me and, well, he said, 'No, no, no, I'm just going to have my family take care of them.'"

Chuck could tell that wasn't the end of the story. Debbie Caldwell was on to something. Something big.

"Josh stopped payment on a check I should have received on December eighth," she said, leaving her words hanging in the air.

That got Chuck's attention. Judy's, too.

"Hold on, Debbie, say that again?" Susan's father asked.

"Right." Debbie took a breath. "He knew the kids were not going to be in day care the following week. It means what you think it does."

Debbie went on to explain that all the other parents paid her on Monday mornings, so she deposited their checks on Monday afternoons. Because Josh's check always arrived on Tuesday from a credit union in Spokane, Washington, she would hold on to it and deposit it the following Monday with the other checks. On Monday, December 7, after alerting Jennifer and Terri that she couldn't reach Josh or Susan, Debbie went to her bank with that day's checks, plus Josh's from the week before, which she had received on Tuesday,

December 1. When she didn't receive a check on Tuesday, December 8, she talked to her bank about it.

"The bank told me that Josh would have had to stop the check from being sent, by Thursday, December 3, at the latest and maybe earlier," she said.

Chuck's pulse quickened. He looked over at Judy. He knew she was thinking the same thing.

"He'd premeditated the whole thing," he said. "This is hard evidence that proves premeditation."

Debbie nodded. "I think so, too."

None of them—Judy, Chuck, Debbie, Ken—felt happy in that sad, sick moment. There was no excited jumping up and down over the fact that they could now prove something that they'd already known. But there was some satisfaction in that moment. No denying that. Every one of them gathered in the Caldwells' comfortable home loved Susan.

Every one of them wanted Josh to answer for what he'd done.

Chuck was convinced that the day-care check was evidence that Josh had arranged Susan's disappearance. It was proof that she wasn't injured in a scuffle with Josh, that she didn't just hit her head and bleed, that Josh didn't panic and dispose of her body.

It was planned.

The next day Debbie collected the bank statements from her day-care business that showed the Powells' payment history and handed them over to the police.

According to the code that the WVCPD and Chuck had between them, the police told him what category the evidence fell into: "They said it is part of the case," Chuck said, hoping Josh would finally be arrested.

And once more, the West Valley City police cautioned patience.

"We're working it, Chuck and Judy. Trust us."

Chuck liked to drive out into the Utah desert. It made him feel closer to Susan. When he was in Utah meeting with the police, following up on leads or attending vigils, Susan's father drove for hours, sometimes by himself and sometimes with Ken Caldwell. Both had licenses to carry a concealed weapon, and both were trained shooters. Chuck would take his Smith & Wesson M&P Compact .40 caliber pistol, and Ken his Springfield XD Sub-Compact .40 or his Dan Wesson .357 Magnum, and do a little target shooting while they looked for Susan. Chuck had a hunch about an area north of Salt Lake City with dozens of little-used farm roads.

They drove every farm road off Interstate 84 from Tremonton north to a rest area in Idaho.

"We thought that would be a good meeting place for Josh and Steve," Chuck said. "And we wanted to check out the area because I'd always felt kind of weird about that area. So we drove every ranch road that would have been accessible to a minivan." They stopped and got out and walked the fields. Chuck also searched areas to the south, including Simpson Springs, where Josh said he had been camping, and investigated how roads that barely appeared on a map met up.

Rumor and gossip and police investigations had it that Steve may have helped Josh cover up the crime. That's why Josh had needed the rental car, and perhaps why Steve had taken off work December 8–9: there was some unfinished business. But Chuck thought that Steve might have done more than that. Maybe he had instigated it. There was a rumor that Steve had made a trip to Utah a couple of months before Susan disappeared. Was he along on the short camping trip that Josh, Charlie, and Braden had made in the minivan in September—cut short because the boys got cold and uncomfortable and wanted to go home?

Chuck's thoughts wandered to the possibilities.

Maybe Steve and Josh had prepared a grave for Susan before December, in the fall when the ground was soft enough to dig? If Josh covered it with a piece of plywood, then he could return to the spot with her body, remove the plywood, place Susan's body in the grave, and cover it up. Or maybe he went looking for a bottomless, abandoned mine so decrepit that it would be impossible to search?

And if Josh was really lucky, the two boys in their car seats would be asleep during a midnight excursion to dump their mother's body in such a desolate, sad place.

Chuck's mind also went right to Steve Powell. No one would know until much later that it was someone else who had come to his aid.

The body was a female, maybe as young as thirty. She had had light brown hair, had been five-two to five-four in height, and had been wearing pink underwear, a jeans jacket, and a pink tank top. Dead since late 2009 or early 2010, her mummified remains were found on a remote corner of a sheep ranch near Laramie, Wyoming, in September 2010. WVCPD sent Susan's dental records. It was not Susan.

The next month, a woman's body was found near a highway in Los Lunas, New Mexico. She had reddish brown hair and was wearing a black sundress and a silver cross around her neck. The New Mexico police had a hunch it might be Susan. While sending Susan's dental work to them, WVCPD detective Ellis Maxwell e-mailed: "You're right, the similarities are so close it's eerie! The eyes, lips, nose, cheeks, forehead and hair," looked like Susan's. He did point out, however, that members of LDS do not wear crosses.

It was not Susan.

A Cox family friend said, "Every time police let us know they've found a body, it's a lurch in your throat. If it's her we don't want to know she's dead, and if it's not her, it means she is still missing and we don't have closure."

27

Someone needs to take the velvet gloves off and treat
[the Coxes] like an investigative subject.
—JOSH POWELL TO *SALT LAKE TRIBUNE*,
NOVEMBER 8, 2010

Those who loved her had vowed they would never forget.
They promised one another that whenever it made sense, they
would band together to remind the world that Susan Powell
was missing. On October 16, 2010, Susan's twenty-ninth
birthday, twenty-five friends from her Utah neighborhood and
church met at West View Park to have cake and release 150
purple balloons, each carrying a photo of Susan. At the same
time, purple balloons were released in Puyallup by friends
and family led by Chuck and Judy Cox.

While Susan was in everyone's hearts at both venues, it
was Steve and Josh Powell who were on their minds. Con-
siderable discussion was made not only of their absence, but
of any role either might have played in the scenario that
played out on December 6–7 the preceding year.

Over in Country Hollow, Steve and Josh did the bare

minimum on the occasion of Susan's birthday. Steve admitted as much in his journal on October 18:

I helped the boys get started on some drawings and Josh put their artwork on SusanPowell.org. It's nothing more than a half-assed effort on our part, but the boys enjoyed doing it . . .

Soon after, Josh and Steve announced that they were changing the "focus" of SusanPowell.org. Its new mission would be to respond to rumors and "correct the record."

. . . At this point, we recognize that we cannot remain silent forever in the face of rumors and lies being spread by individuals associated with the Cox "Friends and Family."

One step Josh took to correct the record was to "break his silence" and agree to an interview with a reporter from the *Salt Lake Tribune*. In the interview, which took place at Steve's house, Josh described Susan as "extremely unstable" and said that mental illness drove her to leave her family. It was another round in Josh and Steve's crusade to blame Susan's disappearance on *Susan*. They claimed she was sexually motivated, that she abandoned her husband and sons and ran off with a boyfriend and that maybe she had embezzled from her job. Josh blamed the Coxes, wondering out loud if Susan had inherited her mother's tendency to emotional outbursts; he called Chuck controlling and manipulative and implied that the Coxes should be investigated, too.

Jennifer Graves told the same reporter that her brother and father were accusing Susan of "being a slut," and that it was offensive to her. "She was not," Jennifer said. "She was frustrated with her marriage."

By then, Jennifer was openly saying that she thought her brother and father had conjured up a tale of Susan's mental imbalance to cover up their role in her disappearance. And she pointed out that, ironically, it was *her* side of the family that had the history of psychological problems, not the Coxes.

Steve Powell's purported proof that Susan was unstable came from her diary. In her diaries, written when she was a teenager in Puyallup, Susan agonized over her love life—much as Steve did over Susan in his own journals. At age fifteen, Susan wrote about being with a boy and worried if the relationship had gone too far. She promised to pray on it, to steady herself, to ensure that whatever troubles had befallen other young women *wouldn't* happen to her. She also wrote about a time when she accidently took an overdose of an over-the-counter pain reliever. It was not, she insisted to family and friends, a suicide attempt. A physician agreed. It was just a mistake, nothing more.

Steve, however, twisted Susan's words and claimed it was more proof of her propensity for erratic behavior. He wanted the world to believe that there was something dark and dangerous lurking in her past. She was not the pretty woman in the photos they'd seen on TV.

Neither Susan nor her friends nor her parents had ever said she was perfect. She was a complex woman, a mother, a devoted wife and friend. Susan became those things by living life, which included making her share of mistakes along the way.

The Coxes shrugged off most of their daughter's diary entries as a teenage girl's ramblings. Susan was never some out-of-control teenager. When they thought about it, they could come up with only one time that Susan had semirebelled, and then just a little bit. She snuck out of the house to talk to a boyfriend in the front yard late one night. Later, she confessed the forty-five-minute adventure to her parents.

And yet the Powells seemed to wallow in the mud they slung at Susan's reputation.

Even Josh's sister Alina got in on the act. She and Susan had never been close, even when Alina lived for a few months with her sister Jennifer in West Jordan, Utah, not far from Josh and Susan. In addition to calling her a "player," Alina told her father that she thought Susan was "a bitch and not very pretty or smart, and with a poor personality." After Susan disappeared, Alina said she had "walked in on intimate moments between Steve and Susan," including when Susan waxed her legs, then asked Steve to feel how smooth they were. Alina said that it was Susan who made the sexual advances to her father. Steve just "went along."

For her part, Susan had always told friends that she felt sorry for Alina, and hoped Josh's little sister would be able to extract herself from her dad's toxic household.

Steve's possession of Susan's diaries ratcheted up the growing bitterness between the two families. He had "borrowed" the diaries from Josh and Susan's storage unit in 2003. Chuck and Judy wanted to keep the diaries and give them to Susan's sons one day. Steve insisted that they remain with her husband and sons "until she returns." Of course, that way he could continue to read them and fantasize about Susan.

That fall, Steve told people that federal agents had been at his house in an attempt to get Susan's diaries. He sent an e-mail to the *Salt Lake Tribune.*

Of course, we are happy to cooperate with law enforcement in any way we can.

He added that he had made a copy of the diary entries for federal investigators and was waiting to hear back from them before he dispatched it to them.

He never did. In the meantime, he decided to talk about the diaries on television and publish them online. They would help convince people that Susan had run away and that Josh was a lonely, abandoned husband and father.

On the first anniversary of Susan's disappearance, December 6, 2010, Susan's family and friends decided to volunteer their time instead of holding another vigil. About thirty-five people gathered at a car dealership in Puyallup to wrap Christmas presents for Santa Cops, a nonprofit that delivers toys and food to needy families. Chuck saw it as a kind of distraction, in addition to something to help those who needed it. Susan had always joined in such activities—it was the mom in her.

Each milestone—holiday, birthday, anniversary of her disappearance—served only to remind Chuck and Judy and their other daughters of all that they were missing. Susan had been gone for a full year. Christmas was approaching, and Chuck and Judy had been kept from their grandsons for eight long months.

28

Chuck: The police were very confident that Josh was going to be arrested. We thought he'd be arrested within three months at the most.
Judy: And then we thought six months.
Chuck: And then we were told "not today." What about next week? "Well, no."
— CHUCK AND JUDY COX, AUGUST 27, 2012

The giant billboard with Susan's face on it beamed over the roadway. Under her photo, the sign said MISSING in huge letters, the date she had disappeared, a phone number to call with information, the Web address of the Susan Cox Powell Foundation, and at the bottom, three words:

HOPE, PRAY, HELP.

Chuck and Judy Cox had passed that sign a dozen times. So had half the people in Puyallup. The sign above Meridian Avenue, Route 161, looking down on one of the state's busiest roads, was just a half mile from Steve Powell's house in Country Hollow. It reminded thousands of motorists that Susan was still missing. It would help Charlie and Braden remember their mother's face. Most of all, it sent a message to the inhabitants of Fort Powell that there would be justice.

Fort Powell.

That's what Chuck called Steve Powell's house. Josh's father and siblings—except for Jennifer, who was convinced that her brother was responsible for Susan's disappearance—were all living at Steve's, along with Charlie and Braden. West Valley City police and the Pierce County sheriff's department wanted to step up the pressure on Josh and thought that getting in his face with billboards and having run-ins with the Coxes would help.

The advertising was as much about making Steve and Josh squirm as it was about the expectation someone might have new information.

Chuck and Judy Cox didn't need any reminders, but when they passed by the enormous billboard it always renewed their discussions of what might have really happened. Chuck couldn't stop himself, and no one would blame him. Judy was his best ear. Over and over, in front of his wife he'd play out those theories of what happened to his daughter that frigid night in December.

Judy agreed, but mostly kept it all inside. She busied herself with her other grandchildren and friends from church, and she supported Chuck every step of the way. Her heart was broken and only very occasionally did she allow herself to consider the very real possibility that Susan was never coming home.

"Maybe they had a fight," Chuck said to Judy.

She nodded. "I can see that happening."

"Yes, and he hurt Susan accidentally. He stashed her someplace."

"And she's hidden somewhere?" Judy asked.

"Maybe Josh didn't kill her. He's a wimp, I don't think he could have killed her."

"Yes, he is a wimp," Judy said. "Always has been."

Chuck took a breath. "You know, Judy, if it was a reasonable, fair fight he would have lost. Susan's stronger than Josh any day of the week."

When that theory ran its course, Susan's parents would edge toward a darker scenario.

"Maybe Steve really did have a hand in this?" Chuck asked.

Judy knew what her husband was getting at, but she waffled a little. "You mean, hiding Susan?"

"Worse," he said.

Judy swallowed hard. "Maybe killing her." Those last words barely came from her lips. Each syllable hurt.

Chuck again went over the evidence as he saw it. Thinking about all the years Josh's twisted father had loved and lusted after his daughter-in-law and all that pornography made Chuck sick. Added to that was the fact that Josh apparently wanted to be free of his wife.

"Josh needed a nudge from someone," Chuck said.

"I can see that, yes."

Chuck went on, recounting how Josh had probably phoned someone for advice on poisoning or sedating Susan.

Jennifer Graves had questions as well. "I don't think he ever made dinner when Susan was around; he simply wasn't that considerate of her," she told the police. "Why would he suddenly do it that night? And why would she then go to bed ill after? It seems fishy to me."

Chuck said, "If she had been poisoned or sedated, it wouldn't be a fair fight."

Judy knew that her husband was right—Susan *was* a fighter. "Right, that's how Josh was able to put her in the back of the minivan."

And then, as if it was too much to bear, too hard to believe that Josh purposely killed Susan, Judy gave him an out.

"Or maybe Josh accidentally killed Susan, put her in the back of the van, strapped the boys into their car seats, and went looking for a place to leave her body?"

Chuck wasn't sure, but there was a piece of the puzzle that always pointed to the possibility that he didn't act alone.

The 800 miles. Chuck had a theory about that.

"When Josh rented the car and disappeared, he was running home to Puyallup but turned around and returned to West Valley City when his dad reminded him the boys were with Jennifer Graves and Josh would lose custody," he said.

Judy could see that. Steve had always been a big stickler for the importance the law placed in "possession" of something, even children.

Susan's parents went over every possible scenario. It was almost as if talking about the worst possible outcomes made them get used to the darkest ideas—like dipping one's toes into the hottest bathwater.

"Or Josh drugged Susan," Chuck said, "but she was alive and he kept her hidden."

That was what Chuck had wondered when they saw Josh in January 2010, crying uncontrollably. Josh had arrived at the Coxes to drop off the boys for a visit. He couldn't stop sobbing. Relations weren't good enough—they'd never been good enough—for Chuck or Judy to reach out to Josh and to ask what was wrong. Later, they could come up with only one reason: *What if Susan had been hidden, and Josh had been told that she had died?*

It must have been something big to trigger Josh's sudden emotional breakdown.

The Coxes had begged the police to arrest their son-in-law, even if it was on a lesser charge than murder.

"I told them the only way to break Josh is to put him in jail because he is weak. We were afraid of what he might do to the kids. But the world did not listen to what we said about Josh," Chuck said years later.

The police had an idea about how to keep the pressure on Josh. It was something Chuck and Judy had never heard of before, but is known to many who search for missing loved ones—a "honk and wave."

29

Putting this in my neighborhood is not appropriate.
They're trying to push an agenda.
— JOSH POWELL, AUGUST 20, 2011,
TO MEDIA AT HONK AND WAVE

The morning of the honk and wave was a sunny one with beautiful blue skies and Mount Rainier looming over Puyallup's South Hill neighborhood. Judy wore what had nearly become her uniform for a second summer: a T-shirt emblazoned with Susan's photograph and the words SUSAN IS MISSING. Chuck wore the same shirt. He also brought along a copy of the temporary restraining order that allowed him to be in the same store or on the same street corner as his son-in-law. He just couldn't approach Josh.

But he *could* approach his grandsons, which was what he and Judy wanted anyway. There really was very little to say to Josh. The Coxes only cared about two things: those little boys and finding Susan.

Chuck, Judy, Chuck's mother Anne, and friends, all dressed in purple, held signs and a big banner:

REMEMBER ME? SUSAN COX POWELL, $10,000 REWARD.

That week, at the suggestion of the police, Chuck had called Kiirsi.

"You need to do a honk and wave," Chuck said.

"What's a honk and wave?" she asked.

"You get big signs and you stand on the corner and you say, 'Honk if you remember Susan.'"

"Never heard of that," Kiirsi said. "We'll do it."

Kiirsi had been ill—in fact, she'd been in the emergency room—and would remain ill all fall. It had started, she was sure, with the stress of Susan's disappearance and worsened when Steve threatened to publish Susan's diaries. It literally had made Kiirsi sick. Despite that, she began calling Susan's friends and organized a honk and wave to take place simultaneously to the one in Puyallup.

The West Valley City police had encouraged the Coxes to stage their honk and wave near the Fred Meyer store at Steve Powell's end of Puyallup. So they did. Television crews arrived on cue to interview Chuck. A microphone was clipped to his collar. And then, like a scene from some Lifetime movie, Steve Powell drove up, jumped out of his car, and brandished a video camera of his own. Josh's father seemed to be in a mood for a confrontation.

Chuck stood there with his arms crossed and looked at Steve, whose face was red and twisted in anger. The two had not said a word to each other since before Susan and Josh had moved to Utah in 2004. In fact, it might have been their only exchange since their children married.

Steve pointed a finger at Chuck and then turned to the TV cameras.

"That guy is violating a restraining order!"

Barely blinking, Chuck reached for his copy of the document in his pocket.

Steve continued. "We were going to get a picture of Chuck Cox. We believe he's in violation of a restraining order because Josh shops at this store."

"We only want to find Susan," Chuck said, leaning a little toward the microphone on his collar to make sure that every word was picked up. The cameras were obvious, but Steve seemed not to notice that Chuck was wearing a mic.

Steve didn't say it in so many words, but it seemed clear to him that the agenda of the honk and wave was all about putting pressure on the Powells.

He was probably right about that.

"How is you coming here helping to find Susan?" Chuck asked Steve.

"It isn't helping to find Susan," Steve admitted. "How is your standing at *our* neighborhood market helping to find Susan, Chuck?"

"People see the flyers," Chuck said, gesturing to the banners that Judy and his mother held.

Steve, dressed in a black shirt and jeans, looked around. All eyes were on him—the volunteers', their children's, shoppers', and newspeople's. He took a breath and issued an invitation to the television cameras.

"Is there any other question I can answer for anybody? I'm totally open to anything. We've got a lot of information about the Cox family, about Susan, a lot of it from her journals . . ."

Later, the Coxes would say a silent thank-you to Steve. His mention of Susan's journals opened a Pandora's box that would change everything for Fort Powell.

If Josh's father thought that he could change the course of the dialogue by trashing Susan, he was mistaken. Instead, reporters kept circling back to the same question they had been asking for a year and a half: Why wouldn't Josh meet with West Valley City police?

Steve grew increasingly irritated. He said that Josh had, in fact, cooperated with the authorities the day after Susan went missing. He pointed the finger of blame squarely at the West Valley City police.

"They handled it wrong," Steve said. "And they know they handled it wrong. They know they screwed it up. I don't think Josh will ever talk to the West Valley City police again. But he'll talk to the FBI! They just have to call! They know our number! They have my e-mail!

"They [the FBI] believe she's alive, they've told us that. And they said Josh had nothing to do with her disappearance," Steve said.

If all that was great theater, *great TV,* it was about to get a whole lot better.

A familiar light blue minivan drove up and a shaky Josh Powell got out. Charlie and Braden remained inside the van, their faces pressed against the glass to take in the commotion around them. It was the first time that many of them had seen the boys in months.

It was the sad, broken Josh, the one who'd been photographed when his wife first went missing. His eyes were hollow and pooled with tears. Tears fell and he fidgeted nervously with his keys.

"Chuck Cox uses my sons as pawns in the media to drive whatever message he is trying to drive," he said to a television camera.

His voice broke a little as he insisted that he *had* cooperated with the Utah police. He said that he stopped cooperating, however, when police in West Valley City tried to get his sons to talk about what they had seen the night their mother vanished.

"They have attacked my sons," he said. "I will protect my sons from anyone and everyone."

Two young female cousins holding hands, Denise's daughters, Clarissa and Dakota, approached the minivan, wanting to talk to Charlie and Braden. Steve stood between the girls and the vehicle and prevented them from saying hello to the boys.

"We just want to see our cousins," Clarissa said.

"It's not a good time," Steve said, both hands raised, palms forward, forming a barrier between them and Josh's minivan.

The girls stood there, confused. *When was it going to be a good time?*

During the volatile exchange between Steve, Josh, and Chuck, at least two plainclothes police officers, one from the

West Valley City PD and one from the Pierce County sheriff's department, looked on. Chuck knew he had been used by the police. They hoped that Josh would show up. He didn't care. "I don't mind that if that's what it takes to find my daughter. But by the end of it I realized I was bait!" he said.

Two days later, on August 22, Alina Powell sent copies of seven pages of Susan's childhood diary to the Associated Press. In an accompanying e-mail, Steve Powell wrote:

> *Susan is a lot more vulnerable emotionally than Chuck and Judy Cox would like people to believe.*

That same week a judge temporarily barred the Powells from publishing any more of Susan's diaries. On behalf of the Coxes, Seattle lawyer Anne Bremner, working pro bono for Susan's parents, filed a civil lawsuit against Josh and his family.

The standoff between the Powells and the Coxes was now an out-and-out war.

Susan was still missing.

30

It is painful to me to be so in love with her and to want
her so badly while she says she is committed to a
marriage to someone who despises her.
—STEVE POWELL'S JOURNAL, JUNE 26, 2008

A couple of days before Chuck and Steve faced off on the
Puyallup street corner, police had received a credible tip
Susan's body might be found in an area of abandoned min-
ing tunnels and shafts near Ely, Nevada. And, as silent as
they had been about the ongoing investigation and any progress in making a case against Josh or anyone else for that
matter, the West Valley City police did something totally out
of character. They invited the media to observe the search.

A caravan of satellite trucks and news cars snaked out of
Salt Lake City to eastern Nevada, 250 miles away.

The West Valley City PD let reporters, the Coxes, the
Powells, Susan's friends, and many others think that there
really *had* been a "credible" and "important" tip.

In reality, they were all being used once again, as Chuck
Cox put it, as "bait," although later the department would de-
fend itself, saying there was merit behind every search.

Nearly fifty detectives and searchers set up a base camp at the historic Ward Cemetery, near the Ward Mine. It was desolate, a ghost town. The mine had operated until the 1960s but now abandoned mine shafts were all that was left behind a gravel pit off Highway 50, aptly known as "The Loneliest Road in America." The area had been used as a dumping ground. Over the years people had abandoned old refrigerators, scrap metal, and other garbage. Someone had dumped a body, too. In 2010 the remains of a man were found.

The police cautioned the reporters to watch out for rats and rattlesnakes—and more important, not to fall down any mine shafts.

An odd news conference held in the desert was another clue that the search might have been intended to get a lot of coverage and "turn up the heat" on Josh. Sergeant Mike Powell—no relation to Josh and Steve—the spokesman for the West Valley City Police Department, was new to the job. Rapport between a police department and reporters is pretty common, but it was in short supply at the Ward Mine that day. The department was not sharing information about the search for Susan with *anyone*. They were on the defensive, with Susan's friends, the Coxes, TV talk show hosts and others wondering when they were going to arrest Josh.

Sergeant Powell tried joking with the media but in the end he didn't have much to say and the reporters weren't permitted to ask questions. They soon began to suspect that they had been led on a wild-goose chase.

The *Salt Lake Tribune* called the news conference "awkward."

A few days later a deputy editor of the paper wrote that it was clear that the police had "oversold" the search, and a columnist called it a "sideshow."

Josh said that not only had he never been to Ely, Nevada, he didn't know how to pronounce it. Both Josh and his father said they assumed the police had found Susan and Steve Koecher and were headed to Nevada to pick them up.

No such luck.

"We thought they really had something, and they just wasted everyone's time," Steve said.

After Susan vanished and Josh and the boys moved back to Puyallup, he used to take them along to meetings of the Gem and Mineral Club. The tip turned out to be about Josh's "unusual interest" in a bag of rocks from Nevada that was raffled off during a fund-raising auction at the club. A club member had called the police and said Josh and one of his sons were "obsessively preoccupied" with the rocks.

What the police didn't say is that a phone tap had picked up Josh talking about Ely, Nevada. That's why they publicized the search for Susan and hoped it would "turn up the heat" on Josh.

Even with credibility issues, another search got attention. Although it was conducted by the same police department that seemed incapable of advancing the Susan Powell case, this one didn't seem staged.

About a month after the Nevada search, the attention shifted to an isolated desert near Topaz Mountain, 135 miles from West Valley City and about thirty miles southwest of Simpson Springs. It's another popular rock-hounding area, and friends said that Josh and Susan had visited the area. In fact, police were taking their cues about where to search from photos they had found when they searched Josh and Susan's home and one of Josh's computers.

The news media covered this search, too, but this time there was no caravan arranged by the police. More than one hundred search-and-rescue personnel from two counties and various agencies volunteered. With ATVs and search dogs, over several days teams scoured trails and dirt roads looking for rocks or sagebrush that had been disturbed, clothing, or anything else that seemed out of place. While searchers wearing hard hats with lights rappelled into old mine shafts, other teams dropped cameras into two silver mine shafts at least a half mile deep.

On the third day of the search, Chuck Cox arrived. Searchers had found something—maybe human remains. It was at least the fifth time in twenty-one months that hopes were raised that Susan had been located at last.

But the week ended in more heartbreak and confusion. Initially, the media reported that dogs had found human bones. Headlines around the world speculated they were Susan's. Then there were reports that they weren't bones but, more accurately, human remains.

Finally it was explained that the dogs did alert, but on charred wood. The wood was in a hole that had been used as a fire pit, about two feet wide, two feet deep, and three feet long. Police speculated that the wood may have been used to burn human remains or bloody clothing. Despite the police stating that they were "disappointed and frustrated," Chuck Cox believed the finding might be important. The police told him the charred wood was "part of the case."

He was sad and hopeful at the same time when he phoned Judy to tell her the news.

"How do we know if it is Susan?" Judy asked.

Chuck let out a quiet sigh. "We don't. I think they might have found the place where Josh burned the clothes or burned something."

Police sent some of the wood to be analyzed to determine if accelerants had been used to start the fire. Chuck was told that it was possible to get DNA from burned wood, although it depended on the heat of the fire and how long it burned.

After they had excavated the fire pit, Chuck picked up a nearby rock. It was a little bigger than a fist. It was not particularly interesting, although when held in the right light, it sparkled a little. For some reason, the rock seemed important and Chuck took it home to Puyallup. He knew it had nothing to do with his daughter's case, but somehow it seemed a part of her. He'd always felt sad, lonely, whenever leaving Utah, as if he was leaving Susan behind. By bringing that rock home, it felt like he was bringing Susan home.

He put it next to his computer. He needed no reminders of Susan, but the rock with its little sparkle told him that even if she wasn't found, she was with him.

31

In several of these images the two females are un-
clothed and taking a bath, using the bathroom or
getting ready for the day.
— PIERCE COUNTY SHERIFF'S DEPARTMENT
INCIDENT REPORT, SEPTEMBER 23, 2011

On a sunny August afternoon a few days after the honk and
wave and three days after the search of the Nevada desert,
more than twenty detectives from the West Valley City Police
Department and the Pierce County sheriff's department de-
scended on Country Hollow and Steve Powell's house. This
time they had warrants. Calling it "part of the ongoing hom-
icide investigation," they were after Susan's diaries and more.
That morning a judge had issued a search warrant on the
grounds that it was "very reasonable to infer that Josh and
Steve discussed the disappearance" of Susan. That and Steve's
decision to show her diaries on national television and send
pages to the media had given the police what they needed
to get inside.

Police had done a little conniving and arranged for Steve
to be out of town on business. A defiant Josh Powell answered
the door. An officer patted him down and instructed him to

sit in a chair on the lawn. While the police searched his 2005 minivan for the fourth time, Josh called his father to let him know what was going on at home.

The day wasn't going at all as Josh and Steve had expected. It had started so well. They'd both given early-morning network TV interviews and were scheduled to do more. It was going to be their day to drive the message of what was happening in Puyallup and Utah. It was supposed to be their opportunity to tell the world once more that Susan had been a tramp and an unstable one at that.

That's not how it turned out.

In short order, the television news trucks began arriving and the news helicopters hovered overhead. As the raid unfolded, the Powell family members were moved to the backyard, secluded from view by a fence. The police had a little trouble with Alina, who left the house when they asked, but tried to go back in and argued with them.

Josh, Alina, Johnny, Charlie, and Braden spent the afternoon in the backyard with an officer assigned to watch them. Johnny never moved from his chair. Josh wandered around the yard, talking on his cell phone.

As the police searched the house, several of the officers noted one thing about the boys: Charlie and Braden were starved for attention. They were talkative with the police and seemed mostly oblivious to what was happening inside the house. Instead, they played with a ball in the yard. When Braden got tired, he climbed onto an officer's lap. Charlie showed the officer a science book and bugs in the yard, and said the helicopter overhead looked like a dragonfly. The officer wrote in a report later that the boys were hungry and thirsty but Josh was oblivious to them and preoccupied with reading the search warrant.

When the officer asked if it was okay if they got some pizza and water for the boys, Josh was quiet for a long time before he finally agreed. Later that day, when Josh said he was taking the boys to McDonald's, Charlie wanted the officer to go, too. The officer wrote that the boys seemed "thrilled" when a detective played catch with them. Charlie sometimes had one eye on his father and seemed "particularly anxious and worried." Braden didn't interact with any of the family members, the officer wrote—not his father, not his uncle, not his aunt.

Investigators found Susan's diaries and much, much more. From Steve's bedroom they recovered laptops, computer towers, cameras, boxes of photographs, a book titled *When Opposites Attract,* and his own journals, ten years' worth of writings about his sexual obsession with Susan. A videotape from Josh's college graduation—a ceremony for a degree he'd never finished—consisted almost exclusively of scenes panning up and down Susan's body. From hundreds of still photographs Josh had of the graduation day it was easy to surmise that the operator of the video camera was Steve.

This time they didn't overlook Steve's "porn cabinet." As described in a police report, Steve's room held a plethora of the mundane and perverted:

> *Ziploc baggie of hair, [women's] undergarments and hygiene products, photos of Susan Powell, 15 desk top and lap top computers, video tape of two minor females using the bathroom taken through an open window without their knowledge, blue/green winter gloves, the book "Dreams of Love and Fateful Encounters," CDs, flash drives, video cassettes, digital video recorder, packets of photographs, CDs with encryption keys, multiple notebooks, hard drives, three-ring binders, a box of journals, photo albums.*

From Alina's room, they took her parents' 1992 divorce documents and her father's financial records. The police also took CDs, flash drives, and "miscellaneous documents" from Josh's room.

After more than nine hours, investigators left, but they weren't finished.

Still determined to find out what Steve and Josh knew about Susan, shortly after the raid police exercised a search warrant on Steve's safe deposit box at a Bank of America branch in Puyallup. Inside, they recovered an internal hard drive in a plastic bag with handwritten notes with a number of dates and Josh's name on them.

Despite the events of the day, Josh kept a date to sit down with a reporter from *Dateline NBC* that evening.

That morning, Steve had made new claims about his flirtatious relationship with his missing daughter-in-law. He said that his only regret was that the sexual part of his relationship with Susan hadn't gone further. In an interview on ABC's *Good Morning America,* Steve insisted he and Susan were falling in love and even implied some type of sexual relationship had existed.

"Susan was very sexual with me," he said. "We interacted in a lot of sexual ways because Susan enjoys doing that. There's no question in my mind that the feelings were mutual."

Nothing could shut Steve up about his thing for Susan. "It was definitely a romantic obsession. Yeah. You know, Susan's a beautiful woman, and when a beautiful woman comes on to you like that, it is really hard to resist that kind of thing."

In his *Dateline* interview, Josh, still wearing his wedding band, contradicted his father, admitting that yes, Susan had a flirtatious personality, but stating that she had *not* had a sexual relationship with his father. He did not seem too happy with his dad. Brother Mike admitted later that there was "tension" between Josh and Steve after the raid, because of the attention it brought to the family and because Josh was sick of hearing about his father's obsession with Susan.

Both father and son once more affirmed that they'd had nothing to do with Susan's disappearance and said they believed she had run away with another man.

Chuck and Judy were among the millions of Americans transfixed by the disturbing revelations. The Coxes watched the interviews downstairs in their family room, among quilts and comforters that people had made for them in honor of their missing daughter. On the wall above the sofa were portraits of their four daughters, who appeared to be watching the parents as they tried to make sense of the latest revelations. Both knew that Steve had been inappropriate enough with Susan that she and Josh had moved hundreds of miles to be free of him.

Chuck's pulse quickened. "The man is sick," he said, as Steve's interview played on the TV screen.

"Sick and perverted," Judy said. "He can't get away with all of his lies."

"He won't," Chuck said. "We won't let him."

Chuck had made that vow before. But as the darkness that had enveloped the Powell household for many, many years began to be revealed, he knew he'd had only an inkling of just how bad it was.

"He wanted to have Susan for himself," Chuck said. "She told us that. She told us how Steve hinted that he'd wanted to share her with Josh. That she could be a wife to both."

While there are some fundamentalist splinter sects of Mormons who practice polygamy and are fodder for cable TV dramas and sideshow TV, the Mormon church does not condone it, and most members are disgusted by the idea.

Judy shook her head. She was revolted by the suggestion. "Susan would never have done that."

Chuck remembered how Susan had told him that Josh shrugged it off as if it were nothing more than one of his father's outrageous statements.

"Steve was testing Josh and Susan to see how far they might go," he said.

Chuck didn't say everything that was on his mind. He worried about Judy. It was like she was being crushed, rock by rock, and would be unable to take all the nastiness that was coming out. He wondered to himself if Steve and Josh had conspired to kill Susan because she refused to submit to both of them.

"It was like the old saying, 'If I can't have you . . . no one can.'"

Mike Powell had been worrying. Had his car, the 1997 Taurus he'd been driving in December 2009, really been destroyed? That's why he'd had it towed 100 miles on a winter day in Oregon. How could he get proof?

He didn't just phone the salvage yard. He did what the Powells always do: find the most complicated way around a situation. And because of it, the WVCPD caught a rare break.

A detective was at a Boulder, Colorado, imaging company when Mike happened to call wanting to buy a high-resolution satellite image of the salvage yard so he could see whether his car had been cut up and sold in pieces, as he hoped it had been. It was the first the police knew about Mike abandoning a car in December. They rushed to Pendleton, Oregon.

The car had been stripped of some parts, including the right front passenger door, taillights, and steering components. They brought in a cadaver dog that "intensely searched" the back of the vehicle and then indicated a positive "hit" for the scent of a body. The car was sealed in plastic by police, towed to a holding facility, and later processed by a forensics unit. Mike didn't learn until later that the police had his car.

32

When they were going to arrest Steve, they called me.
"We're going to be there, call your attorney, it's time."
They were taking the kids, and we should get things
in place.
— CHUCK COX, OCTOBER 3, 2012

On Thursday, September 22, 2011, a month after the honk
and wave and the raid, the same neighbors who had decorated Country Hollow with purple streamers and photos of
Susan looked on wide-eyed as a caravan of police cruisers
pulled up to Steve Powell's two-story house. Sirens didn't
sound, but the strobe of the cars' blue lights indicated that
something was about to go down. Something big. A few
people stood outside to watch what was transpiring in the
house that had become a lightning rod for trouble, the media, and the police. Others had front-row seats in their swivel
recliners perched in front of family room windows.

A moment later, Steve was arrested in the driveway, read
his rights, and placed in handcuffs. If he said anything, none
of the bystanders could hear it. He seemed calm, almost as
if he'd expected it. They confiscated his wallet and keys, his

phone in case he kept more images on it, as well as a key fob security device for computers.

The charge was a doozy: possession of child pornography and fourteen counts of voyeurism.

For the past month, investigators in Utah and Washington had sifted through the thousands of photographs they had removed when they raided Steve's house. Some were images of Hollywood stars. Some were graphic, like the images of Britney Spears and Lindsay Lohan caught by the paparazzi without any panties under their short skirts. Others were random and strange. A folder was filled with video stills from hair removal commercials. In an orderly fashion, Steve had labeled many of his photos and files, so one titled "Neighbors" caught the eye of investigators. Not only had Steve taken pictures of women and female minors without their knowledge—including Susan—but he had taken photographs of two neighbor girls, eight and nine years old at the time, using the toilet and taking baths. The sub-folders of "Neighbors" were titled "Taking bath—1," "Taking bath—2," and "Open window in back house."

Comparing nearby homes in Country Hollow, police were able to determine which house he'd targeted. The family with the young girls had moved by then, but when the police tracked them down and showed the girls' mother the photos, she recognized her daughters—and herself.

She had no idea that they had been the object of desire by a neighborhood creeper. It made her sick, angry, and determined that Steve Powell would never do that to any little girl again.

Steve, who left some neighbors with a disturbing vibe, was not just a weirdo living with a collection of adult kids. Steve was the neighborhood voyeur, maybe even a pedophile.

No one knew exactly what had gone on in that house, but it was curious that Charlie and Braden couldn't wait to leave. To Susan's boys, it might as well have been the arrival of the cavalry.

From a report written by a detective at the scene:

A detective called out to me and as I turned around I saw Braden running for me with his arms reaching out and a big smile on his face. He immediately hugged me and I picked him up. He told me that he was happy to see me again. I saw Charles near the van and he went to [another detective], who picked him up. Charles was interested in seeing the police lights and did not want to be put down. Neither of the boys had shoes on . . . I then went just inside the door, where I knew the shoes were kept . . . I saw Mr. Powell [Josh] in the garage and he glared at me, but he did not call out to Charles. Charles took no notice. Once inside Charles helped pick out shoes for him and Braden . . . Braden was chatty and giggly. He hugged me and told me he loved me. I explained that [a CPS caseworker] was going to take them to a babysitter for a sleepover. Neither of the boys seemed concerned and they were never upset. In fact, they were quite happy to be going. They did not ask for their father or any other family member. Charles did ask if [the babysitters] were Mormons. I told him no and he seemed pleased.

Charlie and Braden, in their pajamas, were placed in a police car. The boys went as though they were off to a friend's for a night's stay, not two little boys being dragged from their home.

Josh didn't come out of the house—not when his father was arrested, and not when the boys were taken into protective custody. Alina, however, was agitated and loud in her protestations about what was happening. The police asked Johnny to get his brother, and Josh finally emerged from the house. To the observers in the neighborhood, it did not appear that Josh was upset by his father's arrest. Even stranger, he didn't seem bothered by the police taking his sons.

Josh did not ask to hug Charlie or Braden or even tell them good-bye.

When the police left, the neighbors watched Alina and Josh stand in the driveway. And then, for the next half hour, they watched Josh repeatedly kick his van.

33

Josh hates her so much he even wishes she were dead. He even talks about it occasionally, fantasizing that she might have an accident. That worries me too, since couples who die in murder-suicide are not that rare.

—STEVE POWELL'S JOURNAL, JULY 1, 2008

Alina stood transfixed while her brother took out his frustration on the vehicle. To many of her neighbors, Alina was a tragic figure, a kind of overweight Wendy to a band of Lost Boys, which included her dad. She was there to do whatever it was they needed. And she did so with a sullen expression and fierce loyalty.

Josh paid Alina 800 to 900 dollars a month to watch Charlie and Braden, a little more when she added piano lessons. Sometimes Josh had jobs for a few weeks here or there, but often he did not work. He could afford to pay Alina and cover incidentals because he had closed the bank accounts in Utah and he had cashed out Susan's IRA.

Alina had her own mind, though many thought she was completely under the sway of her father. After Susan went missing, Alina wondered if her brother was responsible for her disappearance. In time, however, she rejected that outright. She became his great defender, joining Josh in his belief that the West Valley City police were harassing him and that the Coxes were telling lies about her family.

That she would side with the men in her family was no surprise to any who knew her background.

Alina was born into emotional chaos. Terri Powell was pregnant with Alina when she learned of Steve's fantasies about another woman. It made her ill and her doctor ordered bed rest. Terri waffled on her plans and desires for a divorce and by the time of Alina's birth, Terri decided Steve had "changed."

The couple stayed together for seven years more. Terri finally gave up and filed for divorce. It was a nasty one, lasting a grueling two years and having a devastating effect on the five children. Jennifer, the eldest, was working and saving to attend junior college. The two older boys, Josh and Johnny, were already influenced by their father in ways that had observers worried. Mike, ten, and Alina, just seven, were caught in the middle of the mess. Terri held nothing back. She was desperate to protect her youngest child from her brothers and father. According to letters from family members and Terri's own statements in the Powells' 1992 divorce records, the older boys regularly tormented Alina, one time resulting in bruised ribs. The environment was hostile in every way, and that hostility manifested itself in the ways it often does. Alina gained a lot of weight, and began to act insecure and "clingy." Terri, who filed for custody, said that Alina was "afraid to be left with Steve and the boys." Terri wrote that Josh and Johnny had "examined" Alina with her panties off when she was four.

Steve's influence on his kids didn't weaken after he finally moved out. Terri was horrified to learn that Mike was sleeping in Steve's bed. By age ten, according to divorce papers, Alina was hiding her father's pornography in embarrassment when she visited his house. Steve made her sleep in his room and Alina confided to her mother that she was afraid of taking a bath there.

In an affidavit, Terri wrote that Alina had said:

Mama, I know that Daddy and the boys really don't hate me. They just act like they hate me. I know that in their hearts they really love me. Someday they'll act like they love me.

In trying to win custody of her two youngest, Terri wrote that Steve

. . . made many promises, telling her [Alina] that she would never be lonely, and that she would have far more freedom with him.

While Terri prevailed and retained custody of her daughter, it was only short-lived. There were too many rules at her mother's house, and it was emotionally hard for both Alina and Terri when the girl went back and forth to her father's on weekends. Eventually, Terri gave in and let Alina go live with her father and her brothers. Later, like Mike and Josh, Alina attended college. And, like her brothers, she always moved back home.

Now, she was in her mid-twenties, caring for her young nephews, watching over schizophrenic/bipolar Johnny, and living at her father's house.

Still waiting to feel loved and still hoping not to feel lonely.

34

He's got a pretty sick problem there.
—JENNIFER GRAVES ON HER FATHER'S
ARREST, SEPTEMBER 22, 2011,
TO THE *SALT LAKE TRIBUNE*

None of the Utah contingent was surprised that someone at Fort Powell had been picked up by the police. Kiirsi had heard from a Facebook friend in Canada that someone—no one knew who—had been arrested at Steve's house. Kiirsi held her breath, hoping it was Josh. When a Salt Lake City television station phoned her for a comment, the producers said it was Steve who had been led away in handcuffs.

Kiirsi was glad that at least one of the Powells had been arrested for *something*. Susan's close friend hoped that with Steve in jail, Josh would "crumble and talk."

At least the children would be safe, Kiirsi and others thought when they found out the reason behind the arrest. Thankfully, Steve's stash of sordid, voyeuristic photographs had been cause enough to remove Charlie and Braden from the home. The boys were placed in foster care with plans to reunite them with Chuck and Judy.

Soon after the arrest, however, Josh had a visit with his sons. He wasn't about to let go so easily.

A state social worker observed father and sons and wrote about that first visit:

> *When they came out from the visit room, Charlie was crying, but it only lasted a couple of minutes. Braden did not cry at all and did not show separation anxiety . . . foster dad reported that the boys did not want to go into the visit . . .*

Until his arrest, the police had urged Susan's friends not to talk about Steve Powell, although there was plenty they could have said. Susan had given them an earful. Now that he was sitting in jail, they were given the go-ahead by the police, via Chuck, to tell what Susan had disclosed over the years. For the first time, they went public. Debbie Caldwell described how Susan had said that she refused to sleep in the same house as her father-in-law and didn't want her children in his house. Debbie also knew about the time Steve suggested that he and Josh "share her" and how that "freaked her out." Susan's friends knew that she had insisted they move to Utah to get away from her creepy father-in-law.

Now that they were free to talk about Steve, Kiirsi explained on her blog that Susan's dad had asked them to be careful about pointing fingers at Josh, and to keep the focus on finding Susan. Kiirsi wrote how the only thing Chuck had ever accused Josh of was not cooperating with the police:

> *I have done the same. Josh was my friend, too. I have never said he is "guilty" or that he "made Susan disappear" or anything like that. I have only said, "Josh, if you are innocent, PLEASE TALK TO POLICE and clear your name!"*

As Debbie, Kiirsi, and others began to talk about Steve and the sickness that followed him like a shadow, Alina Powell took shots at each of their claims. And although Alina was never close to Susan, she called her "the daughter that Jennifer Graves never was" to her dad.

As for Jennifer, she said she wasn't astounded to hear about her father's arrest. She had known since she was a girl that he kept a sizable stash of pornography. What she'd seen disgusted and haunted her. She'd vowed never to leave her own children alone with him.

And she never, ever did.

A smirking Steve Powell was transported in handcuffs to the South Hill precinct, not far from Country Hollow. The sixty-one-year-old wore a light jacket, a black shirt, khakis, and running shoes. But he wasn't going anywhere. The handcuffs were removed, then he was read his rights again, and asked if he would answer some questions. When he declined, he was moved to the Pierce County jail in Tacoma where he was booked. The police report made note of a "mocking grin" on his face.

The next day, detectives checked the jail's phone system to see if Steve had made or received any calls. Steve had, in fact, called home. Inmate conversations are routinely taped so police listened to the recording. Steve talked to Alina and Mike but spoke the longest with Josh, who repeatedly told his father not to say anything without an attorney present and to be aware that they were being recorded.

Josh, it appeared, had been reading up on inmates' rights.

Cox attorney Anne Bremner called it "hell week" for the Powells, but most of it really happened all in one day. Hearings related to Susan's disappearance were held in three courtrooms in the County-City Building in downtown Tacoma.

On September 23, 2011, Bremner served a temporary restraining order on Josh, stopping the Powells from publishing Susan's diaries. Next came the child custody hearing, which seemed to go in the Coxes' favor. Then Steve was arraigned on pornography and voyeurism charges. He pleaded not guilty to multiple counts and was held on

$200,000 cash-only bail. His children did not have the money to spring him and they did not try to raise it.

Bremner had learned about Steve's arrest the night before from a jubilant Chuck when he texted:

STEVE HAS BEEN ARRESTED! YAY!

While there was cause for celebration, there were still many unanswered questions.

35

I know she is comfortable with me physically by her
body language, and I think she would enjoy letting me
see her all, but she has some mores that prevent that.
—STEVE POWELL'S JOURNAL, MAY 3, 2003

Sometimes the diarist is a liar and a big one at that. With her
beloved orange and white cats at her feet, Cox family attorney Anne Bremner looked down at the journal entries logged
by Steve Powell and shook her head. In a legal career that
had spanned nearly three decades and put her on the front-
lines of tabloid TV as an expert on outrageous crimes, she
thought she'd seen it all. Steve's dark fantasies and misguided
attempts at literary redemption were too, too much. She
looked out the window next to her desk as the sky around
Seattle's Space Needle turned dark. It fit her mood just then.

In fact, she felt a wave of nausea. Every image, every word
on her computer screen made her ill.

Bremner flipped through the journals that detectives had
seized in the raid on Steve's house. It didn't take her long to
see that Steve was in a league all by himself, a Perv with a
capital *P*.

Shortly after Susan's disappearance Steve may have stopped his incessant journaling about Susan's unmatched beauty and his deep desires for her. Anne found it interesting that Steve's journal was mysteriously missing the months just before, during, and after Susan went missing. Or maybe the police had kept those key months. Anne thought his yearnings and ramblings fell somewhere between a schoolboy crush and the worst possible pervert—the kind that ends up with a "peter meter" attached to his private parts by criminal and mental health professionals to gauge what excites him most. Who knew what sick images Steve would respond to?

    . . . *A picture of a naked boy?*
    . . . *The image of a dog in heat?*
    . . . *A little girl on a swing set?*

There were all kinds of deviants out there. Bremner knew that. She also knew that sometimes deviants don't look the part. A lot of women would have found Steve Powell attractive. He wasn't necessarily the creep in the trench coat. He had gray hair with a trendy spike, a slender build, and blue eyes. He'd have fit right in at the CPA's office just down from her law practice. He appeared harmless. But how he looked didn't matter. Looks never did. Bremner had once defended police officers in a civil lawsuit surrounding the fallout of Seattle's infamous schoolteacher and convicted child rapist, Mary Kay Letourneau. Letourneau was a pretty blonde with big eyes and a sweet smile. She served seven years for child rape.

When Steve resumed writing his journal in March 2010, three months after Susan disappeared, he began to leave a trail about what could have happened to Susan in the pages of his Office Depot 3-Subject notebook.

He would sit in his car and write during breaks from his job. He wrote one entry in Steilacoom, a Washington town south of Tacoma, famous for its proximity to Western State Mental Hospital and the landing to McNeil Island, the site of one of the state's most notorious prisons. Both were places where he conducted business as an employee of the Department of Corrections, selling furniture made by inmates to schools and offices. As the light reflected off the gray sheen of Puget Sound, Steve wrote how Josh and the boys had taken a trip to Mount St. Helens, the volcano that had blown its top exactly three decades before. He pondered why Susan had fled.

> . . . if she is running due to criminal activity she may have settled into a comfortable assurance that she's committed a "perfect crime." Now whatever she did may prove her undoing.

He went on to ruminate about how the FBI and U.S. Marshal had cleared Josh. It was only a matter of time before Josh would be "vindicated."

As Bremner read on, she saw the journal entries post-Susan's disappearance as a bread-crumb trail to Steve's vision of the truth, yet oddly juxtaposed with masturbatory fantasies.

> We believe that when she's found, and even if she's done something criminal, these same people will continue to blame Josh . . .

To Steve, "these people" were the Coxes, the police, and Susan's Mormon friends.

While he decried the media's prejudice against Josh on one page, he took the entirety of another page to chronicle what he called a "jerk off" session to a photograph of "Susan's beautiful face." He wrote how many seconds it had lasted and added an exclamation point to cap off the memory.

Bremner had seen the sickest of the sick as a DA and in private practice defending victims. Steve was far off the charts. His sole existence seemed to be comprised of fantasies related to Susan.

Another day, Steve filled the pages of his journal with more theories about what might have happened to Susan. Bremner saw this as theater of the absurd. It was hard to know who the journal was written for—Steve, or others who might read it later?

He wrote how the recent visit with the FBI had left him with the feeling that they were holding back some crucial information about her.

> . . . *something they were not telling us and that they had found her . . . maybe Susan and her boyfriend know they are being watched.*

Ultimately, Steve appeared to be full of hope. The feds had talked about Susan as if they knew her whereabouts. Steve could hardly contain his joy over the possibility that Susan was still out there, and better yet, on her way home. His muse, his inspiration, the love of his life, was probably still alive! Her return would be none too soon. The months since her disappearance had been the darkest time of his life. He noted how her vanishing had devastated him and almost ruined his health. He'd lost about twenty pounds the month she went missing.

> . . . *Susan has been my reason for doing everything.*

Anne Bremner set aside the pages. She felt disgusted and angry. She thought of Chuck and Judy Cox and how they'd been kept in the dark about Steve's obsession with their daughter. Susan had hinted at being uncomfortable at the Powells' house but she hadn't said anything that approximated her father-in-law's own words on the plain pages of that Office Depot notebook.

Every entry was about Susan.

It was always about Susan.

The veteran lawyer wondered if Susan had ever really confided in anyone about the depth of her father-in-law's interest in her. Had she told anyone of the true twisted nature of his sexual obsession?

Or had she even known?

As far as Bremner could tell, the word *mudslinging* was defined by the parties in Steve and Terri's divorce case. Both sides unblinkingly fired point-blank at each other. Steve had insisted Terri was nothing short of a witch—and an unstable one at that—and Terri fired back that she was fearful for her life and for the safety of her children.

Terri's sister, Lisa Martin, was one of many who provided statements on Terri's behalf. She wrote in a 1992 declaration about a conversation she had with Steve, Jenny, Mike, and Alina in the family's living room in Spokane before the divorce. The couple had been fighting over which of the children would live with which parent if it came to that. The boys, it seemed, would stay with Steve. Jenny, an adult, wasn't part of the divvying-up process, but it was suggested that she and her little sister Alina would go with their mother. Terri wanted ten-year-old Mike to live with her, too, away from Steve's influence.

It appeared that Steve wouldn't concede to giving up *any* of the children. They belonged to him—not their mother. They were at a stalemate and the conversation took a very dark turn. Bremner looked down at the transcript of what Lisa said she had overheard Steve tell his children:

> ". . . there are people that can't break up with their girlfriend or wife. These people have the idea that if they can't have that person, then no one can. They go as far as killing them." She noted that when Jenny asked how far he might go if Terri tried to divorce him, Steve said something to the effect of "I'd like to think I wouldn't go that far."

The words were like a balled-up fist, a sucker punch to Bremner's stomach.

Who talks like that? Who says "If I can't have you, no one can?"

Steve Powell *did*. Josh Powell *did*. *That's who.* There was no other way to look at it. The seeds of destruction had been planted in Josh's head by his father, the Powell family's self-appointed puppetmaster.

36

There have been times when I have been afraid of
Steve and/or the boys because of their extremely
hateful behavior.

—TERRI POWELL, 1992 DIVORCE DOCUMENTS

Chuck sat at their big dining room table, lost in thought
about what he had learned about life inside that benign-
looking two-story home with its broad front porch and dark
wicker-style furniture. Susan had always said that Steve's
house in Country Hollow exuded "evil," and now Chuck
believed it.

While Judy quietly made dinner a few feet away, Chuck
ruminated over the events of the day. It had been brutal. He
and Judy had just returned from the first court hearing to
determine who would have temporary custody of Charlie
and Braden. Chuck was completely dumbfounded, a rare state
for a man who'd been on a mission since his daughter's disappearance. Josh and his lawyers insisted that Josh knew
nothing about Steve's unbridled interest in pornography.

As part of the custody case, the state talked to Jennifer and
her mother, Terri. Jennifer told caseworkers that her father's

pornography had been a sick part of her childhood. Her mother claimed to have *forgotten* about Steve's hobby.

Chuck saw the pornography as something inherently dangerous to the well-being of his grandsons and a very good reason—among many—to award custody of Charlie and Braden to him and Judy. Chuck talked it over with Judy and with their lawyer. It was clear that the police didn't have time to look at Steve's history of pornography and the role it might play in the custody battle. The police and caseworkers for the Department of Health and Human Services were mired in their own workloads and couldn't or wouldn't go to the trouble of digging into an old divorce case that had more than a thousand pages of documents.

There was only one thing to do. The day after the custody hearing, Chuck, his mother Anne, and sister Pam loaded up the car and drove the long lonely stretch of I-90 east to the Spokane County Courthouse. At the time, they knew only a little of the story of Steve and Terri's divorce, that Steve had retained custody of his three sons, including sixteen-year-old Josh. The devil, they were about to learn, truly was in the details.

When they arrived, the trio agreed to split the job into thirds as they dissected what had gone wrong in the nineteen-year-long Powell marriage. Over the course of several hours, each of them found things that not only refuted Josh's and Terri's claims of having no knowledge of a serious porn problem, but provided a genuine glimpse into what had made Josh into the man he was.

It all went back to Steve. Indeed, the apple didn't fall far from the tree.

As Chuck began to see it, the divorce records explained the long pattern of family codependency and dysfunction that Steve had passed on to the next generation of Powells.

The cycle began in Steve's childhood. In the divorce documents, Terri wrote that he was the victim of a parental kidnapping. Steve didn't deny the story that began when his mother separated from his father and took Steve and his three siblings to live in Ohio. His father tracked them down and his parents reunited. But a few months later, as Steve wrote, "My dad made a unilateral and secretive decision to separate from my mom."

One weekend while their mother was visiting a relative, the children were taken to Steve's paternal grandparents, who had moved to Idaho without their daughter-in-law's knowledge. When seven-year-old Steve asked where his mother was, his grandmother said he was never going to see her again.

"My older brother, my sister and I were inconsolable," he later wrote. He was overheard telling a friend that the children had been kidnapped by their grandparents; his grandmother punished him by dousing his tongue with cayenne pepper and ordering him to stand in a corner.

Steve was raised Mormon and in the early years of his marriage to Terri he attended church with her. That didn't last long, however. In court papers, Terri wrote that when they were first married, "Steve worked hard, served God and me. He was very thoughtful, very devoted towards me." But a few years later, Steve "began to change in many ways. He is a complete opposite of the man that I married." She wrote that he was "full of himself," "dominating any conversation," "condescending," "dogmatic," and "verbally abusive," taking delight in embarrassing her in front of her children. Terri was worried about Steve's influence on his sons:

> *For those who will listen to Steve, as the older boys have, he seems to have a powerful way of controlling . . . I know that Steve is persuasive in a most harmful, deliberate way. Steve's manipulation of the kids' thoughts and emotions is terribly difficult to deal with. They group together and stir each other up to almost a fever pitch at times.*

In the divorce documents Terri wrote about a time when Josh and Johnny had pushed and hit her, and an incident when Josh had threatened her with a knife. She stated that Steve used "overly harsh discipline" with Josh, but also encouraged their sons to mock and insult her.

Terri read Steve's journal that detailed his explicit fantasies about a woman they both knew in their church. When she confronted him with the journal, he showed no remorse and reiterated that if he could, he'd take a second wife. Steve had veered into the land of Mormon fundamentalists, the outlaws who still practice polygamy.

Terri saw all of it as reasons why she should have custody of the children, but in the end, it was Steve who prevailed. The boys, and later Alina, would be raised under his roof. For her part, Terri was kicked to the curb, penniless and heartbroken.

Little is known about Josh's attempt at suicide when he was a teenager. Family members who were asked about it later seem to have only vague recollections of its occurrence. Even Terri blanked out under questioning by a lawyer when asked if she could recall what had happened and why. Teary-eyed, she conceded she knew *something* had happened, but she was unable to retrieve a single bit of specific information.

It was as if a suicide attempt by a son were something a mother could forget.

Brenda Kay Martin, who was married to Terri's brother, wrote about the incident in a declaration she made in the Powell divorce case. Josh, she said, was about sixteen when it happened. The Powells phoned family members because the troubled teenager was acting strange in a way that indicated he might hurt a family member or himself. Brenda wrote:

> *A few days after this incident he attempted suicide. Fortunately it didn't work and only left a rope burn around his neck.*

On the way back over the Cascade Range which divides Washington in half—the rainy west side and the arid land of the eastern side—Chuck talked nonstop about Josh and Steve and Terri.

He was in shock, as was his mother and his sister Pam.

"Reading this was like a revelation about Josh's true character and his potential for violence," Chuck said later. He was alarmed by Steve's corruption of his own children and attacks on Terri. According to the records they'd just skimmed, Terri had been awarded custody of the two youngest, Mike and Alina, but Steve had constantly disregarded that ruling and his visitation limitations, and used his full-time income to buy his children's loyalty, never missing an opportunity to demonstrate to his children the advantages of living with him.

Steve had no rules. His mantra was "Do anything you want."

It was a game, but an unwinnable one for Terri. She wanted her children to know discipline, love, and the value of a routine.

Not Steve. Chuck saw him as the ultimate Disneyland dad. He bought his children's loyalty by giving them freedom and gifts, and making their mother appear to be a monster.

Chuck felt a little sorry for Terri. She'd been no match for the cruel wrath of her former husband. She had no money, no resources. He knew that she loved her children, but there was no stopping Steve. He used a scorched earth approach in his quest to get rid of her, urging their sons to see her as pitiful and hapless, and encouraging them to ridicule her.

She might very well be lucky to be alive, Chuck thought.

"Josh is much more dangerous than we ever imagined," Chuck said as they were on the interstate toward home. "Susan had no idea how messed up Josh was."

Pam and their mother sat silently. No one could argue against what Chuck was saying; what Chuck had just figured out. No matter what Susan thought she could do with her love for Josh, she could not undo the nightmare that his father had created.

Steve had passed it on to Josh like a toxic gene.

* * *

Steve's influence over Josh waned when he and Susan moved to Utah, but in the months leading up to Susan's disappearance, not only had it resumed, it appeared to kick into overdrive. Father and son spent hours at a time on the phone. During that time, Josh became a mirror of his father. He hated Mormonism and he made threats. The boys, he insisted, belonged to him.

He repeated a warning he'd given Susan before: If she divorced him, she would get the children over his—or her—dead body.

37

The boys were mean and they were wild. They were animals, just vicious. We had to teach them sharing. The psychologist called it "re-parenting." We had to start over and give them some boundaries and teach them "this is how you treat people."
—CHUCK COX, OCTOBER 3, 2012

Now it was time to fight for the boys. The battle over Susan and where she might be—dead or alive—had morphed into something more tangible. It was all about Charlie and Braden. The year before, the Coxes had heard from people who had glimpsed Charlie and Braden in a Puyallup store or in the neighborhood. They were thin, there were dark circles under their eyes, and they had vacant stares. Chuck was worried about their health and about Steve and Josh's influence.

He knew that Josh had undermined the investigation with a refusal to help the police. He wondered if Josh had done anything to keep Susan's spirit alive in that house, for the sake of her sons.

"I'm worried about everything he's trying to do to erase their mother's memory," he told Judy in one of the long hours that makes up the "hurry up and wait" part of child-custody cases.

"All that stuff he's filling their heads with," Judy said.

"We just have to stop it," Chuck said. "We have to for Susan's sake and for their sakes."

There was no argument from Judy or any other person in the Cox family. While there was no evidence that Josh or Steve had molested the boys or that they had been exposed to their grandfather's pornography, the Coxes were very concerned.

During the first hearing concerning temporary custody, Assistant Attorney General John Long told the court about conditions in Steve's house, including how Johnny Powell often answered the door naked or in a diaper, and about the noose that hung on his bedroom wall.

Josh explained to the judge that it wasn't a noose. It was a makeshift handle for a piece of exercise equipment that Johnny had made into part of an art display.

Art display?

Johnny's other artwork included the depiction of a female with a sword entering her vagina and exiting her stomach.

More art?

For the first time in a Washington State courtroom, it became a matter of record that Josh was a person of interest in his wife's disappearance. Long told the judge that Josh had been uncooperative with law enforcement, leading Washington State authorities to believe that he was responsible for his wife's disappearance.

Before the hearing, Child Protective Services interviewed Josh. A much more detailed psychological exam would follow, but the report noted that he'd said there were no major difficulties in his marriage and that he'd told Charlie and Braden that their mother loved them, and showed them pictures of Susan.

"I never hurt Susan, not intentionally," he said in the interview. "We had our problems over the years."

He claimed that he had experienced no depression, anxiety, or sadness in the previous twelve months. Josh said contradictory things about how he was, or was not, supporting himself and his sons. At one point he said that he earned too much money, $5,000 a month, to have health insurance and that's why the boys hadn't had counseling. Another time he contradicted himself, saying that the attention of the media and court appearances dealing with the restraining orders had prevented him from earning enough money to meet all the needs of his sons, including medical coverage and mental health counseling.

He was asked if he was interested in photography, too, like his father. Josh admitted he liked to photograph people's legs in public. He added that he made sure he never got too close or showed faces.

In the end, it went the way of the Coxes, like many believed it would and should.

Josh took the judge's decision hard.

"I was expecting to take my sons home with me today," he told Superior Court Judge Kathryn J. Nelson, in a reed-thin, shaky voice. Josh said he would prefer Charlie and Braden went to foster care than to Chuck and Judy Cox. He considered them "the most dangerous people on the planet" and said the home of strangers would be better for Charlie and Braden.

The blood wasn't just bad between the Powells and the Coxes. It was lethal.

Child welfare experts not involved with the case weighed in, giving their opinions to the news media. The only way for Josh to regain custody of his sons, they all agreed, was to be cleared as a person of interest in the disappearance of his wife, Susan, and prove he had no part in his father's alleged pornography and voyeurism activities.

Braden wasn't *trying* to kill his older brother, but he came close not long after the boys had moved in with their grandparents. After Steve's arrest, Charlie and Braden had spent a few days with a foster family, and then had been placed with Chuck and Judy.

The boys were taking a bath in the upstairs tub that their mother had used as a child when Chuck stuck his head in to check on them.

Braden had his brother in a headlock and was holding his head underwater.

Chuck hurled himself to the tub and pulled the boys apart.

"What's going on here?" he asked.

Charlie's face was red and bubbles streamed from his nose and mouth as he coughed up water.

Judy was right behind her husband and the two of them pulled the boys out one at a time.

Chuck was sure that Braden had only been playing, but that in another minute or two Charlie would have been unconscious or worse.

It was horseplay, that's all, he told himself. Yet he wondered: Were the boys damaged in some deep and profound way by living with Josh and Steve? And when push comes to shove, how could they not be?

Chuck and Judy had let the brothers bathe themselves out of fear and a sense of self-protection. They felt that Josh would make up some kind of hateful story about them abusing them sexually if they bathed them. It was a foolish reaction, but so many vile things had been threatened and said about Susan, and about the Coxes, that Chuck and Judy felt that they had targets on their backs.

Charlie got ready for bed on his own and Chuck helped Braden put on his pajamas.

The Coxes had bunk beds for the boys. Charlie slept in the top bunk and Braden in the bottom one. When Chuck left the room, they started laughing and giggling. A little while later, when the ruckus had gone on too long, Chuck returned to tell them to settle down.

Charlie had stripped off every stitch of clothing and Braden was in his underwear. They were running around the room laughing.

Chuck immediately picked up Charlie's pajamas.

"Why are you doing this?" he asked. "Who told you its okay to be naked?"

"Our daddy," the boys answered in unison as they continued to dash around the room.

Chuck stayed cool, but deep down he felt very, very uncomfortable.

"Okay, you're not doing it here," he said gently, but firmly. "There are rules and you're going to follow them." He helped them to get back into their pajamas and put them back to bed.

That night he and Judy talked about it. They wondered if the boys were mimicking their uncle Johnny, who'd been seen naked around the house.

"Maybe they think its normal," Judy said.

"But it's not. And it's nothing Susan would have ever taught her boys."

A little while later, they learned something else from Charlie. He and Braden slept naked with their father—and he was naked, too.

"What has been going on in that house?" Judy asked, not really wanting an answer.

Chuck knew that whatever it was, it was ugly. He also knew that the boys had come into his and Judy's care just in time.

They would keep them safe.

September in Minnesota was, fittingly, fire and ice. Lawns in Minneapolis were painted white with frost and a summerlong drought had torched tens of thousands of acres across the state when the West Valley police showed up to interview Mike Powell on the Saturday after his father's arrest in Washington.

Just days before, they had recovered Mike's Taurus from a salvage yard in Oregon but they didn't share that information with him until late in the interview.

Mike, almost thirty, was in a doctoral program for cognitive science at the University of Minnesota. It had been nearly twenty-one months since Susan had gone missing and the police hadn't spent much time talking with him. He admitted that he was not close to Susan, although they had known each other casually in middle school in Puyallup. He also said he wasn't all that close to Josh, and most certainly not as thick as thieves as it had appeared when he was in

Utah running interference with neighbors like Tim Peterson or the media. He said he hadn't even attended Josh and Susan's wedding in Oregon, because of other commitments—although he is in photos of their reception the next day. Prior to coming to West Valley City to help Josh with the boys, and then to help him move, Mike said he'd last seen his brother in 2008. Most of their contact had been by telephone when they would talk for a couple hours at time.

And yet, when Josh called "crying" for help in December 2009, Mike Powell was Johnny-on-the-spot.

During the course of the police interview, he offered up nothing more than the Powell party line. He claimed that he was home in Puyallup the day Susan vanished—as was, he insisted, his father, brother Johnny, and Alina. Josh was a good guy, he said. Susan was a good mother—although she occasionally left Josh and the boys alone without saying where she was going. According to Josh.

Mike really couldn't recall much else.

Then the police asked Mike about his 1997 Ford Taurus. What had happened to it? He stammered and he stalled. He was extremely nervous, evasive, and lied about where it had broken down. Then they broke the news to him—they had the car.

At the salvage yard, a cadaver dog, trained to smell human remains, went right to the Taurus. Michael was badly shaken. "He was terrified," Deputy Chief Phil Quinlan said.

38

[Josh] seemed to have a soul-deep hurt because of
his dad's erratic and explosive behavior.
— TERRI POWELL, 1992 DIVORCE DOCUMENTS

Josh was nine years old when Alina was born in 1985. Josh
and his brother Johnny, who was two years younger, were seldom the caring big brothers they might have been had they
been part of a normal family. It was too late. They had already been shaped in their father's image. They had been
exposed to pornography and taught to ridicule their mother,
Terri, and they had no boundaries, including sexual ones.

As their father had groomed them, so they groomed their
younger brother—and eventually their little sister. When
Mike was ten and his parents divorced, he'd already picked
up a slew of bad habits—behavior that their father seemed
to be a model for. Mike learned to swear, hate school and the
government, bad-mouth people, and he dropped out of Boy
Scouts; his father said the Scouts were too aligned with the
Mormon church.

Steve Powell's boys were encouraged to be loners. Steve

equated isolation with being "artistic." The boys were young, impressionable, and they gobbled up everything their father said or did. Steve, who was antigovernment, was "thrilled" by incidents of flag burning. And his sons watched as he was "frantic" over the 1992 Ruby Ridge standoff between federal agents and a family in northern Idaho. As it unfolded over eleven days on television, it was clear that Steve thought the FBI and U.S. Marshals Service should leave survivalist and federal fugitive Randy Weaver alone. By the time the siege was over, Weaver's son and wife were dead, as were a neighbor and a marshal. Steve was all the more angry at the government.

Terri was worried about the boys—all of them. But Steve wasn't. When Johnny wandered around at all hours of the night in a dark hooded cape, practicing a creepy laugh and acting out bits and parts of medieval-type behavior, Steve saw it as his son being creative. Johnny was marching lockstep to the beat of a different drum—Steve's own vision.

Johnny suffered because, according to Terri's affidavits, his father turned a blind eye, interpreting his mental illness as his "artistic" nature. In his early twenties, Johnny suffered a breakdown and was institutionalized. He was also suffering from hallucinations, and as later testified by Alina, he was eventually diagnosed as bipolar with schizophrenic disorder.

By the time they were teenagers, Josh and Johnny would taunt their four young cousins, who were all under the age of five and easily scared. Josh and Johnny liked to disrupt family activities, verbally ridiculing their mother and younger siblings as they watched a children's video. They undressed and "examined" Alina and told her that if she lived with their father she could "watch them."

They didn't say doing what—they just snickered.

At one point, Josh and Johnny were arrested for shoplifting and ordered to do community service. Josh was later arrested a second time, for stealing from a convenience store, and was suspected of arson. Steve laughed when he heard Josh had killed Alina's pet gerbil.

Each item that Terri Powell included in the divorce papers

would have been enough, but taken together, they suggested something more serious than merely acting out.

Chuck Cox later considered what he learned about Josh from the documents:

> *Stealing*
> *Killing his sister's pet*
> *Threatening his mother with a kitchen knife*
> *Hitting and shoving his mother*
> *The suicide attempt*
> *Police called to the house*

These weren't just warning signs of a troubled teen. Chuck believed them to be the genesis of whatever it was that his son-in-law had done to his daughter. He thought it all had begun long before that cold night in December when Susan vanished.

Chuck could easily lay blame at Steve's feet. He'd created a home of misery and dysfunction. He'd set it all in motion so many years ago. And yet, Chuck couldn't completely let Terri off the hook. She'd tried to save Alina and keep her from Steve, but she'd given in and left her children with their father.

And she knew just how sick the household was. She'd been a part of it.

Chuck wondered how Terri felt now that Susan was missing and the revelations of her ex-husband's sexual obsession with her had come to light.

What had she known?

Josh Powell never hid his loyalty to his father. It was born during his parents' divorce. When Terri fought for custody she fought only for the two youngest, Mike and Alina, not Josh. In fact, she thought Josh posed an emotional and physical danger to the younger kids. She didn't think she could handle the boys, but she didn't think they should be left with Steve, either. She told the court that she thought Josh and Johnny would be better off in foster care. Josh never forgot or forgave her for that.

* * *

Chuck Cox had a lot for which he and Judy could be grateful. They came from loving families. The Powells clearly had not. In fact, by looking at the records it was clear that the problems were systemic. There were three generations of parents using their children in ugly, destructive custody fights. Steve's parents had done it to him and his siblings. Steve and Terri's five children got trapped in a similar battle. Josh was threatening the same thing.

It was about winning and controlling.

For the umpteenth time as he sat with Steve and Terri's divorce documents in the office that he'd made of Susan's old bedroom, Chuck wondered what he might have missed. It was like skimming through a bad movie, the kind in which the woman has no idea that she's sleeping with the enemy . . . until it is almost too late. Terri wasn't merely trying to get a divorce; she was looking for an escape. It was as though Steve was the leader of a gang—or a cult—and she needed to figure a way out.

The cult even had a name for itself. It was "The Family," as if they were the mafia or something. Not "our" family, but "the" family. They didn't break ranks. Ever. They were like members of a religion sharing the same twisted beliefs.

Chuck looked down at the documents and read a line that Terri had written in what must have been a moment of clarity:

It seems like there is a sickness pervading the family and I have been powerless to stop it.

Chuck knew that the sickness had moved on to the next generation and that Susan, Charlie, and Braden had been caught up in it.

39

"The Mormons killed my brother and my mom."
"I am going to come to your house at night and kill
you. I hate Mormons."
  —CHARLIE POWELL, FIRST-GRADE STUDENT,
                    FALL 2011

It was mournful and came in waves. What was that sound?
Was it a wounded animal?

Without disturbing Judy, Chuck slipped out of bed, put on
a robe, and went in search of the source of the strange noise.
The home where the Coxes had raised their daughters was at
the end of a street near some wooded land that was home to
forest animals. Maybe a deer had been hit by a car and had
somehow wandered near the vacant land?

Yet it didn't sound quite like a hurt animal. The cries
were a strange, almost otherworldly mixture of sobbing
and moaning.

Chuck quietly padded down the hall to the boys' bedroom
following the sound, which was unlike anything he'd ever
heard in his life.

Without turning on the light, he could pinpoint the sound.
It was Charlie in his bunk bed. The little boy was neither

awake nor asleep but trapped in some terrible nightmare. Chuck went to him, and put his hand gently on his shoulder

"What hurts, Charlie?"

More moaning.

Chuck was worried. He was unsure if he should wake him. The boy was clearly in distress, but he wasn't fully awake or asleep.

He leaned a little closer. "Is it your tummy?" he asked.

Charlie stirred and Chuck took the response to mean no.

"No? Your leg? Let's stretch it out," he said. "It probably went to sleep on you."

The boys didn't often say what they were thinking, but this time Charlie did between his sobs.

"Mommy," he said.

As heartbreaking as that moment was, Chuck felt a kind of relief. With all that Josh and Steve had done to poison the boys' memories of their mother, they couldn't fully erase their love for her.

"You're thinking about Mommy?" he asked.

Charlie looked up at his grandfather. Tears streaked his cheeks. "Yes," he said.

Chuck patted the boy some more. "I am, too."

Susan's father stayed by the bed, stroking Charlie's head and back, feeling the sadness surrounding the child who had seen too much.

The boy was thinking of his mommy, who went camping and stayed with the pretty crystals.

Even after their grandsons came to live with them, Chuck and Judy Cox still didn't have any legal authority. As grandparents, they had no specific rights. The boys were really in the custody of the State of Washington.

The Washington State Department of Social and Health Services (DSHS) is, like similar agencies in other states, a large bureaucracy responsible for everything from the health and safety of children to services for the aging, mentally ill, and sick. In fiscal year 2010, DSHS served nearly 2.4 million people of all ages, about a third of the state's population.

Child Protective Services (CPS) is the division responsible for protecting children from abuse or neglect. After children have been brought to their attention, CPS assigns a social worker who monitors each family. A caseworker—the person who stays nearby during noncustodial parental visitations—is often a contract employee and not necessarily trained in social work.

CPS was involved in the Powell-Cox custody dispute from the beginning. Even before they went to arrest Steve, Pierce County detectives met with CPS staff and an assistant attorney general, and arranged for social worker Rocky Stephenson to meet them at the Powell house.

It was a complicated case, to be sure. What CPS had on its hands was a father, Josh, who was a "person of interest"—a euphemism to protect authorities from saying "suspect" before they're prepared to make an arrest—in his wife's disappearance.

Four days after Steve Powell's arrest, Braden was taken for a "sexual abuse consultation" with a physician. The doctor wrote that Braden's greatest fear was the dark. The boy had a rash—molluscum contagiosum—a common wartlike condition. The conclusion of the exam was that the possibility of sexual abuse could not be ruled out.

Next, CPS ordered routine physical exams for the boys. About two weeks after going to their maternal grandparents, Charlie and Braden were seen by a physician. Charlie told the doctor that he had seen little drops of blood on his genitals, but urinalysis showed no problems. The assessment was that he was a "healthy child." His records indicated that he had been seen in September for a physical; at that time a doctor recommended counseling "given the multiple stressors in his life." He had also been treated for a rash on his elbows and right leg.

Four months earlier, Charlie had been seen for "behavior problems" and "concentration issues." A physician observed Charlie and described him this way:

. . . quite energetic and continuously running around in the exam room, jumping on the exam table, slam-

ming on things, repeatedly making off with the stools, opening drawers and cabinet doors.

The doctor concluded that Charlie had hyperkinetic syndrome, a disorder characterized by excessive activity, emotional instability, and reduced attention span. The doctor wrote in Charlie's records that Josh was trying to apply positive reinforcement discipline techniques and concluded that Charlie might have ADHD or another behavioral problem and if it continued, he should see a child psychiatrist. The rash was a mild fungal dermatosis.

When it was Braden's turn for his physical, he didn't cooperate. He wouldn't sit still to have his blood pressure or his heart rate checked so it was deferred to a later time. Although the physician said that Braden was healthy, he found molluscum contagiosum lesions under the boy's right arm. He was referred to a dermatologist.

Judy remembers that the doctor said something ominous about a venereal disease. Molluscum contagiosum is a viral infection that causes a rash and is most common in children ages one to twelve. It is considered a benign venereal disease. It is also a highly contagious STD that thrives when people live close together. Children can get molluscum contagiosum through direct skin-to-skin contact, but also by touching objects that have the virus on them, such as towels and bedding. It can also be transmitted via sexual contact and by physical contact that isn't necessarily sexual.

Chuck and Judy informed the doctor that the boys had been sleeping nude with their father, also nude. The doctor shut them down. He said he did not want to get in the middle of a family feud over whether Braden had gotten the rash from his father or someone else in the Powell household. Besides, it would be difficult to prove, even if Josh had the same rash.

Not long after the boys went to live with the Coxes, Braden had two visits in one week to an emergency room. He scalded a foot when he stepped into a pot of hot water that a workman was using to set floor tile in the basement—part of a major addition Chuck and Judy had undertaken, in part to give the boys more room. And as an older cousin playfully swung Charlie around by his arms, Braden was knocked to the floor and hit his head. These were fluke accidents, but hospitals have reason to be suspicious, especially when there is an ongoing custody fight. Josh was notified.

The Powells accused the Coxes of "maiming" Braden, and suggested that it might have been done as punishment. It was proof, Josh said, that the Cox home was "not a safe place for children." Josh's Web site showed a gruesome photo of a burned foot—it wasn't Braden's, it was a picture that Josh, Alina, or Mike had found online.

Another part of the children's assessment was conducted during a home visit with a social worker. Charlie was asked if there was anything he would like from "home" (Steve's house) and he said that he missed their pet bird. "His eyes got a little teary when talking about Cryly," the social worker wrote.

In order to determine how the boys coped with stress, they were asked if they had a "comfort item," something they could hold or play with or snuggle with that made them feel a little better when they're upset or sad. Neither boy had one. The report stated that Charlie's coping technique was to pace while talking. Braden hid when feeling uncomfortable.

The Coxes didn't have pets but the report noted that there were concerns that animals might not be safe around Braden.

Charlie's assessment reported that he was inquisitive, and enjoyed catching bugs and being read to. He seemed to be interested in animals and had not been seen being mean to animals. But he didn't like to share, didn't understand other people's feelings, blamed others for his troubles, did not listen to rules, teased others, and took things that did not belong to him.

There were some serious concerns about Braden, who was three months short of turning five at the time of his assessment. Chuck and Judy were concerned that Braden didn't look at them when they addressed him, and that he had long periods of crying, screaming, or tantrums and liked to "destroy or damage things on purpose." He also, according to the report, lacked a conscience and empathy for others. He tried to hurt children, adults, and animals. He also showed an interest or knowledge of sexual language and activity. He was clingy with strangers, and liked to be hugged—that is, when he wasn't biting or hitting.

A member of the Gem and Rock Club, which Josh joined after moving back to Puyallup, wrote to the social worker that Charlie and Braden were brought along on trips that were not meant to include children. The boys often disrupted the club meetings, climbing on and under tables, running up and down stairs, standing in front of speakers, and stealing door prizes off of a raffle table. One even shone a flashlight in the eyes of a guest speaker. The member wrote: "Most of the time Josh just sits with a strange grin on his face and does nothing." The concerned club member also observed Josh dragging one or both boys by the wrist across a room.

It was Braden who was the uncontrollable and impulsive one. The woman wrote:

> Braden has bitten a club member on the bottom. He has head butted someone calling an auction. This boy was also left to scream and cry non-stop, during a class, in a corner for more than an hour. When the instructor asked Josh to do something about his son's crying, Josh's reaction was to say that "sometimes you just need to let them cry and wear themselves out."

When told by his social worker about the complaint from the gem club, Josh said the members were "crotchety."

Braden even sucker-punched a woman he came to love, Elizabeth Griffin-Hall, Ph.D., a veteran employee of the Foster Care Resource Network (FCRN), who supervised their visits with Josh.

One day when she had driven them back to the Coxes, Braden refused to get out of his car seat. She said:

After several refusals I leaned over him to unlatch the buckle. He hit me in the mouth with his fist. I asked Grandpa to help Braden out of the car.

"Chuck Cox is a bad person," Charlie suddenly said one day in the car.

Chuck looked at his grandson. "What do you mean, 'Chuck Cox is a bad person'?"

Charlie blinked his deep blue eyes. "Chuck Cox is evil."

Chuck looked at his grandson, not sure where this was going. Or if Charlie understood just what it was that he was saying.

"*I'm* Chuck Cox," he said. "Am *I* a bad person?"

The little boy thought for a moment. "Why don't you change your name? Then you won't be Chuck Cox, because he is a bad person," he said.

Without blaming Josh, Chuck found a way of explaining to his grandson that not everything he heard was true.

Chuck and Judy heard other bits of what they called the "garbage" that Josh or Steve or both had filled the boy's heads with. The boys said things like "Don't mess with Josh or you'll end up dead," and that their mommy had run away because she was abused by Mormons. Occasionally the boys would voice their own take on things.

"My daddy is a little bit bad," Charlie said.

Chuck kept his mouth shut on that one. There was no argument coming from him.

At school, Charlie was telling other children how he hated Mormons and that they were responsible for killing his mother . . . and his brother, Braden. One time the little boy unflinchingly told an adult staff member at the school how to bury an animal and cover it up so it would never be found.

The Coxes couldn't talk to the media during the temporary custody phase, so they avoided places where reporters might show up. That included vigils and celebrations of Susan's birthday.

On Susan's thirtieth birthday, October 16, 2011, when

hundreds of purple balloons were released at observances in West Valley City and in Puyallup, Chuck and Judy instead released balloons with Charlie and Braden in their front yard.

The two grandparents and the two small boys watched the purple balloons rise into the sky until they were gone from sight.

40

After interviewing Mr. Powell and observing him in-
teract with his two sons, there is nothing to suggest
Mr. Powell does not have the intellect, skill, or prac-
tice to safely and adequately parent his two sons.
—FROM A PSYCHOLOGICAL EVALUATION BY
DR. JAMES MANLEY, DECEMBER 9, 2011

It was pure Josh, and would almost be humorous if it weren't
an alarming sign of how irrational he'd become. Charlie and
Braden's counselor hadn't been "warned" about Josh, so when
she met with him she was unprepared. He hijacked their
meeting, couldn't stay on topic, spoke rapidly, and went on
"verbal rants" about the Cox family and the media. At one
point, the counselor suggested an appropriate way for Josh
to explain to the boys where "Grandpa Steve" had gone.
She said that, for example, he could tell them "Grandpa
made some bad choices and will be gone for a while as a
consequence."

Instead, as soon as the boys joined the session, Josh told
them that the "Mormon police" had made up bad information about their grandpa and put him in jail and that they
were trying to do the same thing to him.

To try to get Charlie and Braden returned to his care, Josh

had to submit to an in-depth psychological exam. Dr. James Manley, a psychologist from Tacoma, was chosen by the state to do the evaluation.

Child Protective Services contributed background information on Josh—including the story about the counselor's meeting with him—and Steve and Terri Powell's divorce records, which Chuck had made available. Josh's mother wrote a letter on his behalf; it said, in part:

> *In my experience, Josh is a loving and very engaged father in the care of his sons, and Charlie and Braden are happy, well-adjusted and vibrant children, even though they miss their mother.*

Josh's mother, now defender, seemed not to remember her ex-husband's pornography hobby and how she had feared it would affect her children. Josh's sister, Jennifer Graves, was so angered at her mother's support of Josh—whom Jennifer was convinced had killed Susan—that Terri was asked to leave the Graves home in West Jordan, where she lived with the couple and their five children.

In the end, Dr. Manley diagnosed Josh with adjustment disorder with anxiety, and narcissistic personality disorder.

Sometimes referred to as "situational depression," adjustment disorders are common. It's the stress people feel when they go through a divorce, lose a job, experience a death in the family, or face other life changes. Normally, people adapt after a few months.

People with narcissistic personality disorder are excessively preoccupied with personal issues, including power, and feel that they are superior to others. People who knew Josh weren't surprised by that; they had seen displays of his know-it-all attitude and control issues for years. The evaluation took two months, but Josh was able to have supervised visits with his sons from the beginning. It was clear to Dr. Manley and CPS social workers that Josh was so preoccupied and fixated on the Coxes—"the most dangerous people on the planet"—that he was completely unaware of how his behavior was detrimental to his sons. He simply could not shut up, even when his parenting skills were being assessed.

During one early visit with the boys, Josh kept telling them how much he missed them, thought about them, and was fighting for them—and then he badgered them with questions.

"Do you remember how much fun we have?" he asked.

The boys stared up at him, taking in every word.

"Make sure you tell people how much fun we have every weekend."

A social worker had to interrupt Josh when his rants turned to the Coxes—"those people who want to take you away from me."

Chuck Cox is bad.

The psychological exam didn't pick up on Josh's repeated lies. With a straight face, he told Manley that he was not aware of his father's ongoing attraction to Susan. He denied sexually abusing Alina and attempting suicide when he was a teenager. At first, he said he had no arrest record—then finally, after some prodding, he admitted that he had spent five days in juvenile detention for theft. He said he didn't know about his father's trove of pornography.

Josh even kept his cool when Dr. Manley said he had learned that five or six images of computer-generated incestuous child porn had been found on Josh's computer in 2009. Josh said it was no big deal. Josh also said there had been no problems in his marriage. He claimed Susan had been suicidal and that he didn't know what happened to her.

He stuck by his story of December 6–7, 2009, the late-night camping trip and the return home to find Susan missing. He added that Susan "had been okay" with the trip.

In the psychiatrist's own words, Josh was defensive, evasive, and glossed over things. It was obvious that Charlie and Braden were beginning to mimic what they heard their father say. The boys had said that their mother "was hiding from her parents because her parents abuse her," and that "the Mormons are trying to steal them."

"God is bad. The police are bad, but God is really bad," Charlie had said.

Josh would talk nonstop about the Coxes, the Mormon church, and the police, yet he would not admit to feeling any stress in his life. He portrayed himself in a positive light in his answers to all the questions, so much so that it threw off some of the testing results. On the measure that determines the potential of child abuse, the "abuse scales" were not elevated because he denied stress, unhappiness, depression, or any other problems.

The conclusion? There were no concerns that he might abuse his children.

Dr. Manley's report indicated that Josh had "excellent parenting and interpersonal skills," although he needed to learn to "consistently place his children's need for an emotionally safe and stable environment ahead of his own [needs]."

He also suggested that Josh seek therapy in order to have a place to vent other than to his children. Josh could continue his weekly visits with his sons—plus he was about to get a second supervised visit each week. State policy mandates that visitations be held in the least restrictive setting, with a caseworker present. Since Charlie and Braden couldn't go near Steve's house—even with Steve in jail—Josh had rented a house nearby. His visitations could be held there.

DSHS never told the police in Pierce County or in Utah that the visits were being moved to Josh's house. And, for their part, the West Valley City police were still silent about the fact that it was Susan's blood that they'd recovered from her house, and that she had left a note saying she was afraid her husband might kill her.

Whether it was policy or safeguarding their own turf, the agencies responsible for finding Susan and protecting her children didn't say much to each other.

41

Charlie, I sure miss you. I was thinking of ways to stay close to you boys. You could tell me in your letters what you want me to bring to our next visit. Perhaps a toy or a certain kind of food. Everything I do is for you. I love you and I'm working hard to see you more. Love, Daddy.
— JOSH TO CHARLIE IN A LETTER, FALL 2011

Josh was in dad mode during a visitation observed by Dr. Manley. He was making lunch and giving Charlie and Braden a tutorial on the merits of cheese at the same time.

"Cheese has protein," he explained as he unwrapped presliced American cheese from its plastic wrapper and started building sandwiches.

"Protein is a part of every cell in our bodies," he said. "What other food is protein found in?"

Charlie and Braden, six and four, didn't know and were more interested in playing with their remote-controlled cars.

"We also find protein in meat, chicken, and fish, like sushi. Also, milk and eggs," Josh went on. He looked over and it was clear that he'd lost his audience. The boys couldn't have cared less.

He tried and he tried, but it wasn't working.

Manley's psychological evaluation noted that Josh was

rigid and overly controlling with the children. In a report, Dr. Manley wrote that in addition to talking to the boys about inappropriate topics, like Mormons and the Coxes, Josh "tends to offer a high degree of structure [to] his and his sons' interactions. At times, his interaction style seems forced or staged. He seems to be trying too hard. Whether this is Mr. Powell's baseline parenting style or is due to his present high degree of stress is unclear."

All visits were supervised by the fifty-nine-year-old Griffin-Hall, who was required to take detailed notes. She noticed right away that this was a man who never relaxed with his sons.

He started many visits by saying, "Charlie and Braden, I have a surprise for you!"

When he made the boys pancakes, he decorated them with faces, eyes and ears.

When a recipe required flour, he went to his supply of 3,000 pounds of wheat—the only tenet of Mormonism he still practiced was food storage—and ground it himself. He explained to his sons that the nutritional value was greater than commercially processed flour because the fiber and oil were left in.

Every visit included an elaborate exercise, proof of his prowess as a teacher, a father.

He demonstrated magnetic force, using a science toy with flashing lights and bells and whistles.

He explained gravity.

He taught the boys the principle of vacuum pressure.

He lectured on the properties of water.

When he forgot the hammers for miniature tool kits he'd organized for each boy, he was distraught. They made do using a wrench to pound the nails with. When the boys lost interest, Josh would say their names loudly and they'd snap back to work—for a few minutes.

Griffin-Hall was impressed with how Josh planned the visitations, which may have been the point. She felt that he was trying to impress her and the court through his interactions with her. That didn't mean that being with his children was some charade. She thought the young father was sincerely interested in his boys.

And yet, she couldn't escape her thoughts on what had happened to Josh's wife.

She was skeptical, but on the "one in a million chance" that he had not killed Susan, Griffin-Hall did the best she could to keep his visits centered in the present and on activities with the boys.

As the weeks passed, she was halfway expecting Josh to be arrested and Chuck and Judy to be given custody. That was, she thought, the best chance those little boys would have of a normal life.

In addition to watching Josh prepare homemade banana cream pie and science experiments, she witnessed a visit when Josh led the boys out to the garage to show them the new camping equipment he had bought.

In many ways, even in the controlled confines of a supervised visit or a psychological exam, Josh was the kind of parent he had always been. The rare occasions he made time for his sons when they were living in Utah often involved a lesson. Without a purpose or a lesson, Josh was awkward. It was as if he needed a script in order to connect with his sons.

While the boys lived with his enemies, the Coxes, Josh wrote Charlie and Braden letters every day. That took some effort, too. Letters had to be sent first to his social worker, Forest Jacobson, who in turn sent them on to the boys. But when Josh asked his sons about the letters, neither Charlie nor Braden seemed to remember getting them. Jacobson tried to explain to Josh that the boys might have read the letters but not paid as much attention to them as he wished. Josh wanted them to write him every day, too, and gave them paper, envelopes, and stamps.

Josh's rental house was a gray-blue, three-bedroom rambler on 189th Street Court East in Puyallup, just a couple of miles from Steve's house. Alina and Johnny stayed put at

Steve's. The rental was close to Emma Carson Elementary School, where Charlie was enrolled in first grade. Though there were neighbors all around, a stand of Lombardy poplars and several tall Douglas firs gave the house privacy. The place was sparsely furnished, but visitors said it was tidy. Josh had set up shelves in one of the bedrooms and unpacked toys for his sons—a playroom in unfamiliar surroundings, like most of the places they'd been since their mother's disappearance.

Between late September 2011, when Charlie and Braden went to live with Susan's parents, and November, when Josh rented the house, his once-a-week visitations were held at the offices of the Foster Care Resource Network (FCRN), one of hundreds of businesses that contract with the State of Washington to provide social services. Griffin-Hall supervised, both there and later when the visitations were moved to the rental house.

Josh brought toys and projects, and lunch, including sushi—which the boys devoured—and pizza and sandwiches. On the very first visit Josh brought his pet bird. While Griffin-Hall tried to explain that the bird wasn't allowed in the offices, the boys had a tantrum. She relented but wrote in her report, "The bird will not attend future visits." She also wrote that at one point Charlie asked Josh "if he was going to get lost, too."

Like their mother.

On that visit—timed so that no other families would be at FCRN at the time—Josh brought a portable campfire and set it up in an outside play area so they could roast marshmallows and hot dogs. As Josh unpacked the van, Griffin-Hall saw a hatchet in the back of the vehicle.

Griffin-Hall, herself the mother of four boys—now grown—and foster and adoptive mother to ten other children over the years, loved Charlie and Braden and they treated her like a grandmother. She had a hearty laugh and the three of them shared stories and told knock-knock jokes in the car as she drove them from the Coxes to Josh's rental house and back. Charlie and Braden loved Griffin-Hall's Prius, and liked to watch the gas and electrical gauges.

"This car's good for the environment," Charlie said.

On the Sunday after Thanksgiving, the boys and Griffin-Hall arrived at the rental house to find that Josh had cooked an entire turkey dinner, with two kinds of pie for dessert. Josh joked that he had been watching Paula Deen and Rachael Ray shows on television.

One of Griffin-Hall's responsibilities was to supervise Josh and make sure he didn't talk about certain topics around his sons—especially the Coxes, religion, and the custody case. But Josh couldn't contain himself. He was so curious about the boys' Thanksgiving that he couldn't put into practice a skill Griffin-Hall had been trying to teach him: to stop and take a few deep breaths and reconsider what he was about to say.

"Did you have any special meals on Thanksgiving?" Josh asked his boys.

Griffin-Hall knew he wasn't asking if Judy had served turkey or ham, white potatoes or yams. Josh was asking *who* had been at the Coxes for the holiday and what they had talked about.

"No," one of the boys said, clueless as to what their dad was fishing for.

"Did you see any special people?" Josh asked.

Griffin-Hall shot him a look. "Josh, that's enough," she said.

Josh ignored her. "Did you pray?" he asked.

Griffin-Hall was on the edge of exasperation, but held it in.

"Josh, let's turn this around and talk about what activity you have planned for today," she said.

Finally, Charlie spoke up. "There was a lot of family there, and Thanksgiving is for family."

Josh couldn't help himself. The door was open for a dig at the Coxes and he pushed it wider.

"You were with the wrong family," Josh said.

Griffin-Hall cut him off. "Josh, you can't tell them they were with the wrong family. Can we get started on their activity?"

What he was desperate to tell his sons was that the day would come when they would never see "the Coxes"—which is what Josh wanted the four- and six-year-old to call their grandparents—ever again.

Josh specifically chose Sunday as his visitation day so Chuck and Judy couldn't take the boys to church. Josh had spoken with Pastor Tim Atkins and his wife Brenda about being an alternative to the Coxes; maybe the boys could live with them. DSHS, however, said it wasn't about to move the boys again but okayed a second weekly visit. So for eleven or twelve weeks, after being fingerprinted and cleared by DSHS, Tim picked up the boys on Wednesday afternoons from school or from the Coxes. They would attend his children's Christian group, the Good News Club, and meet up with their dad at the Atkinses'. On Sundays Griffin-Hall brought the boys to Josh's rental house.

Tim and Brenda had given Josh a Bible, and he often attended the Sunday evening service at Tim's church, Faith Bible Church. They saw Josh laugh, they saw him cry, and they saw him worried and despondent.

The Atkinses asked Josh a lot of questions about the night Susan disappeared and the aspects of his story that didn't add up. They advised him not to attack Chuck and Judy, to work toward reconciliation, and to talk with the police.

They might have been the *only* people in his life who urged him to talk to the authorities. His father hadn't, nor had his brothers, Johnny and Mike, or his sister Alina. They supported his stalemate with the police and often led the attack against both the police and the Coxes through their Web sites, the release of Susan's diaries, and media interviews.

One Wednesday afternoon, Josh and Tim sat at the Atkinses' dining room table as their combined six children played and came and went.

"Josh, what are Chuck and Judy always saying?" Tim asked. "What is everybody saying?"

Josh didn't answer, and just looked at the glass of soda in his hand.

Tim wanted an answer so he prodded Josh. "What are the people at the Bible church saying? What are our neighbors saying? They're saying why don't you just sit down and talk with the police?"

Josh thought for a moment. "I understand that," he said. "But I'm not going to do that because of what happened when I did talk to them."

Tim wanted to hear it once more. "Tell me again. What happened when you talked to the police?"

Josh looked at the pastor. "They tried to twist my words."

"I understand that, Josh. I'm just saying that if you are sincere about reconciling with the Cox family, you have to demonstrate that you want to be reconciled. And one of the ways you demonstrate that is by sitting down and talking with the police."

Tim never learned anything by chance about the night Susan vanished. Josh never slipped up or said anything incriminating. Tim had an understanding with CPS that, as a pastor, if he believed a crime had been committed, he would be obligated to report it. There was a lot Josh kept to himself, but over the two years he knew Josh, Tim never felt that the boys were in any danger.

The most uncomfortable moment occurred during the last visitation at the Atkinses' home. Their three-year-old daughter, Elizabeth, was absent, visiting with her grandparents. They were sitting around a table having a snack. Tim thought he would lighten things up a bit. He looked around at the group gathered at the dining table.

"Charlie and Braden, who is missing?" Tim asked.

Braden spoke right up. "Mommy is missing."

Tim looked at Josh, and Josh looked at Tim. The air was sucked out of the room.

Chuck Cox was curious and a little concerned. He and Judy wondered just where it was that Josh was living, and where Charlie and Braden were spending their time with their father for those three or four hours once a week. Often, before a visit, Charlie and Braden said they didn't want to go see their dad.

Where did they go on Sundays? What was the place like? Were they safe there?

One time when Griffin-Hall arrived to pick up the boys, Chuck the investigator became Chuck the surveillance guy. He tailed her. He stayed a couple of blocks behind and when he sensed that she was about to turn into a cul-de-sac, he cut down a side street. It turned out that it ran behind Josh's rental. Chuck sat and waited. At one point Josh and the boys came out to the backyard for several minutes, without Griffin-Hall.

Josh was never supposed to be alone with his sons, not even for a minute. Josh walked the boys around the yard, where it appeared that he was building an outdoor fire pit.

After the boys came home later that day, Chuck asked them if they had been alone with their dad, and they said yes. In fact, the boys had spied Chuck's truck. He called DSHS and complained. He knew that whatever was said in Griffin-Hall's presence made it into her notes. But if she was out of earshot—and she had been when the boys were in the backyard—then she wouldn't be able to report what garbage, what lies, he might be telling them.

A little while later, a supervisor from DSHS told Chuck that they had talked with Griffin-Hall and that she was always with Josh and the boys, unless she was in the bathroom.

"Don't worry about it," the supervisor said. "The boys are being adequately supervised."

Chuck highly doubted it and said so.

In some ways, Josh had more custodial rights than the Coxes did. He prevented them from taking Charlie and Braden to their ward, and because of the Boy Scouts' long history with the Mormon church, he was able to prevent the boys from participating—just as Steve had stopped his own sons from being Scouts. Josh was also able to mandate that the Coxes couldn't take their grandsons to the YMCA, Lowe's, Home

Depot, or to any event having to do with astronomy or rocks and gems "as these are all things he did/does with his boys."

There were two traditions that the Coxes weren't going to give up, and there was nothing Josh could do about it. They continued to pray at mealtime, and they still held family home evening, a Mormon tradition of families spending Monday evening together playing board games, making crafts, or cooking.

"They found Mommy in the desert," Braden blurted out during one Sunday visit.

Charlie, Braden, and Josh were eating pancakes when Braden matter-of-factly delivered the news.

A lab had finished examining the charred wood found near Topaz Mountain in September, the debris that dogs had alerted on. The West Valley City police wouldn't give any details on what had or hadn't been found. Although the Coxes were careful not to talk about the investigation into their daughter's disappearance in front of the children, Braden must have overheard something.

"What did you say?" Josh asked.

"They found Mommy in the desert," Braden repeated.

"Who said that?" Josh asked.

Griffin-Hall tried to divert Josh from the talk of Susan's disappearance. "Josh, we can't talk about this during the visit," she said.

Braden didn't answer.

But Josh persisted. "Who said that?" he asked again, now agitated.

Both boys were quiet.

Griffin-Hall wrote in her notes that Josh seemed worried and anxious the rest of the afternoon. "He never recovered his equilibrium," she said later.

In late November, Josh's attorney, Jeffrey Bassett, received an e-mail from John Long, the assistant attorney general for Washington State who represented DSHS in the custody case:

We may need to slow up a bit on this case.

Utah police planned to release five or six images of computer-generated child porn found on Josh's computer in 2009. Long suggested that Dr. Manley, the psychologist who had been assigned to evaluate Josh as part of his custody battle, review the images before they proceeded with the custody case. A hearing had already been postponed from mid-November to January, but Long wanted to make sure there would be time for the state, and Josh's attorney, to deal with the child porn.

A few days later, on December 3, 2011, Josh sent a handwritten letter to his brother Mike in Minnesota. The missive was nothing if not specific. It notified Mike about a beneficiary change on his life insurance. If something should happen to him, Mike would receive 93 percent, Alina 4 percent, and Johnny 3 percent of a payout worth 2.5 million. There was no accommodation for his father, though Josh surely would have thought that his father's future as a wage earner was particularly bleak since his imprisonment on the pornography and voyeurism charges. It was doubtful that employers would hire Steve for any but the most menial jobs. *Ever.* Although Terri had emerged during the custody fight as a supporter of Josh's parenting skills, she was also left out in the cold.

According to the letter, the change had been made to ensure that Charlie and Braden would be taken care of if something happened to Josh. It was clear that Josh trusted only Mike. He told his brother that he was afraid Alina and Steve would "squander" any large amount of money he left them.

No one knows for sure what Mike's response was to the letter. He had to know that Josh was unstable. He knew about Josh's teenage suicide attempt.

Despite the scrawled letter from Josh, Mike Powell didn't do anything. Not one thing. He didn't call Josh to see how he was coping with the most recent court setbacks. He didn't reach out to ensure that his brother was doing all right, or that his nephews were safe.

In retrospect, Mike admitted later it seemed that Josh was contemplating suicide again.

When the boys visited Josh the next day—Sunday, December 4—Josh had numerous boxes of ornaments and a Christmas tree ready to decorate. When Charlie looked through the boxes, he found a stocking with Susan's name on it. Josh told him to put it back in the box, but Charlie set it on the floor by the tree where it remained for the rest of the visit, never far from him and Braden.

The police had been tapping the phones of all the Powells for months, long before Steve was arrested. Now that Mike and his abandoned car had the attention of the WVCPD they stepped up their investigation of Josh's younger brother, the one who they thought kept his distance from the family craziness. He defended his father and brother, but he seemed to live his own life. During the first weeks Susan was missing, Chuck Cox wrote the WVCPD worrying that Steve Powell was holding her prisoner. As for other family members, Josh might help his dad but, Chuck added, Mike would never go along with it.

The police got search warrants to increase surveillance of the family and to monitor Josh's and Mike's computers. They knew the two didn't trust phones, but probably discussed the investigation over the Internet. But Josh and Mike were using sophisticated computer encryption to communicate. No one—not the police, the FBI, or even the software manufacturer—could decipher it.

42

The reviewed images indicate someone's fantasy-laden view of having sex with children.
—DR. JAMES MANLEY, JANUARY 31, 2012

James Manley sat in a room at the Pierce County sheriff's office in downtown Tacoma. The psychologist, a sexual deviancy expert, and Detective Gary Sanders looked down at a few dozen of the 400 images that Utah police had found on Josh's computer in December 2009. The pornographic images played out like a kind of twisted, disgusting, version of Cartoon Network. Well-known cartoon characters from the Simpsons to the Flintstones to Superman to Dennis the Menace were depicted in a wide array of sexual activities including incest, group sex, fellatio, cunnilingus, and sodomy.

It was a subset of child pornography, the likes of which are rarely seen by law enforcement, much less by the parents who let their kids watch cartoons.

Captain America, Catwoman, Teenage Mutant Ninja Turtles, Rugrats, characters from *Family Guy*, and *Jungle Book* and SpongeBob SquarePants—every one of them doing the nastiest things imaginable. Some were hand drawn, others were computerized, anime, or photographs. Some had identifying logos indicating where the cartoons and 3-D images had originated. Web sites trumpeted exactly what they were.

Toon porn.

The majority featured depictions of incest or child molestation. There were also photographs of female frontal nudity. One had the head of Harry Potter actress Emma Watson Photoshopped onto a nude figure. Some drawings showed bondage. Some showed beasts having sex with a woman. Others depicted sex involving mother on son, mother on daughter, or father on daughter. In one, there were two adults on a bed praising a girl who was fellating a boy. In another, a girl was fellating a penis with a caption that read "Come on Daddy, come on, let me finish what I started, you're gonna like it."

While these were not photographs of real children and couldn't be legally defined as child pornography, Dr. Manley wrote that they communicated an approval of sex between an adult and a minor.

"The fact that such a collection of images from different sites were collected suggests a high degree of interest," he wrote. The collection of images revealed a pattern of "poor sexual boundaries between the [Powell] family members. If these are Mr. Powell's images, it gives rise to great concern."

A Utah judge had specified that eight people were permitted to see the images that had been found on Josh's computer; in addition to Dr. Manley and Detective Sanders, Assistant District Attorney John Long, and a CPS social worker viewed the toon porn.

Josh's attorney, Jeffrey Bassett, wasn't there because he wasn't told of the viewing until after the fact. Neither was Steve Downing—the Coxes' attorney in the custody case— who wasn't notified until February 9 that he could have seen the images. If he had, he said he might have asked to change the terms of Josh's supervised visitations with his sons, so that the visits would return to the FCRN offices or another public office.

Using what he had seen, as well as what he knew about Josh—from Josh's parents' divorce records and from Josh's psychological evaluation—Dr. Manley recommended that Josh undergo a psychosexual evaluation, the "peter meter" test. He also advised giving Josh a polygraph.

No one expected those requirements to be met with much enthusiasm.

Aside from his letter to his brother Mike notifying him of the change of life insurance beneficiary, there were no signs that Josh was contemplating making a life-or-death decision.

On the supervised visit of Sunday, January 29, Charlie and Braden jumped out of the car and ran to greet their dad, beating Griffin-Hall to the front door as they liked to do. It was to be a four-hour visit, extra-long to make up for the visitation that had been cancelled because of snow the week before. Griffin-Hall noted that the house was tidy as ever, with a classical music station playing in the background.

Both boys said "I love you" to their father.

Braden was limping slightly from the hot-water burn on his foot that he'd gotten at the Coxes' home.

With Josh doing his best to teach and engage them, Charlie and Braden ate some of the candy used to decorate a gingerbread house they had assembled on a previous visit. Then they played with remote-controlled cars for a while, and Josh gave them guidance on how to better work the controls. They also drew flowers and animals with crayons and watched a Leap Frog learning video about outer space. For snacks, Josh gave them hot dogs and breakfast sandwiches.

Then it was over.

"I love you," Josh said. "I'll see you as soon as I can. Be happy and have a good time."

That night, Josh called Tim Atkins. Josh admitted to Tim that some questionable images that might be considered child pornography had been found on his computer. But Josh was feeling optimistic. He didn't think Chuck and Judy would ever give up their custody fight, but he felt the state was leaning to restoring custody to him. He was thinking of extending an olive branch to the Coxes.

"Tim, can you just tell Chuck and Judy that I want things to be different?"

Tim felt some progress was in the offing. *Finally.*

"You need to go into that courtroom and you need to show them you want to be different, in the way you respond," Tim said.

As Tim saw it, Josh had it in his mind that if he didn't put up a really strong fight that somehow he would communicate to the world that he didn't want his boys back.

Fighting proved he was a good father.

Tim told him he was wrong. "No, Josh, you're showing them that you want to fight. Do what they want you to do and be the dad."

Two days later, on January 31, Josh had his last scheduled visit with his sons at the Atkinses' home in Steve's Country Hollow neighborhood. Josh was certain he was going to get his sons back that week. He and Tim talked about the long-awaited hearing the next day.

Charlie and Braden played with Tim's four children and they all had a snack. Josh sat on the couch and read a book to the boys, and helped Charlie read a book about different kinds of insects. They all sat on the floor and played with blocks, and Josh asked Tim to take some photos before they knocked down the blocks.

They ate a Tater Tot casserole. Then Tim broke some news to Josh: He and Brenda had decided they needed to stop helping Josh with his supervised visits. Not only had some of Tim's parishioners complained, but for months DSHS had implied that there was something the Atkinses didn't know. As Tim later recounted, "They would say, 'Well, Mr. Atkins, there are things we can't talk about in this case.' And I always told Josh, 'Josh, they know something they're not telling you and they're not telling me.'"

In an e-mail to Josh's social worker, Forest Jacobson, Tim

wrote that it was clear the police were "actively building a criminal case against Josh."

Josh would still have two visitations a week with his sons. Both would take place at the rental house in Graham and not at the Atkinses'. Tim insists that Josh wasn't upset that the only people to befriend him since Susan's disappearance—the minister, his wife, and their four children—had decided to limit their contact with him.

43

Having demonstrated my fitness as a parent, it is time
for my sons to come home.
—JOSH POWELL, IN AN AFFIDAVIT,
FEBRUARY 1, 2012

On February 1, 2012, the child custody hearing originally
scheduled for November, and then for January—postponed
because of a rare Pacific Northwest snowstorm—commenced
in the Tacoma courtroom of Superior Court Judge Kathryn
Nelson.

Chuck and Judy Cox were sitting near the back. Their attorney in the custody case, Steve Downing, was in an obser-
vational role only. This hearing was between the State of
Washington and Josh Powell.

Josh, who was all smiles, walked Griffin-Hall and her
supervisor, Lyn Okarski, from an elevator to the courtroom,
then went to meet with his attorney. He had told the two
women that he "expected to take the kids home that day."
Josh was confident. Josh's attorney was confident.

Suddenly there was a wail and raised voices from outside
the courtroom.

Judy turned to see where it was coming from; so did Griffin-Hall and Okarski. It seemed to be in an alcove adjoining the courtroom.

It was Josh, being warned by his attorney that he was not going to get custody of the boys. He already knew that Dr. Manley was suggesting further psychological testing. He hadn't known, however, that the testing would delay the custody proceedings for months, possibly forever.

Despite the news, Josh argued that he should regain custody of his children. In an affidavit filed that day, Josh wrote that he missed his wife, and would remain strong for the boys.

> *A lesser person would fall under the intense scrutiny I am facing, but apparently my inherent resilience as a person makes it increasingly difficult for them to pursue their agendas. I am standing tall for my sons, but it deeply hurts to face such ridicule and abuse. I know my own heart is free of any guilt regardless of what people claim.*

The incestuous images were mentioned briefly in court but not discussed in depth. John Long argued that a psychosexual evaluation was necessary because of those images, as well as the pornography found at Steve Powell's house when Josh was living there with his sons.

Judge Nelson agreed. Despite a plea from Josh's attorney that such a test was "intrusive" and that Josh hadn't been charged with any crime, the judge would not consider giving Josh custody unless he underwent the exam. She did not change his visitation schedule, which included the supervised Sunday and Wednesday visits. Charlie and Braden, who had recently had birthdays and were now seven and five years old, respectively, would remain with the Coxes for the foreseeable future.

Chuck and Judy Cox sat behind Josh and could see that he was angry.

"I wanted to ask why are they still letting him have

visitation if they have all these concerns?" Chuck said. "It crossed my mind, 'Hey, this is really tightening the screws on Josh.'"

The Coxes were worried about how he would react to the increasing stress.

The hearing was the tipping point for Josh. If he refused to participate in the psychosexual evaluation, he would lose custody of the boys. If he participated in the test, he would still lose custody of the boys, because it was more than likely that he would not pass it. And for the first time, he would have been asked during a polygraph exam about what had happened to Susan.

Josh would have been subjected to a penile plethysmograph, or PPG, an exam that measures the blood flow to the penis. The PPG is administered with a strain gauge, which is a kind of cuff worn at the base of the penis that tests a man's arousal while he is shown photographs and videos of normal sexual behavior as well as deviant acts. The PPG exam takes about two hours; there is also a two-hour evaluation that covers the individual's sexual history and the sexual behavior of his family when he was a child and adolescent. Penile plethysmographs are commonly used in criminal proceedings when judges need to assess how likely a defendant is to reoffend, but they can also be ordered in civil matters. As it had been for Josh.

Josh spoke briefly with Tim Atkins. They made plans for Sunday, February 5. Josh would see his sons, go to church in the evening, then go over to the Atkinses' house. "That would be great," Tim said.

On the night of the pivotal hearing, the Coxes put Charlie and Braden to bed. Susan's portrait—the same image the public would hold in their minds of the missing mom—was propped up next to the fireplace. Susan wasn't there, but the boys still remembered her.

That night was a calm one. There was no fighting or acting out.

Even so, Judy had been uneasy. She had been worried since the court hearing—more worried than usual.

Chuck felt his wife's anxiety. They had been together long enough to know what each other was thinking, even when no words were shared.

Judy was afraid that the court ruling had backed Josh into a corner.

"You're right. The court put him in a spot," he said.

"I know," she said. "I wonder what he's going to do next."

Chuck didn't know. In fact, Chuck Cox could never have dredged up a scenario as dark as what was to come.

Not in a million years.

44

I remember Chuck made a comment to me . . . "Wow,
this is the first visitation after that court date." We felt
he was going to do something, but we had no idea.
—JUDY COX, SEPTEMBER 5, 2012

Those who knew the family always considered Mike Powell
the one that "got away." While it was true that Jennifer, too,
had escaped the toxic household, she'd been able to leave
because she was of age when the family imploded. But Mike
was a kid. He had to bide his time. The young man, who
looked like a younger version of his father—or a healthier
version of Josh—found a roadmap out of Puyallup by serv-
ing in the army for five years and then going to college, where
he majored in International Studies at the University of Washington. Mike was different from his brother. His ambitions
were met with follow-through, though not always to the degree he'd hoped. In 2008 he ran unsuccessfully for state office, but the setback didn't stop him. He still managed to be
one of nine delegates to represent Washington State at the
National Democratic Convention in Denver.

And yet, like Josh and Alina, Mike always sided with his

father, no matter what. His mother had been an outsider since he had moved into his father's house at the age of ten. When Steve disowned Jennifer, Mike did, too.

As tenuous as relationships can be when bound by fear and paranoia, Mike and Josh appeared steadfast. In Puyallup, before Josh married Susan, the brothers even shared a bedroom. They were as close as anyone in the Powell family. When Josh needed help, it made sense that his first calls would be to his father and to Mike. Steve, though absent from work, didn't go to help out in Utah. Mike and Alina did. Mike helped Josh in ways no one knew.

Josh knew whom he could count on. He knew who had his back. He'd changed his beneficiary to Mike in early December. Now, one day after the hearing ordering the psychosexual evaluation, Josh wrote Mike again. In a letter dated February 2, 2012, Josh named Mike the rights holder for any and all the intellectual property pertaining to his life. He specifically called it "life rights" as though he was certain there would be money to be had from a movie or TV film about his story.

And then Josh was gone. It was only later that those closest to him would realize that they hadn't heard from him for a few days. Josh had called Mike on Friday, but his brother didn't have time to talk. Alina didn't see Josh on Saturday, which was unusual.

There were people who did see him, but they were strangers.

Josh Powell was just another single father doing errands on Saturday, February 4, 2012, the day before Super Bowl Sunday. Only Josh wasn't shopping for beer or soda or Doritos. Instead, he had a checklist of errands that would culminate in a surprise he had planned for Charlie and Braden the following day.

At 11:19 A.M., he went to the Bank of America at 175th Street and Meridian and withdrew $7,000 in hundred-dollar bills, leaving $4,500 in his account. The bank's security camera captured a haggard-looking Josh, but he had looked like that for a long time. The teller didn't ask him why he was withdrawing that much money, but he called a bank manager over to approve the transaction.

Josh also visited his storage unit, #141 at Western Self Storage in Sumner, a few miles from Puyallup. He packed some toys and books into plastic bins, but left other items, including a comforter with a blood-like stain.

Next, he returned to Puyallup and the South Hill Fred Meyer parking lot—the location of the honk and wave that had made national news when his father and Chuck Cox got into it over Susan's disappearance. He dropped off the toys and books at a Salvation Army donation center. One of the books had his name in it and said "Testament" on the cover. Other books were gifts to Susan from friends.

The local recycling center was the next stop. Josh arrived there in the afternoon and left a hymnal, a book on calculus, and a map of Utah. A book titled *Footprints* was inscribed and dated May 31, 2000.

> *To Susan from Brittainy Elizabeth—Sister, friend, P.A.W. [sic] for eternity. Love you, God bless you.*

Another book, *Inside the Strength of the Lord,* a wedding gift, was signed.

> *To Susan and Joshua—with our love and prayers for all that's meaningful and beautiful in your eternal walk together.*

Once rid of all that he was going to discard, Josh made a purchase. He filled two five-gallon cans with gasoline.

Finally, his to-do list was done.

He'd taken care of his money, gotten rid of the past, and made sure he had ample gas, as well as his hatchet, two knives, and matches.

Chuck and Judy discussed whether they should try to stop Josh's visit, scheduled for the next day. They were afraid that if Josh felt cornered by the conditions presented to him at the February 1 court hearing, he might kill Charlie and Braden. Chuck had warned the police for as long as Susan had been missing—more than two years by this time—that Josh might murder the boys. Josh would do anything to keep the Coxes from "winning" the custody fight.

Chuck called Forest Jacobson, Josh's social worker—a woman with an ambiguous name—to tell her their fears, but Jacobson wasn't worried. Chuck remembered she said "Well, he's been really good lately." Chuck didn't say as much, but what went through his mind was that Josh was really good just before Susan went missing, too. When he's "good" it means he's up to something.

One time Judy asked Elizabeth Griffin-Hall, who was a petite woman, what she would do if Josh "lost it," or grabbed one of the children.

"I can't touch them. I can't run after them, I can't grab the kids," she said. "All I'm supposed to do is call 911 on the phone."

Judy didn't like the answer and said so. "That's terrible."

But those were the rules and there was no getting around the rules—even when common sense dictated otherwise.

Jacobson had recently finished writing an update on Josh's supervised visits. She wrote that observations showed that Josh had a "firm grasp on parenting skills," and there were no safety concerns. A goal of the visitations remained family "reunification."

On Saturday evening, Susan's sister Denise arrived at the house. She said she had a sudden urge to see the boys. She tucked them into bed and told them good night. One of the boys hugged her and said, "I love you."

The moment would mean the world to her in the days to come.

When Chuck got home that night, he went in to check on his grandsons. He had to get up early Sunday morning because of responsibilities at the ward, so he wouldn't see Charlie and

Braden until late the next afternoon, when they came home from Josh's.

It was just their second night in their brand-new bedroom. The construction was done, the bunk beds were moved in, and next week the Coxes would do more decorating. Braden's bed was covered with a quilt from the movie *Cars* and Charlie's bed had a Spider-Man quilt.

No villains, just heroes.

He watched them sleep. Braden, who looked so much like Susan, and Charlie, named for his grandfather and great-grandfather, were off somewhere in dreamland.

He stood there, feeling something. A need to capture the moment.

He put his hand on their beds and softly said good night.

With all they'd been through, Susan's father recognized the importance of taking the time while they were there; while he could see them; while they were little kids; while they were happy; while they were sleeping . . . just to say good night.

45

People are saying there is not somebody here, but there's a couple of boys, 5 and 7, he has supervised visitation . . .

—ELIZABETH GRIFFIN-HALL, 911 CALL,
FEBRUARY 5, 2012

Sunday morning at the Coxes' had its moments. Charlie and Braden had breakfast with Judy and their aunt Marie and her two-year-old son, Patrick, who were staying there while Marie's husband was at basic training. The boys had teased their cousin to the point of tears and earned a time-out. But as the time approached when Griffin-Hall would pick them up, the three cousins were playing happily.

As Judy helped them get ready for the visit, Braden spoke up.

"I don't want to go see Daddy," he said. Both boys had said that before, but this time Braden was firmer in his resolve to stay put.

"We want to stay here with Patrick," he said.

Judy got their jackets. "But you'll see Patrick when you get home," she said. "Daddy has planned something nice for you."

"I don't want to see Daddy," Braden repeated.

Judy knew that they loved their dad, and she couldn't figure out why the boys were so insistent that Sunday.

Charlie was wearing his favorite corduroy pants and a sweater. Braden had on his very favorite hoodie, which was orange, with a navy blue puffer vest.

At 11:30 A.M. Elizabeth Griffin-Hall arrived. Reluctantly, the boys put on their jackets and shoes and Judy helped them into the car. The two women spoke for a moment about Braden's burned foot.

"The doctor said there are no restrictions," Judy said. "He can play outside if he wants to."

Then Judy told them good-bye.

"See you when you get back," she said. "Patrick will be waiting for you, too."

Charlie was unusually quiet in the car but began to open up during the drive.

Elizabeth Griffin-Hall drove by a house in the neighborhood that she and Charlie often laughed about. The yard was covered with flamingos, gnomes, and strange fountains. The boys were used to the manicured lawn at the Coxes, and its park-like setting. Even Josh's yard was always maintained and mowed.

Griffin-Hall made sure to point out the house as they approached it.

"Look, Charlie, there's the yard with all the statues," she said.

Charlie giggled.

"Charlie, what if it was decorated for Halloween? Would you like it then?"

"Wait. Slow down, Elizabeth," Charlie told her, and she did. She pulled over to the side of the road.

Charlie was silent, studying the yard from his car seat. Then he gave his definitive opinion.

"It would take two million, two hundred thirty-seven lights to make it good, and then it might be funny," he finally said.

Griffin-Hall laughed about the seven-year old's candid appraisal.

Just before his boys arrived for the visit, Josh sent a series of e-mails. Messages went to his boss at the software company that employed him; his attorney, Jeffrey Bassett; his cousin in Texas, Nathan Leach; and finally, to Pastor Tim Atkins.

The e-mails were short, and each carried the same message:

I'm sorry. Goodbye.

When his cousin received his, he feared the worst and called 911 in Washington, but when he said he didn't know where Josh lived, Leach was told to contact the phone company to try to get an address.

Griffin-Hall pulled up at Josh's house at 11:57 A.M. The boys jumped out of the car and ran ahead to their father, who was standing in the front doorway. He looked sheepishly at her and shrugged his shoulders. And then he shut the door. She heard him lock it. She thought it was a mistake. She heard Josh say, "Charlie, I have a big surprise for you!" She banged on the door, rang the doorbell repeatedly, and begged Josh to let her in. She walked to the garage door to see if she could open it but it was locked. Griffin-Hall realized she didn't have her cell phone, and went back to her car to get it. Then she heard Braden scream. She called her supervisor, then quickly dialed 911. It was 12:08 P.M.

The operator who took the call was David Lovrak, an eighteen-year veteran with 911.

GH: I'm on a supervised visitation for a court-ordered visit and something really weird has happened. The kids went in the house and the biological parent, Josh Powell, will not let me in the door. What should I do?
D: What's the address?
GH: 8119 and I think it's 89th, I don't know what the address is, let me get in the car. Nothing has happened

like this before. I'm really shocked, and I could hear one of the kids crying, and he still won't let me in, OK, it's 1, just a minute I have it here, you can't find me by GPS?

D: No.

GH: OK, it is . . . I still can't find it. He's on a very short leash with DSHS. He looked right at me and closed the door. It's 8119 189th Street Court East, Puyallup. I'd like to pull out of the driveway because I smell gasoline, and he won't let me in.

D: He won't let you out of the driveway?

GH: He won't let me in the house.

D: Whose house is it?

GH: Josh Powell.

D: You don't live there?

GH: No, I'm contracted by the state to provide supervised visitation.

[Confusion about who Griffin-Hall is ensues, then gets cleared up]

GH: He's the husband of Susan Powell, this is a high-profile case. I was one step in back of them.

D: So they went in the house and locked you out?

GH: Yes, he shut the door in my face.

D: What is your name?

GH: My name is Elizabeth Griffin-Hall.

D: And what's your phone number?

[Griffin-Hall gives number.]

D: What agency are you with?

GH: Foster Care Resource Network, and the kids have been in there by now approximately 10 minutes, and he knows it's a supervised visit. Braden is 5 and Charlie is 7.

D: And the dad's last name?

GH: Powell.

D: Two L's at the end of Powell?

GH: Yes.

D: And his first name?

GH: His first name is Josh.

D: Is he alone, or was anyone with him?

GH: I don't know, I couldn't get in the house.

D: Are you in a vehicle now or on foot?

GH: I'm in a 2010 Prius with the doors locked. He won't let me in. I rang the doorbell and everything. I begged him to let me in.

D: Elizabeth, please listen to my questions. What color is the Toyota Prius?

GH: Gray, dark gray.

D: And the license number?

GH: I don't know, I can look. [Gets out of the car and tells him the license plate.]

D: OK, we'll have someone look for you there.

GH: Do you know how long it will be?

D: They have to respond to emergencies, life-threatening situations first.

GH: This could be life-threatening. He was in court on Wednesday and he didn't get his kids back and this is really . . . I'm afraid for their lives.

D: Has he threatened the lives of the children previously?

GH: I have no idea.

D: OK, we'll have the first available deputy contact you.

Elizabeth Griffin-Hall was beside herself. The call had eaten up seven precious minutes. She smelled gasoline, so she got back into her car to back it out of the driveway and away from the house. She heard some pops from the house, a loud whoosh, and then a boom. She felt her Prius rock on its wheels.

At 12:16 the house exploded and people in the neighborhood flooded 911 with calls. One caller described seeing the roof "fly off." Another described a "loud, huge boom," "crap flying all over the place" and "dark smoke." Another caller said he thought it was a meth house that had blown up. A neighbor approached the house to see if he could enter it, but the windows began exploding outward and others warned him that it was too hot to enter.

Griffin-Hall called 911 a second time. This time a different dispatcher asked her if anyone was in the house and she explained again that a man and two children were inside. She was put on hold while the dispatcher called the fire department. And then she had to explain again to the dispatcher how Josh had closed the door on her.

D: Do you know if there's anyone in the house?

GH: Yes, there was a man and two children. I just dropped off the children and he wouldn't let me in the door.

D: Stay on the line with me. I'm going to get the fire department. Hang on. Don't hang up. Stay on the phone here with me, ma'am. Fire, this is Rose. I'm transferring the lady who has the exact address.

GH: I can hear the fire trucks, but they're not here yet. It's 8119 . . .

D: We have an engine there.

GH: People are saying there is not somebody here, but there's a couple of boys, 5 and 7, he has supervised visitation and he blew up the house and the kids.

D: The kids and the father were in the house?

GH: Yes, he slammed the door in my face so I kept knocking. I thought it was a mistake, I kept knocking and then I called 911.

D: You saw him go back in the house?

GH: He didn't ever leave the house, he just opened the door, the kids were one step ahead of me, they are 5 and 7, they were one step ahead of me and he slammed the door in my face.

D: Do you think he might have done this intentionally?

GH: Yes.

By then, Griffin-Hall was reduced to tears.

Over in Country Hollow, Alina Powell had received four e-mails from her brother that morning. She considered them a little "weird" but didn't think much about them until they started to detail what she should do with the money Josh had withdrawn from the bank, which bills needed to be paid, and how to cancel the utilities.

Next, she got a disturbing voice mail from Josh.

"This is Josh. I'm calling to say good-bye. I am not able to live without my sons and I'm not able to go on anymore. I'm sorry to everyone I've hurt. Good-bye."

At 12:21 P.M., Alina, now hysterical, called 911. She told dispatchers that she didn't know Josh's new address.

"The only way I can do it is to drive over there, but I'm terrified to drive over there. I'm not afraid of him, he'd never hurt me, I'm afraid [of what I'll find]."

Graham Fire and Rescue arrived at 12:22 P.M. The house was burning so hot there was little that firefighters could do.

The first sheriff's deputies arrived at the house eight minutes later. They interviewed Griffin-Hall, and she explained that this was no accident; Josh had obviously planned in advance to kill his children that day. It was personal to Griffin-Hall. She wasn't just doing a job over the several months she had supervised the visits.

"Those were my babies!" she said.

A chaplain was sent to the scene. It was about 1:30 P.M. before firefighters entered the house and found the bodies.

Three different detectives questioned Griffin-Hall, moving her from police car to police car for the interviews. Once the media began arriving, the detectives tried to keep her out of view. They tried to protect her from seeing the bodies, too, but she watched as first Charlie, and then Braden, were carried out in white sheets in the arms of the same detective they had run to the night Steve Powell was arrested. She did not see Josh's body removed from the house.

Chuck's phone rang while he was in a meeting at church. Someone had seen a posting on Facebook. Josh had blown up his house.

Chuck's and Judy's paths crossed without their knowing it. A friend drove him home to get Judy, but she had just left for church with her daughter Marie and grandson Patrick. The friend drove Chuck to Josh's house and Chuck stood where he had before, the time he had tailed Griffin-Hall so he would know where Josh was living.

The house had burned fast. The roof was gone, the walls were gone, and by the time Chuck arrived it was mostly black smoke.

"I walked up to the sheriff's deputy guarding the perimeter and I said, 'I'm Chuck Cox, I'm foster parent and grandparent to these children. I need to know what happened. I heard stuff on the news.'"

Chuck thought that that the deputy would answer, "Don't worry, the kids are safe."

He didn't.

"Just a minute," he said.

The deputy walked over to a commander and conferred with him for a moment.

When he returned, Chuck didn't need to hear the words. He could see it etched on the man's face.

"They're gone," he said.

Chuck had seen a lot in his career as an FAA investigator. Crashes. Fires. Burned bodies. He didn't stay long. He looked around at the neighbors, the police, the fire crew gathering around the smoldering scene.

"What shall I do now?" he wondered.

The answer was to go home to be with Judy.

Chuck didn't know that at the same time he stood at the back of what was left of the house, Alina was at the front.

46

I kept asking my friends, "How can a father do that to his kids?" And they said, "Judy—he wasn't a father. He's a psycho!"
—JUDY COX, SEPTEMBER 5, 2012

When Judy, Marie, and Patrick arrived at church they got a puzzled look from the bishop's counselor. He stopped and asked if Judy had talked to Chuck, and told her that Josh had burned his house down, apparently with the boys inside. She turned and started running down the hallway back to the car, brushing past people she usually stopped to visit with. She grabbed Marie and Patrick and they got back into the car. Marie wanted to know what had happened, but Judy refused to tell her because she was driving. Judy finally couldn't hold it back anymore and told her youngest daughter what had happened. It was a harrowing car ride but they made it home in one piece.

Chuck arrived home and the family sat and cried and prayed together.

Three hours passed before they heard from the police. Two officers came to the door and sat down to talk with them.

Until that moment, Chuck and Judy had held out hope that maybe the boys had been found unconscious, taken to the hospital, and revived. Instead, they got the official word that they were dead.

The police officers mentioned something about a hatchet. Chuck and Judy wanted to know more, but the officers didn't want to go into detail. They said Josh had hit the boys on the head to knock them unconscious before starting the fire.

The truth was so much worse than that.

Every Sunday, attorney Anne Bremner went to a walk-in Korean nail salon on Queen Anne Hill in Seattle. It was her respite from representing not just the Coxes, but Amanda Knox and other high-profile cases. The routine never varied and neither did the color on her toes and nails—"Privacy Please." On February 5 the polish was still drying when she got a call from a television station in Salt Lake City.

There had been an explosion, Josh's house had blown up, and did she know if the boys were at the house?

She immediately dialed Chuck. She wanted to warn him of the news—which for some reason she thought had been an accident, maybe a natural gas leak. Even though she'd dealt with the worst purveyors of evil as a lawyer, she couldn't imagine right then that it had been deliberate.

"Where are you?" she asked when Chuck answered his cell.

Chuck's words were wrought with pain. Only a few syllables were needed before Bremner knew that he already had heard.

"I'm at the house, Anne. They're all gone. They're all gone."

"Josh, too?"

"Yes."

Bremner's eyes flooded. She was full of anger, hurt.

"Thank God for that," she said.

"We told them so. We told them he'd do something," Chuck reminded her.

"We did," she said.

Bremner spent the day issuing statements for Chuck and Judy, and the next day she went to their house with a huge pan of lasagna.

News of what police called a double murder–suicide spread to Susan's world, and then to the larger world.

In West Valley City, just down the block from where Susan's best friend lived, Kiirsi Hellewell had arrived home from church. A Salt Lake City reporter called her and said there had been an explosion at Josh Powell's house in Washington. She thought he meant a verbal fight of some kind.

"Then he said, 'A fire, a fire. I'm really sorry to tell you if you haven't heard, but we're getting reports that two children are dead, that it happened during his visitation,'" Kiirsi remembered. "And I just started crying and said, 'I can't talk to you right now.'" She immediately called Chuck. He said he would call her right back.

Kiirsi called Jennifer Graves. Kiirsi never would have predicted that she would become close to Josh's older sister, but she had. When Jennifer sounded cheerful answering the phone, Kiirsi knew that she hadn't heard the news. Kiirsi told her and Jennifer started crying hysterically.

Kiirsi knew she had to call Debbie Caldwell, but dreaded it. Kiirsi thought, Oh, I can't call Debbie. She loves those boys like her own children and she had been more vocal than anybody about saying "You have got to get those boys out of there." Debbie had called CPS when Josh moved to Washington. She had begged them to do a well-child check, and they'd said they couldn't without evidence of danger or abuse.

Kiirsi texted Debbie and said she had to talk to her, that it was an emergency. Debbie called her right away. "And I told her. She just said, 'No, no, no, oh, God, no.'"

Debbie, JoVonna, and some other friends gathered at Kiirsi's to wait for more details from Chuck and to talk about Susan, Charlie, and Braden. Kiirsi cried out in grief when Chuck told her it was confirmed. An adult and two boys had died in the fire.

Chuck told Kiirsi that his one consolation was that the boys were with their mother again.

At church, Pastor Tim Atkins prayed that Josh's visit with Charlie and Braden would go well. After the service a group of friends gathered at the Atkinses' house for lunch.

At about one o'clock, someone from the church called and said he should turn on the news.

"My first inclination was that they had arrested him. So we turned on the news and we saw the fire. At first they were talking about two bodies, and then it changed to three. And we were devastated."

It was only later that people realized that Josh might very easily have killed the Coxes, too, or the Atkinses, or Griffin-Hall, as well as Charlie and Braden.

Tim and his wife, Brenda, walked over to Steve's house to see Alina. Her father was in jail. She was estranged from her big sister. Her nephews had been taken away from her. The families had been feuding for two years. And now her brother and his sons were dead.

Tim and Brenda sat at the dining table and talked with Alina and Johnny.

"We were just in shock and horrified, crying. Alina is telling us what happened and how she found out about the fire, and then there's a knock on the door," Tim said. It was two sheriff's deputies, one trained to help families dealing with trauma.

Alina had told the 911 dispatcher about Josh's voice mail, so the deputies wanted to take her cell phone. She played the voice mail message for them, and let them read the four e-mails Josh had sent, but she didn't want to hand over her phone. She cried and called it her "lifeline." The detective said he knew it was a difficult day, but they needed the phone for their investigation. Frustrated, Alina said, "Why do you need it? It's a suicide. You know who did it." The detective reminded her that it was a homicide-suicide. The detective left to get a search warrant and returned to get the phone. The deputies allowed her to retrieve the numbers of friends and family, all the while watching to make sure she didn't delete data from the phone.

It wasn't until that afternoon that Tim wondered if he had received an e-mail from Josh. He found it in his in-box:

I'm sorry. Good-bye.

Elizabeth Griffin-Hall was shattered. She felt that she had, almost literally, driven Charlie and Braden to their deaths.

Her husband Larry Benson, and her supervisor Lyn Okarski, arrived at the burned-out house to take her home. Her five foster children, ages six to twenty, were waiting at her house on the Kitsap Peninsula with questions about what had happened to Josh, Charlie, and Braden.

She went straight to her bedroom, stripped off all her clothes and asked her husband to throw them out. The purple sweater and black slacks were new, but she knew she could never wear them again. The smell of smoke clung to her and to the clothes. Then she took a scalding hot bath.

She never returned to work full-time. She never again accepted the kinds of difficult custody cases she had specialized in throughout her career.

Sheriff's deputies went to inform Steve Powell that his son and grandsons were dead. Steve was an inmate of the Pierce County jail awaiting trial on charges of voyeurism and pornography. If the deputies expected he would show shock or grief, he surprised them. A sheriff's department spokesman said Steve responded with vulgar language and called the deputies a few choice names, but didn't seem emotional or upset when told of the deaths. He was placed on suicide watch.

Within a day or two, he was named a "person of interest" for the first time in the disappearance of Susan Cox Powell. The Coxes said they had a message for Steve: "Anything he knows, he should talk to the police now or tell us about it now. He doesn't need to protect Josh. There is no point in him keeping back anything he knows."

But Steve had nothing to say.

Josh sent e-mails and left voice mail messages before he died—but he did not find a way to tell his father good-bye. He left nothing that mentioned Susan. There was no note, no confession, not a word about his wife, missing for more than two years.

At a vigil in Kearns, Utah, that Sunday night, fifty people gathered at an elementary school and lit candles for Charlie and Braden. Kiirsi and Susan's other close friends were present, but so were many who hadn't known Susan, including the mayor of West Valley City.

At Charlie's school in Puyallup, just up the street from the burned-out house, children, teachers, parents, and neighbors held a candlelight vigil for the boys. Children placed bouquets, candles, and handmade cards at a growing memorial. They told stories about the boys, cried, and hugged.

At the scene of the house fire, a metal fence kept people out and protected the crime scene, but purple ribbons appeared on the fence, on shrubs, and on trees. People also left stuffed animals and notes addressed to Charlie and Braden.

In Tacoma, dozens of people, including children the age of Charlie and Braden, lit candles in paper cups and pushed them out onto McKinley Pond, where they lit the dark sky until their flames died out one by one.

47

I noticed as I turned the body that there were chop marks on the back of the child's neck area. My impression was that the chop marks were consistent with finding the hatchet. Like the first child, this one was missing a large portion of the skull crown area with the brain exposed.
— PIERCE COUNTY SHERIFF'S DEPARTMENT FORENSICS REPORT, FEBRUARY 5, 2012

The first thing the arson investigators did when they arrived at 1:37 P.M. Sunday was to walk around the perimeter of the house. It was clear, sunny, and fifty-five degrees, a beautiful Super Bowl Sunday. The house was still smoldering but there were no visible flames. A light wind was sending the smoke to the east and northeast.

The roof was completely burned away. Siding had blown across the lawn. All the windows were gone. Insulation was blown up into forty-foot evergreen trees. Doors were off their hinges, except for one lone French door near the rear of the house. Part of it was missing but it was still standing, shut. The front door that Elizabeth Griffin-Hall had pounded on, desperate to get Josh to open it, was gone. Plastic blinds from the windows had melted and been blown to a side yard. Josh's minivan, parked in the garage, was a shell of steel. The fire had burned the house down to its two-by-fours. From any angle you could see straight through it.

Through a blown-out window on the south side, investigators could see the bodies of two children. The bodies were partly covered by debris from the fire.

The house was still smoking and firefighters thought there was more accelerant in the house. A couple of firefighters went inside to spray more water on the fire, but stayed out of the room where the bodies were.

Videos and photographs were taken of the house. An exterior wall was removed to give investigators better access.

When the fire was out and the air quality tested, investigators looked again through the window in the back of the house. Two small children were lying on what was left of a box spring and mattress with remnants of a red comforter or sleeping bag. The Coxes were told that the boys' hands were touching; the police were not sure if Josh has posed them, if it happened by accident, or if Charlie and Braden had reached for each other as they took their last breaths.

One of the boys, later determined to be Charlie, was on his left side. The majority of his clothing was burned off.

Debris was removed from Charlie's body, using a hand trowel and broom. He was photographed and turned over. The exposed part of his body was red, burned, and blistered. A lot of his skin had burned away, and his left arm was mostly gone. The back of his skullcap was missing. They placed Charlie in a white cloth, then the sheriff's deputy tenderly lifted Charlie into his arms and carried him outside.

When investigators returned to the room, they found a hatchet bent by heat and two knives on top of the mattress where Charlie had been. They were photographed and packed as evidence.

Braden was facedown, with a lot of debris from the fire covering him. They removed debris from his body and took photographs. As they were turning him over, they saw chop marks on the back of his neck. Like Charlie, Braden was missing part of his skull. Braden, too, was also placed in a white cloth and gently carried outside in the arms of the deputy.

There was so much debris from the fire that at first they didn't see Josh's body. For a few minutes, they wondered if he had fled the house before it blew up. But eventually they discovered him, lying on his back. His body, especially from his waist to his feet, was burned more than the bodies of Charlie and Braden. His penis was exposed and most of the skin on his legs was missing, with only bone and muscle tissue left. They wrapped his body in a cloth and used a stretcher to carry it outside.

After they had removed Josh's body they found a melted five-gallon gasoline container where Josh's buttocks and upper thighs had been. There was a cell phone in the ashes, and among the ruins was a large birdcage, but no sign of the parrot.

Charlie and Braden died of smoke inhalation, but the "chop injuries" also contributed to their deaths. Charlie was struck on his neck, and Braden was struck on both his head and neck. No determination was made about whether Josh had tried to kill the boys before he started the fire, or only meant to subdue them with the blows. He had scattered the gasoline from one of the five-gallon containers in various rooms of the house; the second one he sat on.

The boys were still alive when the fire began because soot was found in their lungs and esophagi. After striking the boys with the hatchet and laying them side by side on the mattress, Josh poured a mixture of gas and ethanol on them. Since they were still breathing, some went down their throats.

48

I think he must have just felt that there was only one
way left to protect his sons from the pain from all the
emotional and physical pain that they've been expe-
riencing.
— ALINA POWELL, FEBRUARY 9, 2012, TO ABC

The double murder–suicide escalated the animosity between
the families. The Powells saw Josh as a victim. The Coxes
knew he was a murderer. The comments that caused the most
head-scratching were from Alina. During an interview on
Good Morning America, she portrayed her brother as a mar-
tyr, saying he had been "damaged by the lack of due process"
and "harassed, abused, and lied about."

"They were our boys. All three of them," she said, as she
fought off tears.

Alina had the support of an aunt and uncle, Maurice and
Patti Leach, and their son Nathan, but no one else. Patti Leach
(Steve Powell's sister), praised Josh for the "restraint, patience
and dignity" he displayed during the "ordeal." They blamed
religious bias, "the Internet kangaroo courts," the news media, and "government agencies' practices" for pushing Josh
to the edge. Josh's cousin, Nathan, called on the FBI to in-

vestigate how Josh had been "cyberbullied" on Facebook, possibly contributing to his decision to kill himself and his children.

Alina said she still didn't believe that Josh had had a role in Susan's disappearance.

It was a confession. That's what the Coxes, the police, and Susan's friends thought. By killing the boys and himself, Josh was admitting that he had killed Susan. One wouldn't have happened without the other.

Jennifer and Kirk Graves were in shock. They had visited the Coxes at Thanksgiving and had spent time with Charlie and Braden. With the Coxes' blessing, they hoped one day to adopt the boys. Chuck and Judy wanted to be grandparents again, not parents to two young children.

Not surprisingly, many people felt rage at Josh. Kiirsi's husband, John Hellewell, who was Josh's closest friend, said that the murder-suicide showed that "all he ever thought about was himself."

Kiirsi was blunt. She was furious with Josh. "If he's going to take such a cowardly and selfish way out of this, I wish he would have left a note to explain what happened [to Susan]. . . . If he wanted to kill himself, he could have done that, but how dare he do something so horrible, so evil as to murder the boys."

On the morning after Charlie and Braden were killed, Chuck and Judy walked reporters through the new addition to their home, the room they had built for the boys. The bunk beds had the *Cars* and Spider-Man quilts on them. A stuffed dolphin was at the head of Charlie's bed. Chuck talked about how Braden loved puzzles, how much he looked like his mother, and how his personality was like hers, "giggly and mischievous." Charlie was very interested in science, and loved to observe bugs.

Charlie had made a paper snowman and hand-cut paper snowflakes. They were still taped to the window in the bedroom. Judy said that she would keep them, but they would give away some of the toys. They were just too difficult to see.

Most people would pull the curtains and turn off the phone, keeping their grief as private as possible, not invite reporters into their home. But Chuck and Judy had surrendered their privacy two years before in hopes that they would find their daughter. Now they wanted to keep the search for her alive and push for an investigation of Fort Powell.

Chuck almost never heard from the police in Utah. But the day after the fire Chuck got a call from West Valley City Police Chief Buzz Nielsen. He and a couple of detectives were in Puyallup to try to talk to Steve Powell, and to see where Josh had killed the boys. Nielsen had been watching the Super Bowl when he got the call about the fire.

Chief Nielsen wanted to talk to Chuck so they met up at Josh's storage unit where investigators were looking for clues to the horrific deaths the day before, and to Susan's disappearance.

The two men were quiet at first, stunned, really, as they looked over the remains of a marriage. The police gave Chuck some of Susan's personal items, including a sewing kit and a drawing of a dinosaur by Charlie. As the men stood there, it was inescapable. The contents of the storage area held mementos of Josh and Susan's life together. There were white and red signs proclaiming SOLD! from Josh's washed-up real estate career in Utah, and hundreds of pounds of wheat in bags and plastic drums, along with gallons of water from the time Josh insisted that he and Susan make preparations for hard times—or maybe the end of time.

It was where most of the belongings ended up that Susan had documented in the poignant video she made detailing their "assets."

Near the front of the locker was a white cardboard box. Chuck noticed it right away. It had "Susan's Things" written on it, but someone had put a large red X through the words.

Susan was gone. Charlie and Braden were gone. And, of course, Josh, too. A large red X through an entire family.

Chief Nielsen and Chuck returned to the squad car. The

veteran cop started to tear up as he spoke. "You were right all along," he said, referring to Chuck's warnings that Josh would kill the boys and himself.

As the chief tried unsuccessfully to hold back tears, Chuck wanted to scream: "I know I was right. I didn't want to be right. How does that help? The boys are still dead. They can't interrogate a corpse. How can this help find my daughter?"

But Chuck didn't scream anything. Instead, his anger mixed with compassion.

Nielsen said that the police wanted to find out who had helped Josh get rid of Susan. "The investigation is far from over," he promised.

"I knew he was talking about Steve and the entire group at Fort Powell—Alina, Mike, and Johnny," Chuck said later. Chief Nielsen said his department was still determined to find Susan.

Publicly, Chief Nielsen said that they had "strong circumstantial evidence" against Josh and had hoped to file charges later in 2012. He said that Josh had *not* been aware of the progress of the investigation, so fear of arrest could not have been a factor in his killing himself and the kids.

Chuck, however, disagreed.

In Utah, grief counselors at University Hospital in Salt Lake City began to get calls as soon as news spread. People not related to the victims were shaken up, and wanted to know how—or whether—to explain the horrifying crime to their children. A lot of people were furious that Josh had escaped "earthly justice" by taking his own life.

Susan's friends were among those trying to figure out what to say to their children, who had known Charlie and Braden. Kiirsi had always been candid. "I told them exactly what happened," she said. "I thought, 'Am I going to try and sugarcoat this or keep things from them?' And I said no. Because it has been such a huge part of our lives."

Debbie Caldwell had not only her own kids to think of, she had a dozen day-care children who had known Braden and Charlie and whose parents had known Susan, Josh, and the boys. Most of the children had seen television coverage of the fire, and were prepared for Debbie to be sad. Debbie and the parents of the younger children decided not to tell them that Josh had killed the boys. "We just told them that the boys died because their house caught on fire," she said. The older children had heard the terrible details at school. "They were allowed to talk freely and we just answered their questions honestly. We also told them that they will probably never meet another Josh in their lives because not all people are that bad. We have worked hard to help them understand that they are safe and their dads would never hurt them."

On Monday, the day after the fire, investigators were still at the crime scene. Pierce County sheriff Paul Pastor—a man who had seen his share of shocking events as head of the second-largest sheriff's department in Washington State— made remarks both direct and emphatic.

"This was something evil," he told a TV station. "Let's not refer to this, please, in public, as a tragedy. This was not a tragedy. This is a horrible murder of two little kids. Let's not dress it up. Let's not sanitize it. Let's not distance ourselves from it. It is something wrong. It is something evil. Let's say that."

49

His funny, bright, compassionate personality lives
on with all of us who knew him.
—JOHN HUSON, CHARLIE'S FIRST-GRADE
TEACHER, FEBRUARY 11, 2012

He had a sharp mind and a big imagination. He was
a budding puzzlemaster . . . with contagious, joyful
energy.
—CHRISTIE KING, BRADEN'S
PRE-KINDERGARTEN TEACHER,
FEBRUARY 11, 2012

In a steady rain, two white hearses pulled up to Tacoma's
massive Life Center church. One brought the Cox family and
the other carried the single casket holding the remains of
Charlie and Braden. Rain was appropriate for the day, Saturday, February 11. Many of Susan's close friends and their
husbands and children from Utah had made the trip—Kiirsi,
Debbie, Michele, and the Marinis. Some two thousand
mourners, mostly strangers, came from all over western
Washington. Alina later called it a "publicity service," rather
than a memorial service.

Some of the Powells were there too, but Terri, Alina, and
Johnny were seated in the balcony section far from the Coxes
and the boys' casket—a request that they understood, but they

felt slighted anyway. Josh's brother Mike didn't attend the memorial service. Steve Powell was in jail, and though state law allows an inmate to petition for release to attend a family memorial, Steve had wisely not done so.

Jennifer Graves and her family had made their choice long ago. They sat with the Coxes.

Many of the mourners wore purple ribbons and purple buttons with photos of Susan and her sons as they looked down at the single blue casket blanketed by a spray of flowers punctuated by Gerbera daisies in orange, Braden's favorite color.

The minister of the Life Center church, Dean Curry, told the gathering that the Cox and Powell families had been drawn together by the tragedy. While Chuck appreciated where the pastor was going with his sentiments, he knew he was wrong about that.

They hadn't been and never would be.

Judy had her six-year-old granddaughter, Dakota, curled up on her lap. The little girl watched intently, while gripping a white stuffed duck and a pink and purple giraffe.

Country Hollow neighbor Pastor Tim Atkins told a story about praying before meals with the boys, and Charlie's and Braden's teachers spoke about how much Charlie loved science and how Braden would leap into his grandparents' arms when they came to pick him up. A children's choir sang "Amazing Grace" and a family friend who sold Mary Kay cosmetics with Susan at one time, Dawnette Palmer, sang an LDS hymn, "Our Savior's Love."

Josh was never mentioned during the service, and his image didn't appear in the photo tribute that showed his sons dressed in Halloween costumes as characters from Disney's *Cars,* and in the arms of their mother and maternal grandparents.

When the time came, Chuck and Judy walked to the front of the sanctuary. Chuck, wearing a dark purple tie, gently touched the casket as he passed by it, then addressed the mourners.

"Throughout this trial we felt the support of so many

people around the world," he said. "We want to express our sincere gratitude. It helps us know there are good people in the world—good people who fight against evil. Everyone was doing everything they possibly could do to keep them safe. We thank you very much. We know they're with their mother."

When it was over, Chuck, Susan's three sisters—Mary, Denise, and Marie—Chuck's sister Pam, and Kirk Graves acted as pallbearers.

Later that evening, a vigil was held at Josh's burned-out house. Kiirsi, Debbie, and others loaded into Jennifer and Kirk's van and drove over. It was a need to be there—to see it, to make it real—that compelled them. But they also wanted to join with others in their grief for the boys. It was raining, as it had been all day, and most of the mourners had left by the time the Graves' van arrived. As candles flickered, the Utah contingent moved toward the yellow tape of the crime scene barrier with the charred remains of the murder scene on the other side.

They studied the tributes strangers left behind. Stuffed animals, baseball gloves, balls, all sorts of little toys and bundles of supermarket bouquets circled the perimeter of the house.

Kiirsi was among the first to notice dozens of little white cards tucked into the wire fence. Gently, she pulled one out. The others did the same. And as the rain fell around them and blended with the tears on their cheeks they read the notes strangers had written on index cards and scraps of paper.

> *RIP you beautiful angels. You are now with your mommy again and forever.*

In its own way, being there became affirming. While no one could deny evil was on one side of the fence, there was proof of goodness, love, and compassion on the other.

On Sunday there was a private, LDS funeral for Charlie and Braden. That morning, Chuck and Judy sat quietly at the dining room table and tried to eat their usual breakfast of oatmeal. They felt so wounded by everything that had transpired, but they could lean on the strength of their Mormon faith. They knew their family would be reunited once more.

"We'll be with her and it will be a great reunion," Chuck said to Judy. "And since we've done everything in our power while we're here to help other people and keep the covenants we made in the temple, we'll be a family forever."

Judy spoke through her tears. "And because the boys were so young they'll go to the Celestial Kingdom and they'll eventually be reunited with Susan and she'll be able to raise them."

Chuck put his hand on his wife's hand. "Something she didn't get to do in this life," he said.

Susan's parents knew many were speculating about Josh's soul. Was he in hell? The police, the community, and Susan's friends—everyone called Josh and his actions evil.

He wasn't going to get to the Celestial Kingdom, that's for sure. And he probably wouldn't reach the Terrestrial Kingdom—home to those who received Jesus but still failed in this life—or even the lowest glory, the Telestial Kingdom, where "liars, sorcerers, whoremongers, and adulterers" go.

"Josh knew what he faced in the afterlife," Chuck reminded Judy. "He'd had instruction in the temple; he'd been married in the temple. He knew he would suffer more than he ever had in this life."

"Well, he can't hurt any of us where he is now—in outer darkness," Judy said.

On Monday, Chuck and Judy buried their grandsons. The families had to negotiate time to pay their respects at the cemetery. After a graveside service at Woodbine Cemetery, the Coxes left and the Powells arrived for their own service. Then the Coxes returned for the lowering of the casket.

Before it was placed carefully into the muddy earth, Charlie and Braden's cousins and a few aunts and uncles gathered around and covered the casket with stickers, mostly Spider-Man and other cartoon characters.

No villains, just heroes.

Only the good guys.

There is room in the burial plot for a second casket, for when Susan is found.

The following week word got around that Josh's family planned to have him buried next to his sons. It wasn't completely true, although Terri admitted she and Alina had looked at a plot up the hill from the boys. She had dropped those plans. But the rumor snowballed. In one afternoon, a local Crime Stoppers organization—a nonprofit composed of civilians and police officers—with the help of Seattle's KIRO radio station, raised tens of thousands of dollars to buy the plots on either side of Charlie and Braden to ensure the boys' murderer could not rest near them. They raised more money than they needed, purchased the plots, and put the remainder of the money aside for future projects.

Chuck and Judy Cox braced themselves for a legal fight. They prepared to file a temporary restraining order to prevent Josh's family from burying him *anywhere* in Woodbine, the only cemetery in Puyallup.

Chuck even warned Josh's mother, Terri.

"If you bury Josh there," he said to her over the phone, "we'll move the boys and you'll never know where they are."

In the end, Josh was cremated. His ashes are—naturally—back home, at his father's house in Puyallup.

If Chuck and Judy Cox had even thought to hold their breath for Steve Powell to tell the truth about Susan's disappearance, they'd have long since passed out from lack of oxygen. To the public, they were stoic and strong. But alone, in the house in which Susan had been raised and her sons had stayed while they'd prayed for their mother's return, both cried a million tears. There were times when it was so painful even to talk about what had happened that the words lodged themselves in their throats. The media was a diversion. The love of friends, family, and strangers, a blessing.

And yet when they could find a moment to talk, a moment

when the words weren't eclipsed by tears, they talked about Susan, and about Steve and what he might know about her whereabouts.

Judy could see no reason for Steve to not disclose what he knew.

"Josh is gone," she said. "There's no need to protect him anymore."

Chuck knew where Judy was going. He could also see the burden being placed on Steve to do the right thing—if ever there was a time in which to do it—was now. His grandsons were dead.

"What would Steve have to lose by telling the police whatever, if anything, he knew about Susan's disappearance?" Judy asked once more.

She only wanted to know where her daughter was.

Steve, incarcerated in the Pierce County jail, refused to meet with West Valley City police chief Buzz Nielsen, the FBI, and the Pierce County sheriff's department. Pierce County prosecutors—about to put him on trial for voyeurism and pornography—said they would even consider making a deal with Steve in exchange for information about Susan's disappearance.

But two days after the fire, sixty-two-year-old Steve exercised his right against self-incrimination and filed a notice in Pierce County Superior Court that he would not speak to law enforcement.

Everyone had hoped that the death of his son and grandsons would soften him up.

It didn't.

50

I don't know why he'd think the marriage is worth staying in, I doubt only myself going to counseling would fix "all the problems."
—SUSAN POWELL E-MAIL, JULY 11, 2008

Nine days after Josh murdered his sons and killed himself, Alina and Mike Powell contacted New York Life Insurance about collecting on the policies for their brother and their nephews. No one—except his brother Mike—knew that Josh had changed his beneficiary, removing Susan's name and replacing her with his brothers and sister.

The Coxes knew about the $1 million policy Susan and Josh had purchased early in their marriage from Beneficial Life. It had been established as a trust. But the Coxes didn't know that in June 2007—one month after filing for bankruptcy—Josh and Susan bought another policy, this one from New York Life, worth $2.5 million.

It was just three months later, in the fall of 2007, that Josh told his father that he fantasized about Susan being killed by a drunk driver. When Chuck learned of the big New York Life policy, he called it Josh's "retirement plan."

"There's no doubt in my mind Josh's plan was to take out the life insurance, she goes missing, and he has her declared dead after six years," he told Judy.

Because Josh removed Susan's name as beneficiary, and because Josh could be considered a "slayer," he (or his family) may not be entitled to the proceeds of the policy. New York Life said it also has concerns regarding his competency at the time he made the changes.

The insurance company decided not to wade into the muck and mire of Fort Powell and asked a Washington court to decide who should get the life insurance money.

Lawyer Anne Bremner is no Barbie doll. It is true that she *looks* like Barbie—slender, long-legged, and blond-haired—a kind of a legal-eagle Barbie brought to life. In a corner of her Seattle office, looking west over Puget Sound, there are several of the famed fashion dolls clad in tiny replicas of the suits Bremner wore in the courtroom in famous cases or as a TV commentator discussing Mary Kay Letourneau, Michael Jackson, Laci Peterson, Casey Anthony, and others.

But anyone who underestimates her learns she is a tough competitor in a courtroom. Since soon after Susan Cox Powell's disappearance, Bremner worked pro bono for the Cox family. Early on, Chuck and Bremner discussed whether Steve might have had a role in Susan's disappearance. It seemed to them that Steve's sexual obsession with her had made him unhinged. They thought he had been nuts for years. Who tells his own children that sometimes people can't let go and murder a loved one? Steve had twenty years earlier.

A co-worker of Steve's had e-mailed Bremner a few weeks before Steve's May 2012 trial, saying that around Thanksgiving 2009, Susan's father-in-law had told her he was going to Utah to go camping with family. In the middle of winter? she asked. He said yes, it was fun. When he returned a week later, she asked about the trip. Steve told her they roasted marshmallows and sat around the campfire and sang songs. It was cold, but great. She said it was a week or so later that news broke about Susan being missing. When she had another visit with him in mid-December, he didn't say a word about his daughter-in-law vanishing. Bremner wondered if they could prove Steve had been in Utah. Police were tight-lipped.

Knowing the way "The family" watched out for each other, it was possible that Steve might have been in Utah in the fall, without Susan or her friends knowing it.

The police found credible the reports of a Utah woman who told police that she had seen Steve and Josh in the Topaz Mountain area that fall—the spot where the dogs alerted on charred wood. The woman told police the men were not dressed for the outdoors, said they were looking for crystals, and were not friendly. She didn't remember or see if there were children in the minivan.

Chuck stared at the debris as he moved slowly through the charred house and around the yard, kicking at the ground gently with the toe of one shoe. It was a couple of days after the funeral.

He was on a treasure hunt, looking for mementoes that might have belonged to his daughter or grandsons.

All he found was a stack of photographs that had barely survived the fire, the firemen's hoses, and the weather since February 5.

The pictures had water damage and more than a few were scorched and melted together. Among them was a photo of Susan and Josh dancing at their wedding reception, and Josh at his graduation from junior college. But there were no photos of their nearly eight years of marriage. There were no pictures of Charlie and Braden, and none of Josh and Susan's life in Utah except for one—a photo of what appeared to be the W. Sarah Circle house with two rose bushes in bloom near the front door.

All the other photographs were of family holidays with Chuck wearing a Santa hat; Susan with her teenage girl-friends; Susan hugging her nieces and nephews and dreaming of the day she would be a mother.

It was her life as if she had never married Josh.

51

This is a case about a secret. A secret that Steve
Powell kept hidden until August 25, 2011.
— PIERCE COUNTY DEPUTY PROSECUTOR
BRYCE NELSON, MAY 9, 2012

It wouldn't have mattered if Steve Powell's trial started at 5:00
A.M., Chuck and Judy Cox could barely sleep and were wide
awake and ready to face him down in court. The family, including Chuck's sister, Pam, and his mother Anne, ate a
breakfast of oatmeal and cold cereal, mostly in silence. All
had speculated about what the day might bring, but that
morning they were inching toward—they hoped and
prayed—some kind of truth. They piled into Chuck's decade-
old dark green Ford Windstar and drove south to Tacoma
around 7:30 A.M. They didn't wear buttons with Susan's picture. There were no MISSING posters to hand out. They didn't
do anything to call attention to themselves.

They were there because they *needed* to be. Not because
it was part of some media event designed to put the spotlight
back on Susan's case, but because there was a chance that

Steve Powell on trial for *anything* might give them new details.

And maybe new leads.

Before the jury was seated, Judge Ronald E. Culpepper threw out the pornography charge against Steve after defense attorneys argued it required proof that Steve "initiated, contributed to, or in any way influenced the victims' conduct"— something prosecutors couldn't prove. Then the judge barred the evidence related to Susan from being presented, saying that the journals and photos were not relevant to the charges against Steve. The judge upheld as proper the search warrant that had led to the raid of Steve's house the preceding summer.

The jurors were seated on May 8, 2012. Most admitted that they had seen media coverage of the Powells. One of Steve's defense attorneys explained to the jury that the trial had "nothing to do with the case involving Susan Powell, Josh Powell, the children, or anything else."

Susan was basically "removed" from the trial, because the judge feared her high-profile disappearance and the murder of her two sons would prejudice the jury.

If only.

Chuck didn't lean over to tell Judy what he was thinking. He didn't need to. Susan's parents could see in the eyes of some of the jurors that now-familiar look of sympathy and recognition. They knew they were Susan's parents. And they knew just what Steve's son had done.

It's lucky for Steve that Susan was excluded from the case, Chuck thought, though he was not happy about it. *The judge's ruling was also par for the course—it seems the prosecution is always handicapped in a system that puts all the rights in the hands of the accused.*

After a few delays and the usual legal wrangling, the jury began hearing the voyeurism charges against Steve. He was accused of taking photographs of two young neighbor girls in 2006 and 2007 while they were bathing and using the toilet. The jury saw the photos Steve had saved on a disk.

It was a messy, sad, and tragic case. A sickening one for any trial watcher.

Chuck and Judy continued to sit in the courtroom every day. Anne Bremner, who had been retained by the mother of the girls, was seated next to the Coxes. A few rows away and to the back sat a stoic Alina Powell. She sat there scribbling notes as though she were a court reporter. She smiled at no one. No spark of recognition passed from her eyes when she looked around the room.

The mother of the girls, who were eight and nine when Steve pointed a telephoto lens at them in their most private moments, testified that she sometimes kept the windows open for cross-ventilation. She knew Steve only to wave to when he was outside mowing his lawn. The family had moved away in 2007. The mother didn't know about the photographs until a detective found her in 2011.

It didn't seem that anything would be learned about Susan's case, unless—as Chuck hoped—Steve got angry and blurted out something incriminating because he was angry at himself, the world, and especially the Coxes. Chuck talked with Bremner about whether they should just bag it and go home.

Bremner didn't think so. "You are standing in for Susan, but also for Steve's other victims," she said.

Chuck saw the point. There were plenty of victims. Some were known, like the girls across from the Powells' house. But Steve had also filmed dozens of girls and women on streets and in parks around Puget Sound who would never be identified. They needed someone there for them.

Steve's defense attorney tried to imply that someone else in Steve's household—maybe his son Johnny—could have taken the bathroom photos. The prosecutor said that Steve had taken hundreds of photographs of the girls in their home where they should have been able to assume they had privacy.

Every day Steve sat at the far end of the defense table, against a wall, wearing a blue blazer, and a shirt and tie. He never made eye contact with the prosecutor, witnesses, or the Coxes, and only occasionally glanced up at the judge. One day he turned and smiled briefly at his daughter as he was led out in handcuffs.

Steve didn't testify during the trial, and he seemed to tune the whole thing out—he appeared blank, emotionless, impassive, sometimes scribbling on a tablet, rarely interacting with his two defense attorneys. When Bremner needed to serve him with a subpoena, he wouldn't look at her or take the envelope. "He was kind of sheepish. I wanted him to look at me, have a little confrontation," she remembered. "I handed it to him and he wouldn't take it, so I put it down and said, 'Here,' and his lawyer said, 'Thanks Anne, he's been served,' because they knew he wasn't going to acknowledge it. But I was surprised at how feeble he was and shy and he knew exactly who I was. You could just kind of tell he drew into himself."

The judge did admit one of Steve's journal entries, from August 17, 2004:

> *I enjoy taking video shots of pretty girls in shorts and skirts . . . I sometimes use these images for self-stimulation.*

The mother of the victims spoke in the courtroom and looked directly at Steve when she told him that her children had lost their sense of security. "Shame on you," she said. "Even though my girls didn't know you were watching them, I know that *someone* was watching you. You better pray that He forgives you because I can't."

While Steve didn't smirk, he didn't acknowledge the witness or what she had to say, either.

Steve's oldest daughter, Jennifer, testified against him. Prosecutors couldn't ask her if she thought he had taken the photographs, but outside the courtroom she said she had no doubts. On the stand she was asked to identify photos of her father's house and talked about its layout. She also was asked to identify a passage from Powell's diary that was shown to the jury. She said it looked like her father's handwriting. She couldn't see her father from where she was sitting as she gave testimony but she and Alina exchanged glances. They hadn't spoken in more than two years.

They looked like a happy family on a sunny winter day, two young boys on playground equipment, their proud parents and grandfather looking on.

On the day her father's case went to the jury, Alina released a Web site with home videos meant to vindicate Steve Powell and show that he and Susan got along just fine. The site, West Valley and Pierce County Malfeasance, with the subtitle "False claims about Susan and Steve," used family moments caught on video showing Josh, Susan, their sons, and Steve at a park, on a state ferry, and at a Puget Sound beach to illustrate that her father had a healthy relationship with Susan, despite the claims of the police, the Cox family, Susan's friends—and Susan herself.

Alina couldn't have predicted the "upside" of her video Web site. Susan's sister, Denise Cox, cried because she had never seen the videos and called them "bittersweet."

Susan was laughing and playing with her children, pushing Charlie on a swing, helping Braden down a slide, and carrying Braden on her shoulders. She wasn't paying the least bit of attention to Steve and seemed to keep her distance from him. She was focused on her children.

Susan was so alive.

After deliberating just over six hours, the jury found Steve Powell guilty on all fourteen counts of voyeurism. Prosecutors wanted Steve sentenced to ten years in prison due to the youth of the victims. Instead he was sentenced to just thirty months behind bars, followed by thirty-six months of probation. He was ordered to undergo sex offender treatment, and must register as a sex offender.

After a recess, Judge Culpepper made an unusual move and addressed what one attorney called "the pink elephant" in the room: the case of Susan Powell. The judge acknowledged that people want someone to punish. "Mr. Steven

Powell—so far as I know—there's no information he was involved in that," the judge said, referring to Susan's disappearance.

Acting on behalf of the mother of the girls, Bremner filed a civil lawsuit against Steve, seeking undisclosed damages on behalf of the two girls for invasion of privacy and "severe emotional distress." Bremner said that the family doesn't expect to get much in the way of damages from Steve, but they hope it keeps the pressure on him to finally talk about what happened to Susan.

Chuck and Judy were disappointed not to learn what, if anything, Steve knew about Susan's disappearance.

"The one thing that really kept me together is knowing that they won't get away with this," Judy said later, after some time had passed. "In the beginning it really bothered me," she said, stopping and searching for the right words. "I wanted, not revenge, but I really wanted justice. And I want justice now but I'm also thinking I probably won't receive it, the way the justice system is."

Not surprisingly, the lone contingent from Fort Powell wasn't happy with the trial's outcome. As the Coxes and the lawyers shuffled to the doors, Alina stayed in the courtroom by herself, in tears. She'd held hope that this mess would go away and her father would come home. On the way out, the Powell family's greatest defender told reporters that her family had been persecuted and what she personally had lost in the last two and a half years: ". . . a sister-in-law, a sister, a brother, two darling nephews, and a great father . . ."

But as grateful as the Coxes were that some justice had finally visited the Powell household, it didn't do anything for their hopes of finding their daughter.

Susan was just as gone as she had been on that December night in Utah, almost three years before.

52

I love my boys, I live for them.
—SUSAN POWELL, HANDWRITTEN LAST
WILL AND TESTAMENT, JUNE 28, 2008

Days after the first anniversary of his brother's and nephews' deaths, Mike Powell committed suicide. Minneapolis police said the thirty-year-old graduate student jumped from a seven-story structure on February 11, 2013, landed on a sidewalk, and died immediately.

It was shocking and confusing. He did not leave a suicide note or a will. At the time of his death, Mike was embroiled in a legal battle in U.S. District Court for Western Washington with Chuck and Judy Cox over Josh and Susan's $2.5 million insurance policy. The day he killed himself, Mike had filed a response to a development in the case. He had been a fierce defender of his brother and felt the voyeurism charges against his father had been "fabricated."

Back at the Monroe Correctional Complex where Steve was jailed, a Department of Corrections staffer had Steve brought to her office. She told Steve that she had received a phone call from the coroner's office in Minneapolis. He immediately said, "Oh my God, oh my God." Just as he had when he learned about Josh's, Charlie's, and Braden's deaths, Steve didn't show any emotion when he heard the details of Mike's suicide. He immediately started to blame law enforcement for his son's death.

The next day, staffers noted that Steve did not appear to be upset or depressed, but did appear to be "pouting."

Federal agents had visited Steve in July 2012 to talk about Susan's disappearance. Steve told Alina they threatened to cut off Mike's graduate school money. After Mike died, Steve concluded that the agents had given his son psychotropic drugs that made him commit suicide. It was all a conspiracy involving the FAA, the FBI, Chuck Cox, and the members of the LDS faith. Naturally.

Alina and her mother Terri are the executors of Mike's estate, which could still profit from Josh and Susan's life insurance. Susan's friends, family, and neighbors have a term for that kind of insurance payout: "blood money."

Josh and Mike's sister Jennifer Graves was informed that she wasn't welcome at a service held for the second brother she had lost in a little over a year. She was crushed.

Mike Powell didn't kill himself over a life insurance dispute. He knew he had become the focus of the Susan Powell investigation.

Chuck Cox had received a tip in January 2013. The caller was a relative of the Powells who said that one of Steve's sisters and her husband had rented a house on 180 acres of thickly wooded forest outside of Salem, Oregon, in late 2009. The entire Powell clan had access to the property. Chuck passed on the lead to the police. Now that they knew about Mike's broken-down car in Oregon, they quickly planned a search.

Just five days after Chuck shared the tip with the police, Mike Powell killed himself. Chuck believes that a relative must have told him about the pending search.

For two days in mid-May 2013, the police, cadaver dogs,

local law enforcement, and volunteers combed the 180 acres. Chuck was on site and was optimistic. It was a huge piece of land, secluded, and familiar to Mike. He could have easily brought Susan's body to the property after he met up with Josh in Utah on December 8–10, 2009. The dogs found some remains on the property, thought to be animal bones. The search warrant for the property did not cover the house or crawl space, so Chuck hopes to return.

It was the last WVCPD search for Susan. The next week, detectives from the WVCPD went to Washington State to meet with Chuck and tell him painful news: They were closing the active investigation into Susan's disappearance. That meant that, finally, they would open most of their files. Chuck and Judy Cox would learn details of their daughter's last day and would hopefully learn just what the police had been doing for three and a half years. Many wondered if the search for Susan had suffered because the WVCPD was embroiled in a scandal involving a rogue narcotics squad and a fatal shooting.

On May 20, a police department spokesman, the West Valley City manager, the deputy chief, the mayor, and others crowded a stage at a news conference. They said they had left "no stone unturned" in their investigation. They searched for Susan on foot, horseback, in the air, and on water and under water. They searched deserts, ponds, rock quarries, a swamp, 400 mines, and a landfill. They investigated 800 tips in eleven states and conducted 900 interviews.

It was the largest missing person's investigation in U.S. history.

Regarding the investigation, there were two bombshells. Steve Powell did not have direct involvement in Susan's disappearance but may have learned about it later. He still refuses to cooperate with police.

It was Michael who, authorities now believe, was "heavily involved" in the disposing of Susan's body. Susan's DNA was not found in the car he abandoned—but dogs did indicate an odor of decomposition.

The police stopped short of saying Josh killed Susan. The most they would say is that Josh Powell was involved in the disappearance of his wife.

None of it helped to find Susan, or explained if Josh planned Susan's death, or if she died accidentally and he disposed of her body. And it doesn't explain why the WVCPD had told Chuck and Judy for years that an arrest was imminent.

Why wasn't Josh Powell arrested? The police said that despite some droplets of Susan's blood on the floor, there was no crime scene, there was no body, and most of the evidence was circumstantial. Two deputy district attorneys worked with the police department during the investigation and neither felt there was enough evidence to prosecute Josh.

The Coxes and Anne Bremner disagree. Bremner said not having a body can make it tougher to prove a murder charge, but prosecutors across the country have won convictions in such circumstances. In this case, she said, the circumstantial evidence was remarkably strong.

There may be future investigations. Bremner said a federal investigation is under way, but the U.S. Attorney's Office in Salt Lake City, the FBI, and the WVCPD said they are not aware of any federal investigation.

Epilogue

We still have a small hope that maybe she is being
held captive somewhere and will be able to get free.
It's not much of a hope, and it's not realistic, we understand that. We still haven't given up.
　　　　—CHUCK COX, OCTOBER 3, 2012

Chuck Cox has taken over the search for his daughter. With
the closing of West Valley City's case, he is driving Interstate
84 from Utah to Oregon, looking for someone who may have
noticed two gray cars on a cold December day in 2009. If
Josh and Mike met up wherever Josh had left her body, put it
into Mike's car, then headed north, they must have stopped
for coffee or gas along the way. Chuck has calculated the time
Josh had with the rental car, from Tuesday evening at 10:26
P.M. to 4:39 P.M. on Wednesday afternoon, when he activated
a new cell phone in Tremonton. Josh drove 807 miles—or to
round it off, about 400 miles away from the Salt Lake City
airport where he rented the car and back in sixteen hours.

At one time the WVCPD prepared a map with a 400-mile
radius that included Oregon, Idaho, Montana, Wyoming, Colorado, Nevada, Utah, Arizona, New Mexico, and an edge of
California. It's a lot of states to search.

Chuck thinks the brothers went north, about 404 miles north. He knows there are dozens of farm roads off I-84 that meander west. Some even drop south, to the Simpson Springs and Topaz Mountain region.

Now it's just Chuck and a private investigator driving the roads. Sometimes the sister that was closest to Susan, Denise, goes along. They hand out flyers with photos of Josh and Mike and their two gray cars. Someone must have seen something. If they did, there are volunteer searchers with trained dogs ready to help Chuck look.

Judy doesn't join him on the rides. It is all so painful, even after the passage of time. She's grateful for his resolve even when it takes him away from the family. He's fighting for their daughter and their grandsons.

If anyone can find Susan, it's her father.

Acknowledgments

Books like these can be written only with the cooperation of those inside the story. We were hamstrung a bit with *If I Can't Have You* because of the ongoing legal issues involving the cases of Susan Powell and her murdered sons. It wasn't until the WVCPD closed its case and released its files in May 2013 that we learned what the police knew and when they knew it.

We were unable to secure an interview with Steve Powell, whom the Coxes—and for a long while, the police—thought had played a part in Susan's disappearance. We did have the opportunity to spend several hours on two different occasions with Steve's daughter, Alina Powell. Alina, an intelligent, thoughtful, and troubled young woman, had lots to say about Josh and what happened in the family. Unfortunately, she declined to go on the record.

We are grateful to the many people who shared their memories of Susan, Josh, Charlie, and Braden, especially

Susan's circle of friends in Utah who have never given up looking for her and searching for answers to her disappearance. They include Kiirsi Hellewell; Debbie and Ken Caldwell; Rachel and Tim Marini; Michele and Stacie Oreno; JoVonna Owings; Amber Hardman; Barbara Anderson; Adam St. Louis; and Mike Khalaji. Thank you also to Charlie and Braden's friends, Madee and Leif Austin; and Salt Lake City journalists Roxeanne Vainuku and Chris Jones. In Washington, Elizabeth Griffin-Hall; Lyn Okarski; Tim and Brenda Atkins; and Laurie Nielsen helped by sharing their time and experiences.

We owe a special debt of gratitude to Anne Bremner, who helped us understand the complicated legal issues.

We appreciate the limited cooperation of the West Valley City (Utah) Police Department; Police Chief Thayle "Buzz" Nielsen; Sergeant Mike Powell; and Detective Ed Troyer and the Pierce County (Washington) Sheriff's Department.

We benefited from the advice of Ginger Adams Otis; Brad Arnesen; Nicole Hardy; Claudia Olsen; Jean Olson, and Sterling Morris.

Thank you to Cox family members, including Anne Cox; Pam Cox; and Susan's sisters, Mary Estep, Denise Cox Olsen, and Marie Moniz for trusting us with their memories.

Most of all, we thank Chuck and Judy Cox for the many hours during which they shared Susan, Charlie, and Braden—and themselves—with us.

—Gregg Olsen
Olalla, Washington

—Rebecca Morris
Seattle, Washington

January 2014

2015 Update

Since *If I Can't Have You* was published, another anniversary has come and gone. Susan Powell has been missing more than five years. Her father, Chuck Cox, continues to explore the roads of Utah, Idaho and Oregon where Josh and his brother Michael are suspected of leaving her body.

After Steve Powell was convicted of voyeurism and lost a civil suit, ownership of his house in Puyallup went to the family of the young neighbor girls he had surreptitiously photographed. After Powell family members moved out, Susan's father searched the house, even digging up areas of the yard, in hopes he would find evidence that Susan had been at the home after she was reported missing. All he found were old clothes that may have belonged to her, Charlie and Braden's bicycle helmets, a sled, and dozens of office chairs dating back to when Steve and Josh sold office furniture.

Steve Powell was released from prison in March, 2014. In

the fall of 2014, the State of Washington reinstated pornography charges against him and he is awaiting trial. If convicted, he could be sentenced to five years in prison. He was also ordered to serve time in jail for refusing court-ordered sex offender treatment. He still refuses to tell what he might know about what happened to Susan.

Chuck and Judy Cox's wrongful death suit against the State of Washington, alleging that social workers did not do enough to keep Charlie and Braden safe from their father, is scheduled to go to trial in 2015.

In March, 2015, Chuck and Judy Cox, and Josh Powell's mother and sister, reached an agreement settling a court battle over some $2.3 million in life insurance. Details have not been made public.

Years after the *Salt Lake Tribune* filed a public information request, the FBI finally released a document showing that it had found child pornography on Josh's computer at least 17 months before he killed his sons and himself. The information, which might have prevented Josh from having visits with his sons, was never shared with authorities in Washington State.

Gregg Olsen and Rebecca Morris
January 2015